U.S. BATTLESHIPS 1939–45

CASEMATE | ILLUSTRATED | SPECIAL

CASEMATE | ILLUSTRATED | SPECIAL

U.S. BATTLESHIPS 1939–45

INGO BAUERNFEIND

CISS0016

Published in the United States of America and Great Britain in 2024 by

CASEMATE PUBLISHERS
1950 Lawrence Road, Havertown, PA 19083, USA
and
47 Church Street, Barnsley, S70 2AS, UK

Hardback Edition: ISBN 978-1-63624-256-9
Digital Edition: ISBN 978-1-63624-257-6

A CIP record for this book is available from the British Library

Design by Battlefield Design

Printed and bound in the Czech Republic by FINIDR, s.r.o.

For a complete list of Casemate titles, please contact:

CASEMATE PUBLISHERS (US)
Telephone (610) 853-9131
Fax (610) 853-9146
Email: casemate@casematepublishers.com
www.casematepublishers.com

CASEMATE PUBLISHERS (UK)
Telephone (0)1226 734350
Email: casemate-uk@casematepublishers.co.uk
www.casematepublishers.co.uk

All photos are courtesy of the United States Navy or Naval History and Heritage Command, except where indicated.

Facing Title Page: Battleships *Texas* (BB-35) and *New York* (BB-34) on the Hudson River, New York, lighting up the night sky with their powerful searchlights in search of imaginary aerial attackers, May 3, 1939.

Title Page: The battleship *New York* (BB-34) leads *Nevada* (BB-36) and *Oklahoma* (BB-37) during maneuvers, 1932. All three ships had been modernized shortly before, as can be seen from the new tripod masts with their observation devices. These masts had replaced the lattice masts.

Contents Page (background image): Japanese Foreign Ministry representatives Katsuo Okazaki and Toshikazu Kase, and Lieutenant General Richard K. Sutherland, U.S. Army, correcting an error on the Japanese copy of the Instrument of Surrender, at the conclusion of the surrender ceremonies. At this historic moment, the ship was crowded with people who all wanted to catch a glimpse of the event.

Contents Page (main image): *New Jersey* leading the American battle line off the coast of Yokosuka, Japan, followed by *Missouri* and the nuclear-powered guided missile cruiser *Long Beach* (CGN-9) with vessels following, 1982. *New Jersey* was modernized first as it was in the best condition of all *Iowas* due to its previous iteration during the Vietnam War in the 1960s.

Contents

Foreword

Prior to the outbreak of World War II most navies throughout the world believed that the battleship would be the deciding factor in engagement on the high seas. However, the advance of the aircraft carrier would change that domination. This is not to say that battleships were not important, but they would be used for other purposes. The United States would see its battleship line crippled at Pearl Harbor; the British would use their battleships to engage the Germans on the high seas. What is important to recall is that these battleships that the U.S. would produce would have improved technology, increased firing range and instrumental accuracy.

U.S. battleships would support bombardment landings in the Pacific and in the European theater. The landings in North Africa were supported by them as well as the landings in Sicily and later Italy. The most pronounced effects of these battleships would be used at the Normandy landings in 1944.

As the war wound down, American battleships turned their bows to the invasion of key Japanese holdings in Guam, Saipan and Tinian and the landings at Iwo Jima in February 1945. The unbridled firepower would reduce the defenses on all these islands but not completely; it would still leave the Marines and Army infantry to land on the beaches and engage the enemy in close-quarter combat. After the engagement at Iwo Jima, battleships returned in support of the invasion of Okinawa. It would be the last use of American battleships in the Pacific in the bombardment of key Japanese strongholds.

The climactic naval battle that took place at Leyte Gulf would be the last action of America's battleships in the Pacific war. The action there was desperate and decisive with the loss of Japanese battleships and cruisers, and it would mark the end of any major naval engagements between the United States and Japan in the Pacific war.

With the dropping of the atomic bomb, Japan was forced to surrender unconditionally. That surrender would be implemented on the decks of the great battleship U.S.S. *Missouri*. It was an iconic moment captured on film. That footage showed the solemnity in which Japanese officials stepped forward to sign the document that would bring the end of World War II upon the Earth.

Today five battleships are preserved in the United States: the U.S.S. *North Carolina* in Wilmington, North Carolina; the U.S.S. *Alabama* in Mobile, Alabama; the U.S.S. *Missouri* at Pearl Harbor, Hawaii; the U.S.S. *New Jersey* in Camden, New Jersey, and now the battleship U.S.S. *Texas* undergoing repairs and rehabilitation in Galveston, Texas.

The author, Ingo Bauernfeind, is an ardent student of the history of the world's warships during World War II. His expertise has been shown with his previous publications and his experience in working as an employee in various departments at the U.S.S. *Arizona* Memorial and the U.S.S. *Missouri* in Pearl Harbor. These are examples of his abilities as a naval historian. It has been my pleasure, as the historian for the National Park Service (now retired), to work with Mr. Bauernfeind on several historical inquiries regarding the Pacific War. It is my hope that you will enjoy this book.

Daniel A. Martinez, Historian, Pearl Harbor Aviation Museum
December 12, 2023

Introduction

On March 31, 1992, when the venerable U.S.S. *Missouri* was decommissioned for the second and final time, the age of the battleship irrevocably came to an end. At that time the "*Mighty Mo*" was the last of its kind, representing a breed of warship that had dominated the world's oceans, particularly in the early 20th century.

During World War II, American battleships played a crucial role in various naval operations. However, as the conflict progressed, their importance began to diminish as aircraft carriers took over as the primary offensive weapon. The rise of the latter was due to their ability to project airpower over long distances and attack enemy ships from a safe distance. In contrast, battleships were limited to their guns' range and vulnerable to enemy air attacks. Nevertheless, they continued to play an essential role in shore bombardment and escort duty throughout the war.

In addition, their development and deployment were significant milestones in the evolution of naval warfare. Advances in armor protection, gunnery, and fire-control systems improved battleship performance and paved the way for future naval innovations. The lessons learned from battleship engagements during the war continue to influence modern naval warfare; their legacy and impact on naval warfare cannot be understated.

While the U.S.S. *Arizona* Memorial, located in Pearl Harbor, is a testament to the sacrifice and service of the men who fought and died on American battleships, *Missouri* has become an enduring symbol of the Allied victory in World War II, as it was on its deck that the Japanese officially surrendered on September 2, 1945.

The *Iowa*-class, in particular, became a symbol of American naval power, as it also played an important role in projecting American strength around the world during the Cold War.

Today, all the world's battleships are gone except eight of the United States Navy's (and the Japanese *Mikasa*) having survived as floating museums, standing the test of time. As a sign of national power and prestige, they have long served their nation as an important factor in both diplomacy and military strategy, much like today's nuclear-powered aircraft carriers and submarines. This is their story.

American battleships steaming in column formation, circa 1914. The leading ship is either U.S.S. *Wyoming* (BB-32) or U.S.S. *Arkansas* (BB-33). Note the dense smoke produced by these coal-burning ships compared to oil-burning vessels.

Comparative Sizes of Battleships

Battleships

Wyoming-class

Pennsylvania-class

New York-class

New Mexico-class

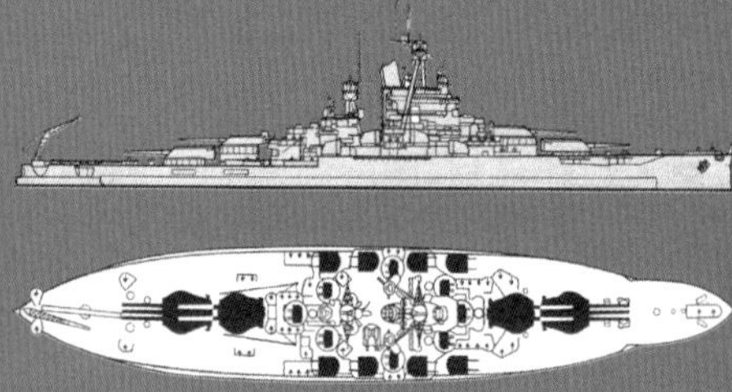

Nevada-class

Tennessee-class

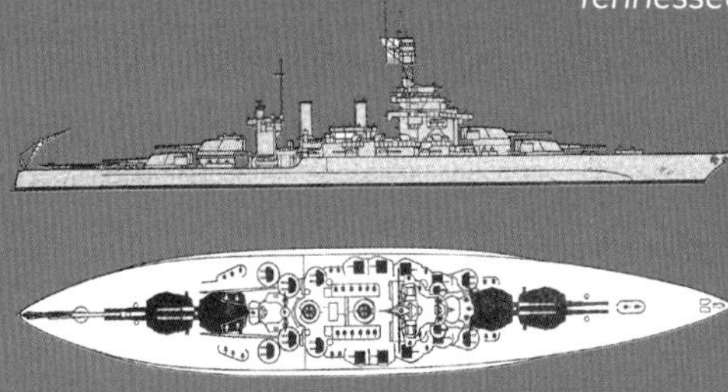

Colorado-class

SCALE

0m 50m 100 m 150m 200m 250m 300m

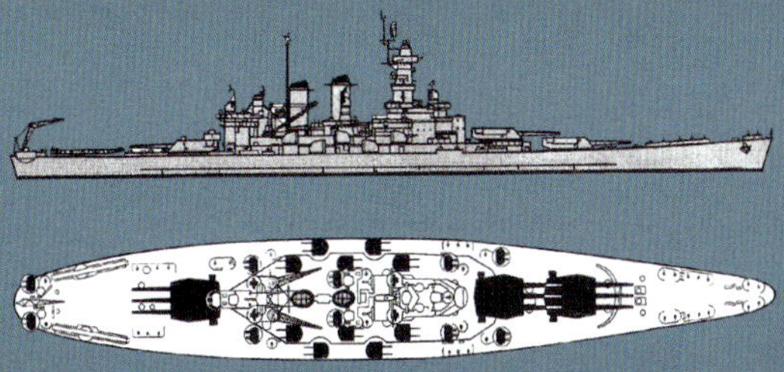

North Carolina-class

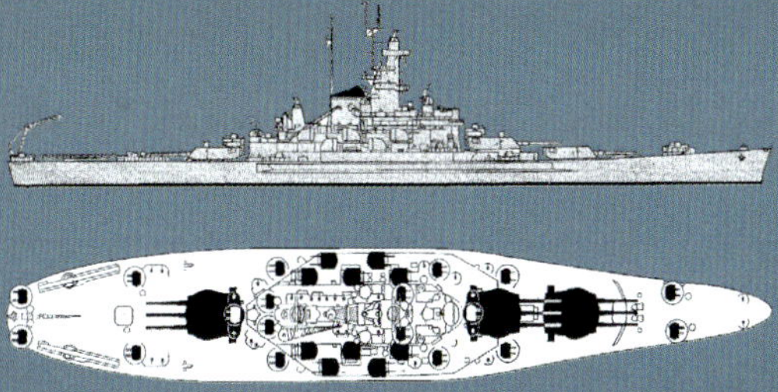

South Dakota-class

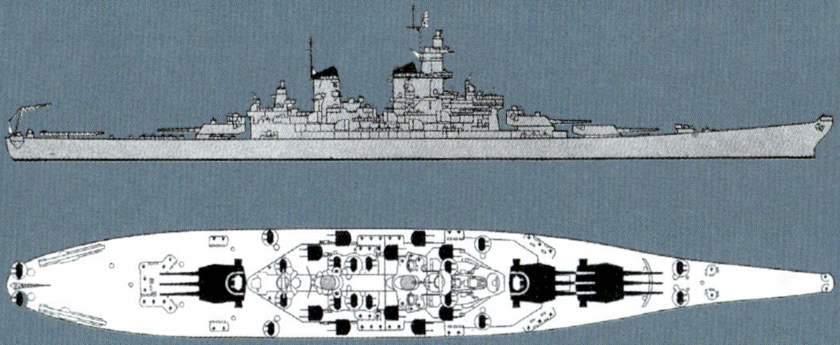

Iowa-class

Battlecruisers

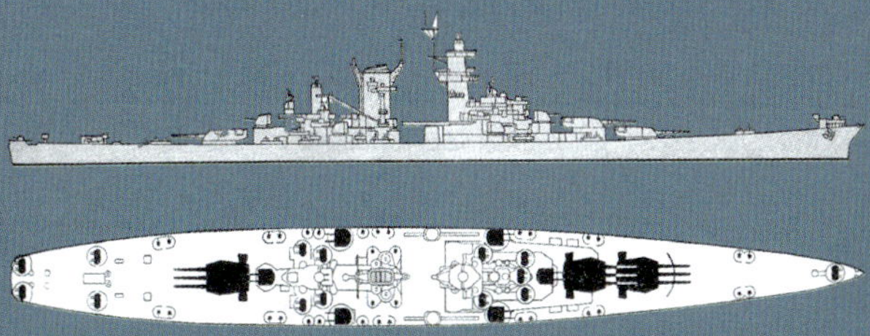

Alaska-class

1 Pre-dreadnought Era

After the British victory over the Franco-Spanish fleet at Trafalgar in 1805, the era of proud wooden sailing ships slowly came to an end. The introduction of steam power in the late 1840s enabled ships to be less dependent on the wind in battle and during maneuvering. This led to the construction of screw-driven ships and the fitting out of several existing ones with this new propulsion system.

However, the career of these unarmored wooden vessels with sails and propellers was short-lived due to the introduction of explosive and incendiary shells which posed a major threat. In addition, the French *Gloire*, launched in 1859, the world's first ocean-going ironclad warship, proved to be superior to all existing ships. However, as it was built with a wooden hull, it was rendered obsolete when the British Royal Navy responded with the *Warrior*-class in 1860, the world's first generation of completely iron-hulled, ironclad warships. Now the naval race was on for the best-protected and most heavily armed warship—the predecessor of the 20th-century battleship.

At the same time, the American Civil War raged on the other side of the Atlantic. On March 9, 1862, Hampton Roads off the coast of Virginia became the backdrop for the first clash between ironclad warships—the Union's U.S.S. *Monitor* and the Confederacy's C.S.S. *Virginia*. While the former carried a revolving gun turret, the latter was a casemate ironclad using the raised and cut-down original lower hull and engines of the scuttled steam frigate U.S.S. *Merrimack*. After fighting for several hours, the battle of Hampton Roads ended as a draw as neither could overcome the other's armor.

The French *Gloire* soon rendered traditional unarmored wooden ships of the line obsolete, prompting all major navies to build ironclads of their own.

Launched in 1859, the French *Gloire* was the world's first ocean-going ironclad. (*La Royale*/Jean Randier)

The superior armored British HMS *Warrior* followed the French *Gloire* by just 14 months, and both nations began building new ironclads and converting existing screw ships of the line to armored warships. *Warrior* has survived to this day and can be visited alongside HMS *Victory*.

The engagement not only confirmed the need for ironclad ships but also proved the advantages of rotating gun turrets enabling the ship to fire in all directions without having to turn the ship around immediately after passing the enemy. Until the end of the 19th century, the rotating gun turret became the standard on warships. With steam propulsion becoming more efficient and reliable, masts gradually disappeared. The mid-1870s saw the introduction of steel as a solid and durable construction material alongside iron and wood. The French *Redoutable*, launched in 1876, was a central battery and barbette warship that became the world's first battleship using steel as the principal building material.

Eventually, the ironclad warship evolved into the pre-dreadnought battleship. The first ironclads, the French *Gloire* and the British *Warrior*, looked much like conventional sailing warships featuring broadside batteries and three masts. Just a few years later, in 1871, the Royal Navy launched *Devastation*, a turreted ironclad showing a stronger resemblance to a pre-dreadnought battleship than previous and contemporary turretless ironclads. *Devastation*, built without masts and armed with four heavy guns in two turrets fore and aft, was the world's first ocean-worthy breastwork monitor (the term *monitor* was derived from U.S.S. *Monitor*). However, designed to attack enemy harbors and coasts and built with a very low freeboard, *Devastation* could not operate as a fighting platform on the high seas as the decks would be swept by water, interfering with the working of the artillery.

The battle of Hampton Roads between U.S.S. *Monitor* and the Confederacy's C.S.S. *Virginia* in 1862. Prior to this clash, *Virginia* had sunk several wooden Union ships proving the superiority of ironclad warships over conventional unarmored wooden vessels. (U.S. Library of Congress)

Monitor's design was distinguished by its revolving turret. It was quickly duplicated and established the American monitor-type of armored warships. This stereo image is an early form of three-dimensional photography. (U.S. Library of Congress)

Great Britain, the dominating sea power, determined to keep its lead in modern warship design, did not rely exclusively on monitors such as *Devastation,* and designed a type of warship that blurred the distinction between a coast-assault battleship and a high-seas battleship. Commissioned in the late 1880s, the six ships of the *Admiral*-class reflected the latest developments in ironclad design. Their protection consisted of iron-and-steel compound armor rather than wrought iron; they boasted breech-loading guns of between 12-inch and 16.25-inch (305 mm and 413 mm) caliber in rotating turrets. They were succeeded by the eight larger and faster ships of the *Royal Sovereign*-class (1889), which were uniformly armed with 13.5-inch (343 mm) guns. Their higher freeboard made them unequivocally capable of the battleship role on the high seas. The nine ships of the *Majestic*-class (1895) eventually represented a mature pre-dreadnought battleship design, serving as a model for future battleships for years to come. Constructed entirely of steel, they were armed with 12-inch (305 mm) main guns with a range of 10,000 yards (9,100 m).

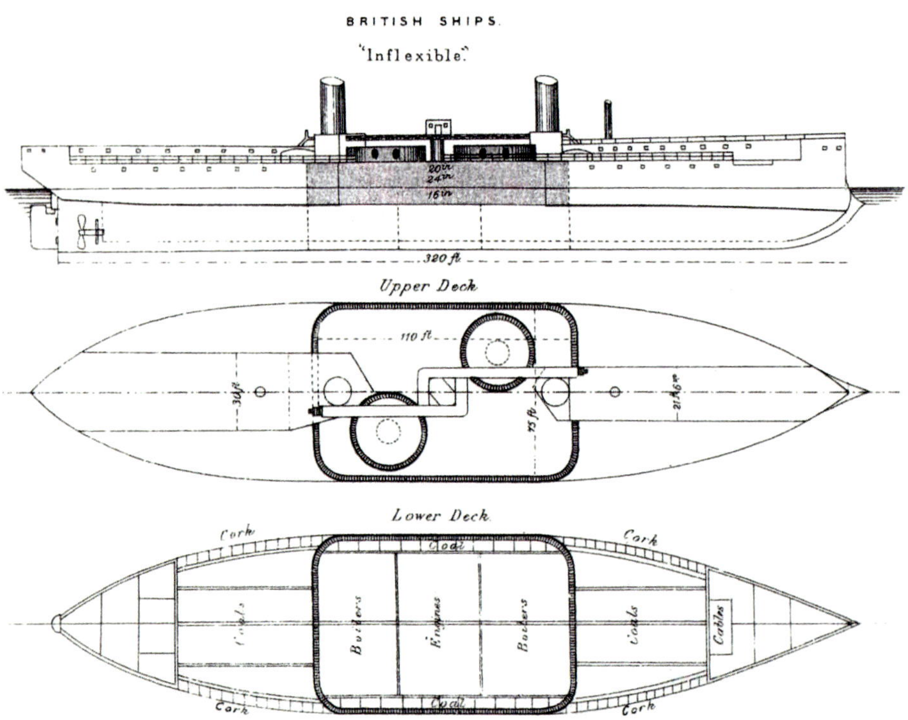

Diagrams showing right elevation, deck plan and below-decks plan of the British ironclad battleship HMS *Inflexible* (1876). A heavily armored citadel was located amidships. It would keep the ship afloat containing the main guns, boilers and engines. (*Brassey's Naval Annual 1888*)

The British *Majestic*-class (1895). Its 12-inch (305 mm) main guns were more powerful and lighter than previous larger gun calibers. (U.S. Library of Congress)

Pre-dreadnoughts battleships were armed with different gun calibers used for various roles in ship-to-ship engagements. Their main armament usually consisted of four heavy guns, mounted in two centerline turrets fore and aft. Although these slow-firing weapons initially suffered from a limited accuracy, they were able to penetrate the thick armor plating that protected enemy ships' engines, magazines, and main guns. While the commonest caliber for the main artillery in British, French, American, Japanese, and Russian pre-dreadnoughts was 12-inch (305 mm), some designs such as the German *Brandenburg*-class carried smaller 11-inch guns (279 mm) to attain a higher rate of fire.

The secondary battery mostly consisted of smaller guns, usually 6-inch (152 mm) to be used against smaller vessels such as cruisers, destroyers, and torpedo boats. Another role was to damage the less-protected parts of enemy battleships. Although their shells could not penetrate the main armor belt, they could hit lightly armored

The American pre-dreadnought U.S.S. *Kearsarge* (BB-5), launched in 1898, carried a powerful main armament of four 13-inch guns and an "intermediate" battery of four 8-inch guns. The latter soon became obsolete. (U.S. Library of Congress)

Installation of a 12-inch gun on a *Connecticut*-class battleship (1904). The subsequent four classes were also armed with this weapon. Its range was up to 20,000 yards (18,288 m) at 15° elevation.

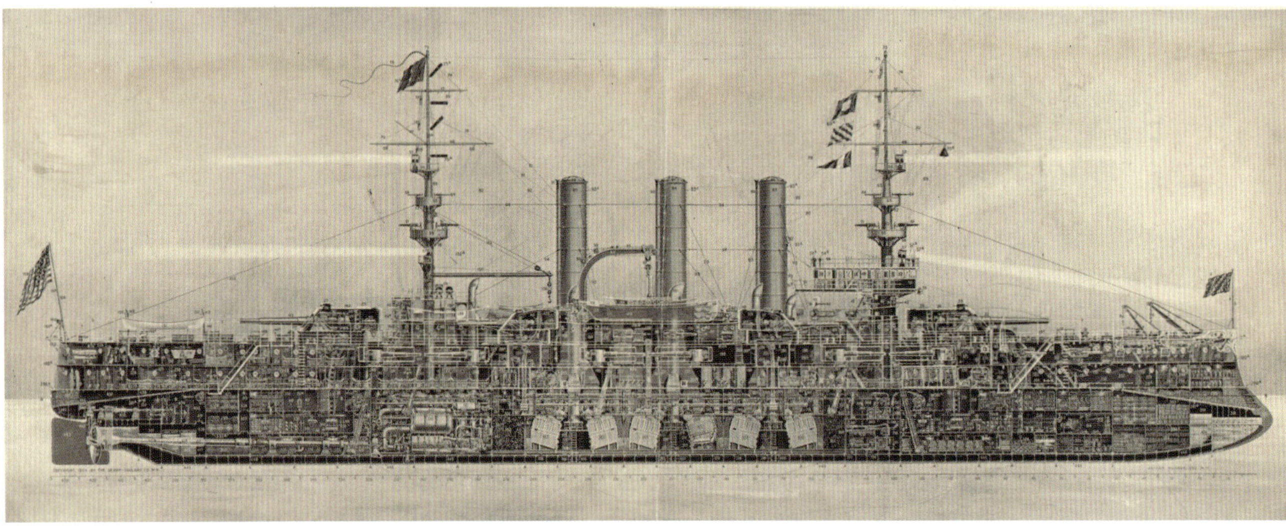

U.S.S. *Louisiana* (BB-19), launched in 1904.

The secondary battery of the *Delaware*-class (1908) consisted of 21 5-inch guns on pedestal mounts in casemates along the side of the hull.

areas like the bridge, or start fires on board. Some pre-dreadnoughts were armed with an "intermediate" battery, typically consisting of 8-inch (203 mm) to 10-inch (254 mm) caliber guns. These lightweight weapons served as a means of adding more firepower to an already well-armed battleship. The armament was completed by a tertiary battery consisting of light, rapid-fire guns ranging from 3-inch (76 mm) caliber down to machine guns. They provided short-range protection against torpedo boats or were used to strafe the decks and superstructure of enemy warships. In addition, numerous ships carried torpedoes located either above or below the waterline.

Armor and Protection

Pre-dreadnoughts carried a considerable weight of steel armor for protection against enemy gunfire. Instead of giving the ship a uniform armor protection, thus making them too heavy, the armor plating was concentrated over critical areas including the gun turrets. The central hull section housing the engines and boilers was protected by the main armor belt (central citadel). With a thickness of up to 18 inches (457 mm) or more, it ran from just below the waterline to a certain height above it. The main armament and ammunition magazines were protected by thick armor from the main belt. The main armor belt tapered to a lesser thickness along the side of the hull towards the bow and stern; and tapered up from the central citadel towards the ship's superstructure. The deck was lightly armored with 2 to 4 inches (50.8 to 101.6 mm) of steel. With the improved quality of armor plating, new ships could be built with thinner armor providing the same protection, thus saving weight.

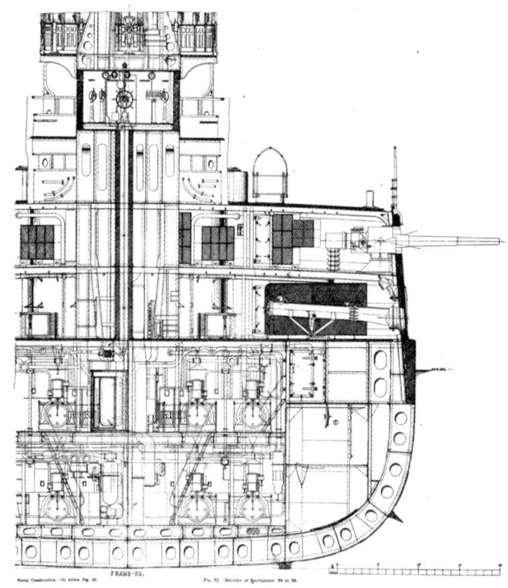

U.S.S. *Kearsarge*'s midship section plan depicting the armor arrangement, along with one 5-inch broadside gun, an 18-inch above-water torpedo tube, and the steering wheels in the armored conning tower and the pilothouse.

Propulsion

Prior to the construction of the turbine-driven British HMS *Dreadnought* virtually every battleship was powered by reciprocating steam engines giving them a top speed of up to 18 knots (21 mph; 33 km/h). While the pre-dreadnoughts of the 1880s used simple compound engines, the following years saw the introduction of more efficient triple or even quadruple expansion steam engines. The adoption of increasingly higher-pressure steam from the boilers resulted in an improvement in engine performance. The introduction of water-tube boilers allowed higher pressure steam to be produced with less fuel consumption and less risk of explosion. (Although coal was almost exclusively used as fuel, early experiments with oil took place in the late 1890s.)

The late 19th century saw the introduction of triple or even quadruple expansion steam engines.

The Great White Fleet World Cruise (1907–9) was a demonstration of American naval power. The tour served additional purposes from goodwill visits to the testing of fleet preparedness.

The United States and Japan

The U.S. Navy started its pre-dreadnought construction in 1891 with short-range coastal-defense battleships, which had poor seagoing capabilities. These early designs, however, ensured American naval dominance against the antiquated Spanish Navy, which possessed no comparable vessels in the Spanish-American War (1898), most notably at the sea battle of Santiago de Cuba. The U.S. Navy's final 13 pre-dreadnoughts, consisting of the *Virginia-*, *Connecticut-* and *Mississippi*-classes, could operate on the highs seas and had a longer range than their coastal-defense predecessors. From December 1907 to February 1909, the Great White Fleet, consisting of 16 pre-dreadnought battleships, along with various escorts, circumnavigated the world by order of President Theodore Roosevelt. The mission was to make courtesy visits to numerous countries, while displaying America's new naval power to the world.

Great White Fleet painting by John Charles Roach (1984), depicting U.S. Atlantic Fleet battleships during their 1907–9 world cruise.

A mascot kangaroo on board U.S.S. *Connecticut* (BB-18) during the world cruise. The animal was presented to the ship by the citizens of Sydney, Australia, when the U.S. Atlantic Fleet visited the city in 1908.

On the other side of the vast Pacific Ocean, Japan had been involved in various naval conflicts. With six pre-dreadnought battleships as the core of its fleet, its navy twice engaged the numerically superior but technically inferior Russian fleets at the battle of the Yellow Sea (1904), and the battle of Tsushima (1905). After capturing several Russian battleships of various ages, Japan ordered additional classes of pre-dreadnoughts. Commander-in-Chief of the fleet during the Russo-Japanese War was Admiral Tōgō Heihachirō, who successfully confined the Russian Pacific Fleet to Port Arthur before winning a decisive victory over the Russian fleet at Tsushima. His flagship *Mikasa*, built in Great Britain, has miraculously survived to this day as a museum ship in Yokosuka and

President Theodore Roosevelt (standing on gun turret at right) addresses the crew on the after deck of U.S.S. *Connecticut* (BB-18), in Hampton Roads, Virginia, upon its return from the world cruise, 22 February, 1909.

Mikasa, flagship of Admiral Tōgō Heihachirō during the battle at Tsushima (1905), is the only surviving pre-dreadnought battleship anywhere in the world.

is the last pre-dreadnought battleship anywhere in the world. Meanwhile, Admiral Jackie Fisher, First Sea Lord of the Admiralty, had begun to modernize the British fleet by conceiving an innovative new battleship type, which upon its launch would render all existing pre-dreadnoughts obsolete. Its name was HMS *Dreadnought*.

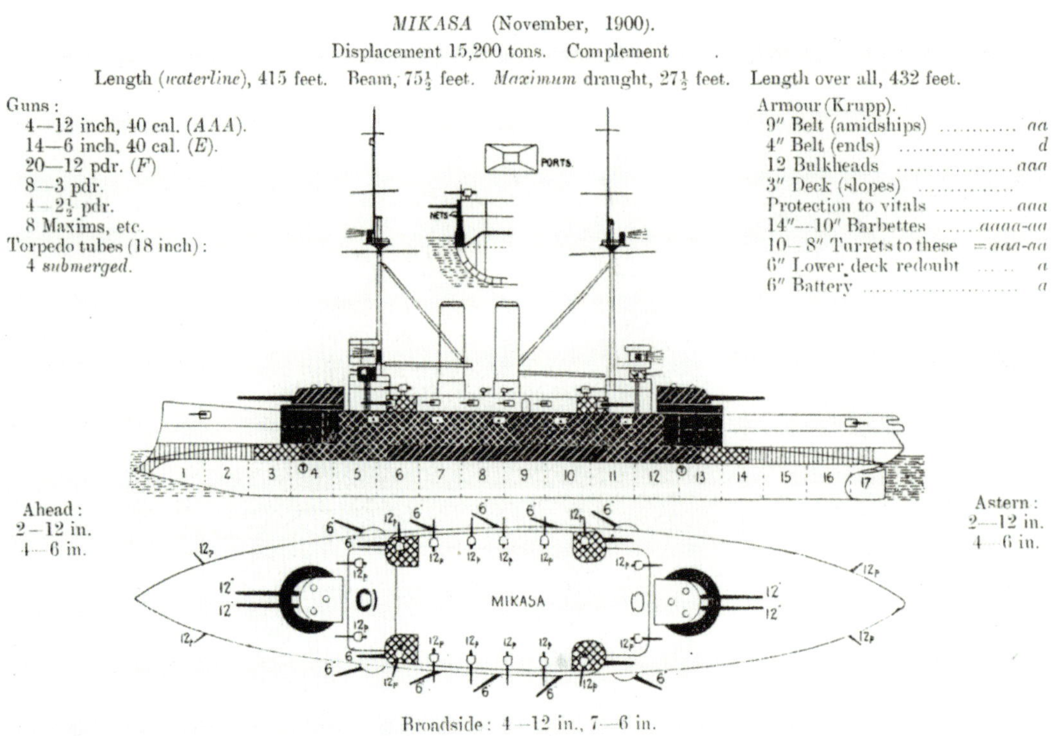

Layout of *Mikasa*'s armament and armor. (*Jane's Fighting Ships 1906–7*)

2

Dreadnought—The All-big-gun Battleship

At the dawn of the 20th century, various sea powers had concluded that battleships would fight each other at longer distances in the future, with accuracy declining with increasing range. In addition, the advantage of a high rate of fire decreased as the gunnery's accuracy depended on spotting the shell splashes of the previous salvo to adjust the guns for a more precise follow-up salvo, thus slowing the rate of fire.

Experts took notice when pre-dreadnoughts exchanged volleys at ranges up to 12,000 yards (11 km) during the Russo-Japanese 1904–5 conflict, thus operating beyond the range of secondary batteries. As an evolutionary step, naval designers reduced the number of these weapons and instead added more heavy guns, typically 9.2 inch (234 mm) or 10 inch (254 mm), complementing the main artillery of 12-inch (305 mm) guns, thus leading to "all-big-gun mixed-caliber battleships", later labelled semi-dreadnoughts. These included the British *Lord Nelson*-class and the Austro-Hungarian *Radetzky*-class.

The Austro-Hungarian *Radetzky*-class carried a mixed main armament of 12-inch and 9.4-inch guns. (Fortepan/ ID 19490/Saly Noémi)

By the turn of the 20th century, the effectiveness of heavy artillery saw significant improvements—in 1895, a 12-inch gun might have fired one round every four minutes; by 1902, up to two rounds per minute was common.

As the next evolutionary step, navies began experimenting with the idea of a capital warship design carrying a uniform armament—the all-big-gun battleship. Soon several experts, such as the Italian Navy's chief naval architect, Admiral Vittorio Cuniberti, began defining such warships as having a single caliber of 12 12-inch guns, carrying a 12-inch armor belt, displacing 17,000 long tons (17,270 t), and being capable of a top speed of 24 knots (27 mph; 44 km/h). Now, the first true battleship was taking shape—at least in published articles written by those who envisioned its advantages.

What is the advantage of an all-big-gun battleship? Naval designers stressed that the use of a uniform caliber would provide homogeneity in terms of ammunition supply and the transfer of crews from the disengaged guns to replace gunners wounded or killed in action. It also helped streamline the complex procedure of fire control as it meant only one set of calculation systems for the gun range adjustments. One single caliber also would reduce the risk of confusion between shell splashes of bigger and lighter guns, which in the past had made accurate ranging more difficult. Ultimately, the likelihood of future engagements at longer ranges proved to be pivotal in the decision-making process that the heaviest possible guns, 12-inch instead of 10-inch, should become standard. Moreover, the latest improvements in the design of 12-inch mountings resulted in a considerably higher rate of fire, thus eliminating the previous advantage of smaller calibers.

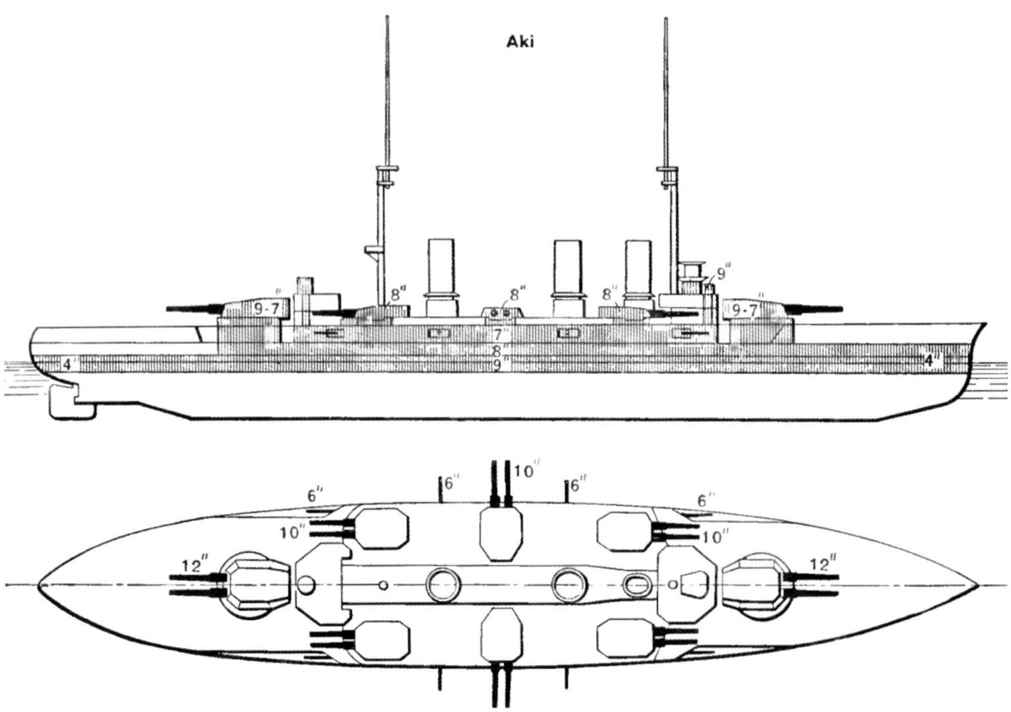

Length, 460 ft. ; 19,800 tons ; Speed, 20·5 knots ; Completed, 1910 ; Armament, 4—12 in., 12—10 in., 8—6 in., 8—12 pr., 8 small.

Diagram of the Japanese battleship *Aki* (sister ship of *Satsuma*) depicting the layout of the armament. (*Brassey's*)

The Japanese *Satsuma*-class *Aki* launched in 1906–7, could have been the world's first all-big-gun battleship.

In 1905–6, Japan, a rising naval power, was the first to lay down two all-big-gun ships, *Satsuma* and *Aki*, to be armed with 12 12-inch (305 mm) guns in four twin- and four single-gun turrets. However, the financial burden of the recent Russo-Japanese War and the shortage of 12-inch guns, manufactured in Great Britain, forced the Japanese designers to change the armament's layout. Eventually, both ships were built with a mixed caliber consisting of four 12-inch guns in two twin turrets and 12 10-inch (254 mm) guns in six twin turrets. Although planned as all-big-gun battleships, both were completed in 1910–11 as semi-dreadnoughts due to their mixed armament. Whereas *Satsuma* retained traditional triple-expansion steam engines, *Aki* (like *Dreadnought*) was built with the then-new steam turbines.

At the same time, British Admiral Jackie Fisher, a long-time advocate of technical innovations, shared—along with his naval designers—the Japanese vision of an all-big-gun battleship. In early 1905, Fisher's "Committee on Designs" evaluated the available reports of the battle at Tsushima, and examined various possible armament, armor, and propulsion configurations for an improved version of Japan's *Satsuma*. The "dreadnought breakthrough" eventually occurred in October 1905 when the keel for *Dreadnought* was laid in Portsmouth. With a standard displacement of 18,000 long tons (18,300 t), its main armament consisted of 10 12-inch guns in five twin turrets and its secondary battery of 27 single 12-pounder (76 mm) guns. *Dreadnought* was powered by two paired sets of Parsons direct-drive turbines driving two shafts. The greater power and lighter weight of turbines gave *Dreadnought* a speed of 21 knots (24 mph; 39 km/h), making it 2 or 3 knots faster than existing battleships. Thanks to the efficiency of Britain's shipbuilding industry, *Dreadnought* was commissioned in December 1906—just 14 months after its keel was laid. All subsequent battleships following or resembling its concept would be labelled "dreadnoughts." Moreover, *Dreadnought*'s introduction almost without exception halted further construction of intermediate-battery ships and rendered the existing ones obsolete.

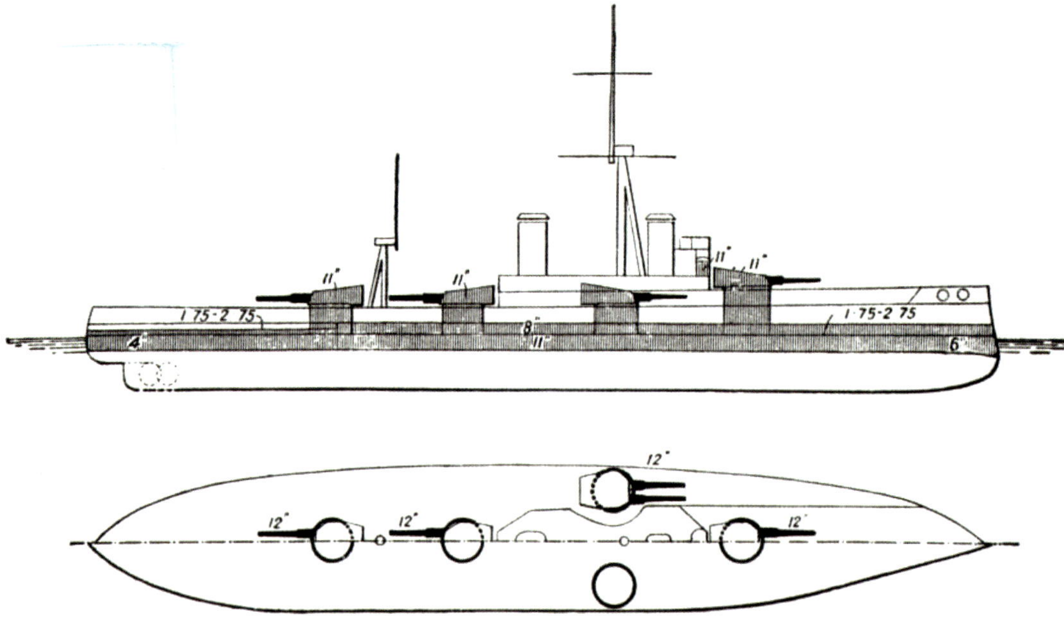

Diagram of *Dreadnought*, the world's first all-big-gun ship, depicting the layout of the armament. (*Encyclopedia Britannica*)

The name *Dreadnought* or *dread nought* means *fear nothing*. HMS *Dreadnought*, launched and commissioned in 1906, gave its name to the first generation of all-big-gun ships.

Dreadnought's 12-inch guns had a range of up to 25,000 yards (22,860 m). The weight of a shell was 850 lb (385.6 kg). *Dreadnought*'s guns never engaged an enemy battleship, but it rammed and sank the German *U-29* during World War I. (U.S. Library of Congress)

Parallel to, but independent of *Dreadnought* and *Satsuma*, was the conception of the American U.S.S. *South Carolina* (followed by its sister ship *Michigan*), which was in many ways equally innovative. Although retaining traditional triple-expansion steam engines, it introduced a superfiring main battery. Although *South Carolina*'s design had been approved in 1905, it took until December 1906—the month in which *Dreadnought* was commissioned—when its keel was laid, and until 1910 to be commissioned.

U.S.S. *South Carolina* (BB-28), launched in 1908, was designed in parallel with but independently of HMS *Dreadnought* and was in many ways equally revolutionary. It introduced a superfiring main battery, which became the standard for future battleships.

U.S.S. *Michigan* (BB-27), *South Carolina*'s sister ship, dressed with flags for a naval review off New York in 1911. The secondary armament, placed in casemates, consisted of 22 3-inch guns.

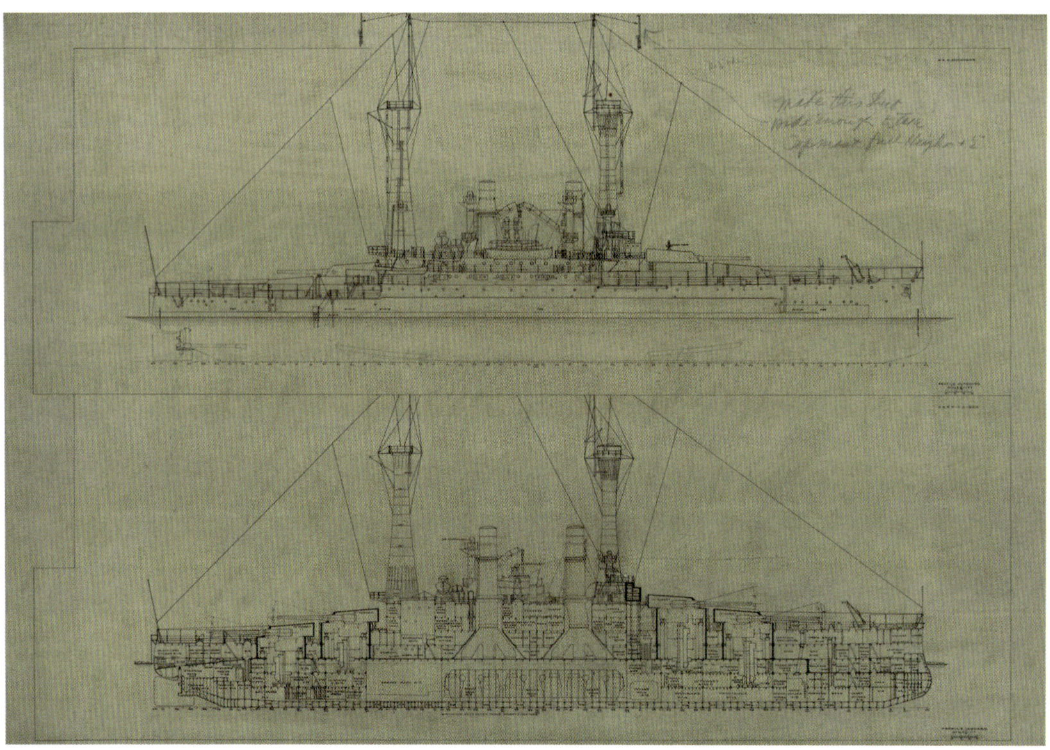

Detailed drawings of *Michigan*'s exterior and interior details. (U.S. National Archives)

All-big-gun designs commenced almost simultaneously in three navies. In May 1905, Japan was first, and began the construction of *Satsuma*. Great Britain followed with *Dreadnought* five months later. Finally, the U.S. Navy's construction of U.S.S. *Michigan* (*South Carolina*-class) commenced in December 1906. *Dreadnought*, however, was the first to be completed and commissioned, in 1906.

When *Dreadnought* was commissioned in 1906, 12-inch guns had been the standard in most navies. Numerous dreadnoughts were fitted with torpedo tubes, thus, in theory, enabling a line of battleships to unleash a devastating salvo on an enemy line of warships. In practice, however, this very rarely happened. Besides the low effectiveness of this weapon, there was a considerable risk that stored torpedoes could explode if hit by enemy shells.

The artillery's effectiveness depended to a certain extent on its layout. *Dreadnought* and its immediate successors carried a total of five turrets—one forward, one aft and one amidships on the ship's centerline, and two next to the superstructure (wing turrets). This layout enabled three turrets to fire ahead and four on the broadside.

With all turrets placed in the ship's centerline, all guns could fire on the broadside, although fewer could fire end-on. In this case the hull would be longer, thus requiring significantly more armor weight. However, firing centerline guns would cause less stress on the ship's frames compared to firing the wing turrets which were closer to the frames. A superfiring layout was first adopted by the U.S. Navy with U.S.S. *South Carolina* in 1906. This involved raising one or two turrets enabling them to fire over a turret immediately forward or astern of them. This configuration meant that either forward or aft turrets could fire at any target within their arc of fire.

Early dreadnoughts carried a very light secondary armament for the protection against torpedo boat attacks. For example, *Dreadnought* carried 27 12-pounder (76 mm) guns with a maximum range of 9,300 yards (8,500 m) capable of firing 15 rounds a minute against these vessels. Foreign battleships featured similar guns. In these early years, torpedo boats were expected to attack separately and individually from any major fleet actions. Therefore, secondary guns did not need any extensive armor, and they were placed in partly armored positions

Michigan's two aft 12-inch gun turrets. Their superfiring arrangement gave both turrets a wider arc of fire.

An early portable antiaircraft gun aboard U.S.S. *Michigan*. Before World War I, aircraft were not yet considered a threat.

high on the ship, reducing weight and maximizing the arc of fire. Within a few years, however, destroyers would become the principal threat to battleships as they were more heavily armed and harder to sink than torpedo boats. As destroyers were expected to launch a torpedo attack as part of a major fleet action, the battleship's secondary guns had to be protected against the blast of heavy guns and shell splinters, while simultaneously firing at the other enemy vessels. The secondary armament ranged from 12-pounders (76 mm) to 5.9-inch (150 mm) guns.

Protection and Armor

Much of a dreadnought's displacement was taken up by its armor consisting of steel plating. Only a certain amount of weight, generally 30 to 40 percent, was available for protection without compromising the ship's speed, firepower, and seakeeping capabilities.

The armor's bulk was concentrated around the "armored citadel." Based on the design already used in pre-dreadnoughts, this box featured four armored walls and an armored top enclosing the most vital innards of the ship. The citadel's sides—the armor belt of the ship—started on the hull just in front of the forward turret and ended just behind the aft turret. Both ends of the citadel, fore and aft, consisted of two armored bulkheads stretching between the ends of the armor belt. The citadel's top was an armored deck. The citadel contained the ship's engines, boilers and the ammunition and powder magazines for the main armament. The protection of these systems was vital because a hit to any of these systems could disable or sink the ship. Although the citadel's bottom was not armored, it consisted of (up to) three compartments, making it a triple bottom. According to naval strategists and designers, early dreadnoughts were to fight against other battleships exchanging salvoes at ranges up to 10,000 yards (9,100 m). During such engagements, the shells would fly on a flat trajectory hitting the enemy warship on its side at or just above the waterline. If they penetrated the side, they would cause damage to the ship's vital systems. As a result, the thick armor belt was placed around the waterline. When *Dreadnought* was conceived, its designers were well aware of the threat posed by shells hitting the side of the ship, and thus gave it an 11-inch (279 mm) armor belt.

Technical development continued rapidly through the dreadnought era, with steep changes in armament, armor, and propulsion. Ten years after *Dreadnought*'s commissioning, much more powerful ships, the super-dreadnoughts, were being built.

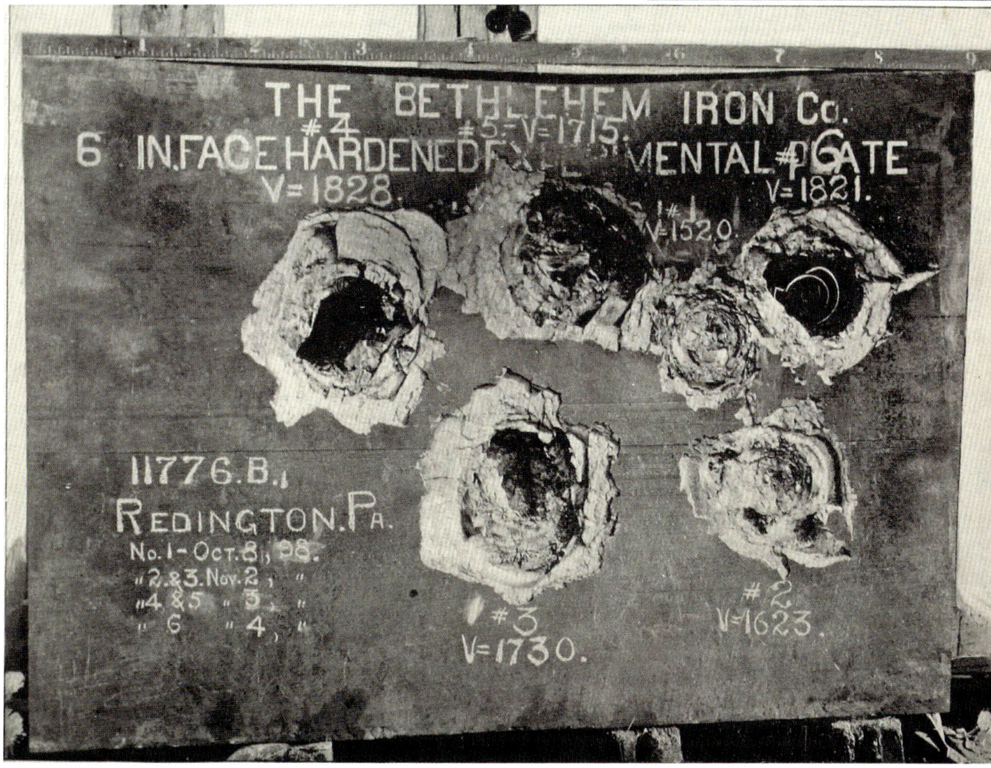

An experimental 6-inch Krupp armor plate (1898) used for testing purposes to determine the penetrating power of various types of projectiles and the resistance of the armor. (U.S. Library of Congress)

A turbine-driven Bliss-Leavitt torpedo. Alcohol was mixed with super-heated compressed air to provide motive power for the turbine. Prior to 1914, American and foreign battleships were fitted with submerged torpedo tubes in addition to their artillery armament. The battleships' underwater protection was limited against torpedoes.

During naval engagements, enemy shells not only could penetrate the ship's side, but also pose an additional, even though lesser, threat of indirect damage to the ship's innards. A shell exploding after hitting the armor belt, deck, or superstructure could send fragments flying in all directions. To protect the ship's innards from these dangerous splinters, much thinner steel armor was used to cover the decks. In general, all navies dedicated the thickest layer of armor to the central citadel's sides. Some navies, including Great Britain, Germany, and France, extended the ship's protection beyond the citadel by also covering the hull's fore and aft sections with a tapering belt and deck amor.

To allow a long armor belt running from bow to stern with a tapering on both ends, many early dreadnoughts only had a thin strip of armor above the waterline for the purpose of weight. During an engagement in rough seas, with the ship tending to roll, its side armor belt would temporarily submerge, thus exposing the unarmored upper part of the ship's opposite side to incoming enemy shells. Moreover, if heavily laden, the armor belt would be entirely submerged. In addition, rudders and propellers were still the battleship's Achilles' heel. Another concern was the increasing risk of plunging fire (shells hitting the deck vertically) from long-range fire, as well as the new threat posed by armor-piercing (AP) bombs dropped by aircraft—an enemy to be reckoned with in the future.

Dreadnoughts—and warships in general—were exposed to various threats capable of disabling or sinking them. These included shellfire, mines, torpedoes, collisions, or even internal explosions caused by accidents in the magazines or gun turrets. As a result, a subdivision of the hull below the waterline was conceived to keep battleships afloat and operational if their hull was holed, because, in theory, the compartmentalization was to allow only one area to be flooded at a time, thus keeping the rest of the hull watertight and ship buoyant. A considerable improvement in the underwater protection against torpedo or mine damage came with the designing of a torpedo belt (torpedo bulkhead)—an inner bulkhead along the side of the hull. It was generally lightly armored to capture splinters caused by torpedo or mine explosions and placed inwards from the outer hull by one or more compartments. The compartments in between were either left empty, or filled with coal, water, or fuel oil, thus serving as an absorption space for the torpedo's or mine's explosive force.

Propulsion

When *Dreadnought* was launched in 1906, it was the first all-big-gun battleship driven by steam turbines, followed by subsequent British (and foreign) designs. Early dreadnoughts built by other naval powers featured slower triple-expansion steam engines, which had been standard in pre-dreadnought designs. The main advantage of turbines was their higher power output compared to reciprocating engines of comparable size. At cruising speeds, however, the former were considerably less fuel-efficient than reciprocating engines. As a result, some naval powers requiring ships with a long range at cruising speeds, continued to build battleships with this propulsion system. This included the U.S. Navy depending on a battle fleet capable of cruising across the vast Pacific and engaging the Japanese in the waters off the Philippines in the event of war. France transitioned to turbines with the *Danton*-class in 1909, and Germany followed with its *Kaiser*-class two years later. For several years the U.S. Navy, however, simultaneously built dreadnoughts with turbine and reciprocating engines.

Coal had been in use since the introduction of the very first steamships. Early dreadnoughts carried tons of coal to fire their boilers, thus heating water and feeding the turbines with the generated steam to drive them. One advantage of this fossil fuel was that it could be used as part of the ship's protection scheme due to its quite inert condition in lump form. However, coal also had some disadvantages. It was very labor-intensive to load into the ship's bunkers and eventually shovel it into the steam boilers. After some time, the boilers got clogged with ash, so they had to be cleaned by hand. The use of coal also was dangerous because airborne coal dust and related vapors were highly explosive. Moreover, burning coal produced thick black smoke, thus likely giving away the position of a single ship or an entire fleet. Smoke also interfered with visibility, signaling and fire control, thus impairing the ship's overall capabilities.

Cruising turbines were used up to 15-knot speed, showing the single-wheel cruising turbine and reduction gear on the forward end of the main spindle. When HMS *Dreadnought* was launched in 1906, it was the first all-big-gun battleship driven by steam turbines.

Men stoke coal-burning power plants of a pre-1914 battleship. Loading coal and shoveling it into the boilers was hard, dirty work.

1909 cartoon in *Puck* showing (clockwise) the United States, Germany, Britain, France, and Japan engaged in a naval race in a "no limit" game. Founded in 1876, *Puck* was the first successful American magazine of contemporary caricatures and political satire. (Keppler & Schwarzmann)

As an alternative, oil-fired propulsion offered several advantages for naval designers and crews operating the ships. Oil reduced the ship's smoke trail making it less visible on the horizon. It also could be pumped directly into the steam boilers making a large complement of stokers surplus. With oil having twice the thermal content of coal, oil-fired ships could be fitted with smaller boilers giving them a significantly greater range for the same volume of fuel than coal-fired vessels.

Except for the United States, all other naval powers—including Great Britain—had to import their oil, thus prompting them to adopt a propulsion scheme consisting of dual firing boilers capable of burning coal sprayed with oil in case the latter was in short supply—a factor which could become relevant in wartime, thus limiting the operational range of the battle fleet.

With the United States having large reserves of oil, their navy was the first in 1910 to make the decision to abandon coal in favor of oil for firing a ship's boilers, shortly followed by the Royal Navy two years later. However, the lead ship of the British *Queen Elizabeth*-class, commissioned in December 1914, was the world's first oil-fore battleship instead of the American *Nevada*-class, which did not enter service until 1916.

Development in the United States

The first dreadnoughts completed by the United States were the two ships of the *South Carolina*-class, *South Dakota* (BB-26) and *Michigan* (BB-27), commissioned in 1910. To save weight due to a limited displacement, all eight 12-inch (305 mm) guns were mounted along the centerline, in superfiring twin turrets fore and aft. This arrangement allowed a broadside equal to *Dreadnought*, but with fewer guns. Its efficient distribution of weapons would eventually become standard in future generations of battleships. With its triple-expansion steam engines, the *South Carolinas* were only capable of a top speed of about 18.5 knots (21.3 mph; 34.3 km/h), compared to the 21 knots of the turbine-driven *Dreadnought*, therefore being forced to operate with the older American pre-dreadnought battleships. For this reason, the two ships of the subsequent *Delaware*-class, *Delaware* (BB-28) and *North Dakota* (BB-29), capable of 21 knots, could be considered the first adequate American dreadnoughts with regards to their speed. While expanding its battle fleet by laying down two ships, in most subsequent years until 1920, the U.S. Navy continued to use reciprocating engines (tripe expansion engines) as an alternative to turbines until the *Nevada*-class was laid down in 1912. The *South Carolinas* and the *Delawares* were broken up in the interwar years. Between 1906 and 1923 the U.S. Navy completed 22 dreadnought battleships in 10 classes.

Firing its 12-inch guns during battle practice, U.S.S. *Delaware* was one of American battleships that operated as part of the British Grand Fleet during World War I. This postwar photograph gives a sense of the power of the ship's main battery guns.

From left: U.S.S. *Delaware* (BB-28) and its successor, U.S.S. *Florida* (BB-30), face-to-face at New York Navy Yard, 1913.

Florida-class

The two dreadnoughts of the *Florida*-class, *Florida* (BB-30) and *Utah* (BB-31), were designed from pre-dreadnought experience and observation of foreign designs, as no U.S. dreadnought had yet been commissioned at the time of the *Floridas'* conception; all ships were either at some stage of construction or in design. In addition, American capital ship design was also heavily influenced by various war games (relatively realistic simulations of naval operations) conducted at the U.S. Naval War College. The *Floridas* were an improvement over the preceding *Delawares*. Their larger beam improved buoyancy and reduced hull stress, which was a deficit of the latter. While *Utah* was built with a heavily armored fire-control tower atop a standard-sized bridge, *Florida* received a larger bridge than was then standard housing both ship and fire-control personnel under armor protection. This proved especially successful and became a blueprint for the bridge design of the subsequent *Nevada*-class.

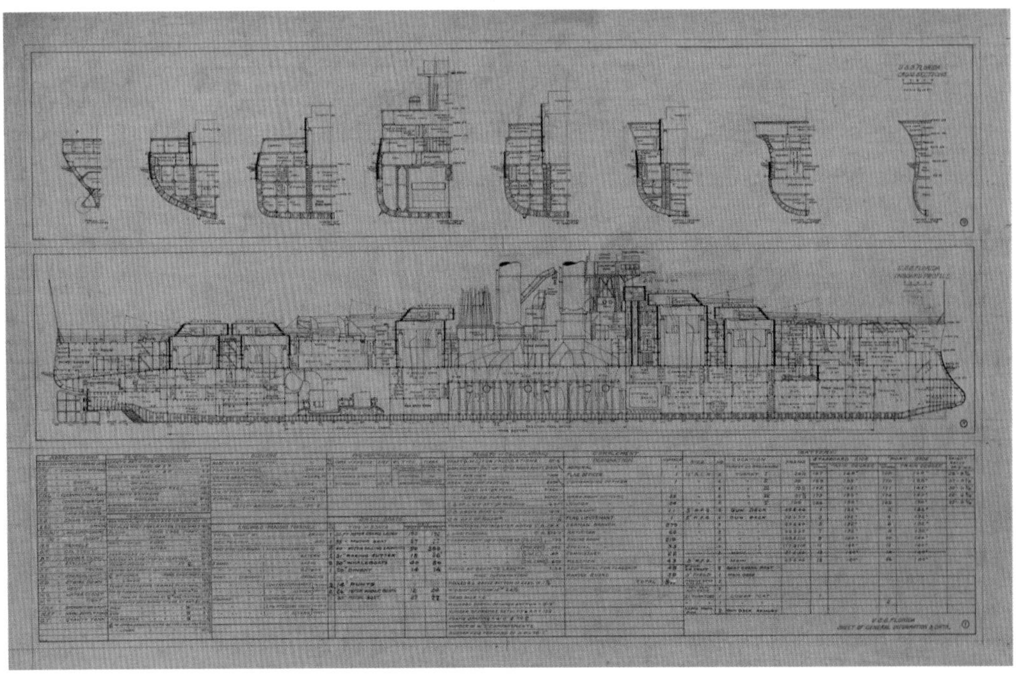

Drawings of U.S.S. *Florida* (BB-30) detailing the interior of the ship with its layout. (U.S. National Archives)

One of the massive hawse pipe castings for U.S.S. *Utah's* (BB-31) anchor chains. The man is used for size comparison. (U.S. National Archives)

New-York Tribune.

PART II. SUNDAY, MAY 8, 1910. EIGHT PAGES.

UNCLE SAM'S NEWEST DREADNOUGHT, THE FLORIDA, AS SHE WILL LOOK WHEN CLEARED FOR ACTION.

THIS 22,000 TON BULWARK OF PEACE WILL BE LAUNCHED AT THE BROOKLYN NAVY YARD THIS WEEK.

The *New York Tribune* praising *Florida*'s impressive firepower as part of its title story which announced the ship's launching in 1910. (U.S. Library of Congress)

Propulsion

The *Floridas* were propelled by four-shaft Parsons turbines. Their steam was provided by 12 Babcock & Wilcox coal-fired boilers. Rated at 28,000 shaft horsepower (shp) (20,880 kW), the engines gave the ships a top speed of about 21 knots (24 mph; 39 km/h). The engine and boiler room arrangements remained the same as in the *Delawares*, but the engine rooms had to be lengthened to accommodate the larger turbines, which meant the after-boiler room had to be eliminated. Funnel spacing was therefore closer. During modernization in 1925–27, the 12 coal-fired boilers were replaced with four more efficient White-Forster oil-fired boilers. The reduction in the number of boilers allowed the twin funnels to be trunked into one single larger funnel, thus changing the *Florida*'s silhouette. The ships had a range of up to 5,776 nautical miles (6,650 mi; 10,700 km) at a cruising speed of 10 knots (12 mph; 19 km/h).

Florida's bow with its three massive bow anchors. Due to the low freeboard, the decks would be swept by water and spray, interfering with the working of the artillery.

Florida (depicted here after the removal of its aft lattice mast) and its sister ship *Utah* were armed with 10 12-inch guns in five gun turrets placed in the centerline. (U.S. Library of Congress)

Armament

Originally, the *Floridas* were designed with eight 14-inch (356 mm)/45 caliber guns in superfiring fore-and-aft mountings. As this new weapon, the under development, did not become available until 1914, the ships were instead armed with 10 12-inch (305 mm)/45 caliber Mark 5 guns in five twin-gun turrets like in the preceding *Delawares*. The guns had a rate of fire of 2 to 3 rounds per minute. They fired 870 lb (395 kg) shells; the propellant charge was 310 lb (141 kg) in silk bags. The barrels were expected to fire 175 rounds before being replaced. The *Floridas* carried 100 shells per gun, or up to 1,000 rounds in total. At an elevation of 15°, the artillery had a range of up to 20,000 yards (18,288 m).

Both ships were fitted with 16 new 5-inch (127 mm)/51 caliber guns as secondary batteries in individual casemates with increased armor protection compared to the *Delawares*. They fired a 50 lb (23 kg) AP shell at a rate of 8 to 9 rounds per minute. In 1917, the *Floridas* received two 3-inch (76 mm)/23 caliber guns for antiaircraft (AA) defense. This was increased to eight guns during the 1920s. At an elevation of 75° and a rate of up to 9 rounds per minute, these guns fired a 16.5 lb (7 kg) shell to a maximum range of 8,800 yards (8,047 m) and ceiling of 18,000 feet (5,486 m).

Both ships were also armed with two 21-inch (533 mm) submerged torpedo tubes mounted one on each broadside. Capable of a speed of 26 knots (30 mph; 48 km/h) and carrying a 200 lb (91 kg) warhead, the torpedoes had a range of up to 4,000 yards (3,658 m).

Protection

The armor layout strongly resembled the preceding *Delaware*'s design. The thickness of the armor belt ranged from 9 to 11 inches (229 to 279 mm) in the more vital areas (ammunition magazines and machinery spaces) of the ships. The barbettes of the main gun turrets had an armor protection ranging from 4 to 10 inches (102 and 254 mm). The turrets were protected with up to 12 inches (305 mm) of armor. The conning tower was 11.5 inches (292 mm) thick. Compared to the *Delawares,* the armored deck was slightly reduced in thickness, from 2 to 1.5 inches (51 to 38 mm).

Operational History

Both *Florida* and *Utah* were involved in the 1914 occupation of Veracruz, Mexico (second battle of Veracruz), deploying Marines as part of the operation. After the United States had entered World War I in 1917, both

U.S.S. *Utah* in its original configuration during World War I, with camouflage patterns painted on its hull and triangular baffles attached to its masts. Both were intended to confuse enemy rangefinders. Camouflage was common in all navies and developed over time.

ships were deployed to European waters. *Florida* was assigned to the British Grand Fleet and based in Scapa Flow, Scotland. Following the end of hostilities, it escorted President Woodrow Wilson to France for the peace negotiations in December 1918. *Utah* was based in Ireland, from where it was tasked with protecting transatlantic supply convoys as they approached European waters.

Retained under the Washington Naval Treaty of 1922, which limited the size of international fleets after World War I, both ships were significantly modernized from 1925–27. This included the installation of oil-fired boilers and additional bulges designed to increase resistance against torpedo or mine damage, thus increasing the beam to 106 ft (32 m). A catapult for launching reconnaissance aircraft was mounted on the No. 3 gun turret. The *Floridas* also had their rear lattice masts (cage masts) removed and replaced with a pole mast.

However, both ships were eventually demilitarized under the terms of the 1930 London Naval Treaty. While *Florida* was scrapped, its sister ship *Utah* was converted first into a radio-controlled target ship, then into an antiaircraft gunnery trainer, serving in that role until the attack on Pearl Harbor.

During a period of increasing tensions with Japan over the Second Sino-Japanese War and Japanese expansion in the Pacific in 1940, the U.S. Battle Fleet was moved from California to Pearl Harbor, Hawaii, to deter further aggression. In early December 1941, *Utah*, after having completed another round of antiaircraft gunnery training, was moored off Ford Island in the heart of the naval base of Pearl Harbor (Oahu, Hawaii), on the opposite side of the active battle fleet (Battleship Row). Shortly before 8 a.m. on the morning of 7 December, the Japanese began their attack. Several Nakajima B5N torpedo bombers from the aircraft carrier *Soryu* launched their torpedoes against *Utah*, with two of them hitting the hull.

Utah (renamed *AG-16*) underway at sea in 1936, while serving as a target ship. Note timbers arranged on the weather decks to cushion the impact of water-filled practice bombs.

Utah capsizing off Ford Island after being torpedoed by Japanese aircraft during the attack on Pearl Harbor; photographed from the cargo ship U.S.S. *Tangier* (AV-8), which was moored astern of *Utah*.

Serious flooding caused the ship to list to port and settle by the stern. As the crew abandoned *Utah*, one man—Chief Watertender Peter Tomich—remained below decks to ensure as many men as possible could escape safely, and to keep vital machinery running as long as possible, thus endangering his life. Tomich received the Medal of Honor posthumously for his actions. At 08:12, *Utah* rolled over onto its side. Commander Solomon Isquith heard knocking from men trapped inside the capsized ship. He called for volunteers to secure a cutting torch from the badly damaged cruiser *Raleigh*; four men were rescued. In total, 58 crewmembers lost their lives, though 461 survived.

Following the complex yet successful righting (rotation to upright) of the capsized battleship *Oklahoma*, an attempt was made to right *Utah* by the same parbuckling method using 17 massive winches. As the ship was slowly rotated, it failed to grip the harbor bottom and instead slid towards Ford Island. The recovery effort was eventually abandoned, with *Utah* rotated 38° from horizontal. Unlike the battleships sunk or damaged at Battleship Row, it had no military value, so there was no further attempt to raise it. After formally being placed out of commission, it was stricken from the naval vessel register in November 1944. To this day, the wreck remains where it sank, partially above water. The crewmembers killed during the attack were never removed, and as such, *Utah* is considered a war grave.

Utah during a salvage attempt.

Utah Memorial

In 1972, a memorial was built on the northwestern side of Ford Island, near *Utah*'s wreck, which is now part of the Pearl Harbor National Memorial. It consists of a 70-foot (21 m) white concrete walkway extending from Ford Island out to a platform in front of the ship, where a brass plaque and a flagpole are located. In 1989, *Utah* and *Arizona*, the other remaining wreck in the harbor, were added to the National Historic Landmark registry. Several former crewmembers, who

Aerial view of *Utah*'s wreck today showing the conning tower and forecastle.

were aboard *Utah* at the time of its sinking were cremated and had their ashes interred in the wreckage. Relics from the ship are also preserved in the Utah State Capitol building. These include pieces from the ship's silver service and the captain's clock. The ship's bell is on display at the University of Utah.

Albert T.D. Wagner was the chief yeoman aboard *Utah* when it sank. When he served in the Philippines, his wife gave birth to two girls, Mary and Nancy. Born premature, each weighed three pounds. Nancy had the umbilical cord wrapped around her neck and died two days later. Wagner took his daughter's ashes aboard *Utah*. Nancy was supposed to be scattered at sea in a ceremonial burial in the old Navy tradition. The somber plans were interrupted by the attack on Pearl Harbor, and while Wagner was able to escape with his life, the urn containing his daughter Nancy went down with the ship off Ford Island, where it remains to this day. Every December, Mary Wagner Kreigh, the twin sister of Baby Nancy, visits Pearl Harbor, gazing out at the rusted hull of *Utah* plucking a flower from a wreath: "I throw it over into the water and thank the sailors for watching over her. She couldn't have better guardians."

Close-up view of *Utah*'s superstructure remains.

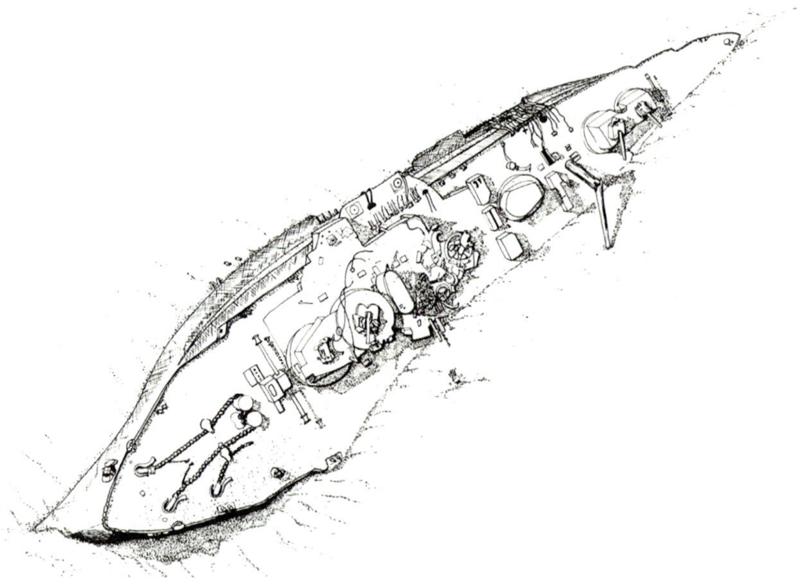

Drawing of *Utah* as the wrecks looks today. (Drawing by Jerry Livingston)

Members of the Navy Region Hawaii Ceremonial Guard march in formation at the conclusion of a ceremony in honor of a Pearl Harbor survivor and U.S.S. *Utah* crewmember.

Nina (left) and Mary (Wagner) Kreigh (right) prepare to raise the American flag at the *Utah* Memorial in Pearl Harbor at sunset on December 6, 2005.

Florida-class General Characteristics (as built)

Class	*Florida*
Name	*Florida* (BB-30) *Utah* (BB-31)
Shipyard	New York Navy Yard (BB-30) New York Shipbuilding Corporation, Camden (BB-31)
Commissioning	September 15, 1911 (BB-30) August 31, 1911 (BB-31)
Displacement (normal) Displacement (full)	21,825 long tons (22,175 t) 23,033 long tons (23,403 t)
Length (overall)	521 ft 6 in (159 m)
Beam	88 ft 6 in (26.9 m)
Draft (max)	30 ft 1 in (9.2 m)
Propulsion	4 × steam turbines (28,000 shp / 20,880 kW)
Maximum speed	21 kn (39 km/h)
Range	5,776 nmi (10,697 km) at 10 kn
Complement	1,001
Armament	10 × 12-in (305 mm)/45 cal. Mark 5 16 × 5-in (127 mm)/51 cal. 2 × 21-in (533 mm) torpedo tubes Various AA guns
Fate	Broken up 1931 (BB-30) Sunk in Pearl Harbor, December 7, 1941 (BB-31)

Wyoming-class

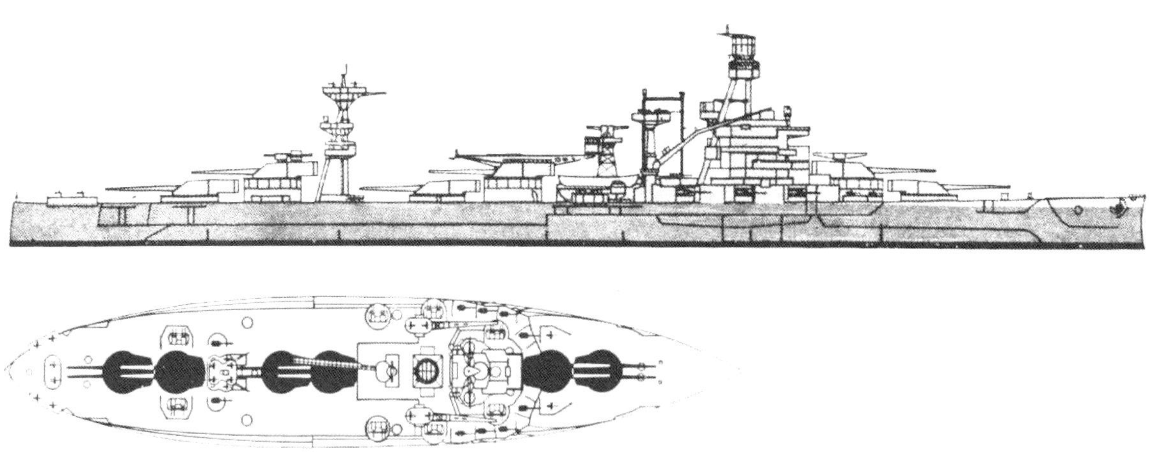

U.S.S. *Arkansas* in its original configuration, probably photographed before World War I. (U.S. Library of Congress)

In 1908, the General Board (the advisory body to the U.S. Navy), representatives of the Naval War College, and President Theodore Roosevelt—known for his keen interest in naval and military affairs—held the Newport Conference. This gathering examined various issues relating to existing and proposed battleship designs. The results of the conference led to the conception of the *Wyoming*-class, to be armed with 14-inch (356 mm) guns as the Royal Navy had already adopted the 13.5-inch (343 mm) caliber. Although the introduction of the new 14-inch gun would take at least two years, Secretary of the Navy Victor Metcalf showed strong interest in it. However, the Bureau of Construction and Repair (C&R), responsible for supervising the design, construction, maintenance, and repair of ships, argued that there was no need for this caliber as the existing 12-inch gun was powerful enough to penetrate existing armor plating at battle ranges of 8,000 to 8,500 yards (7,300 to 7,800 m). Based on the *Florida*-class, C&R submitted three individual design proposals to meet Metcalf's request: *Design 404* armed with eight 14-inch guns, *Design 502* with an additional twin turret (total of 10 14-inch guns), and *Design 601* with 12 12-inch guns.

The General Board approved two ships, *Wyoming* (BB-32) and *Arkansas* (BB-33), to be built under *Design 601*. The reason was that work on the 14-inch gun had not begun yet, and its introduction would have caused a considerable delay in the ships' completion. In addition, adopting the larger and heavier guns would have increased the displacement significantly, thus requiring the enlargement of existing harbor and dry dock facilities. *Design 502* would later become the basis for the subsequent *New York*-class.

Propulsion

The *Wyomings* were propelled by four-shaft Parsons steam turbines rated at 28,000 shp (21,000 kW). Steam was provided by 12 mixed oil-and-coal-fired Babcock & Wilcox boilers. The ships were capable of a top speed of 20.5 knots (23.6 mph; 38.0 km/h). Fuel capacity was 1,667 long tons (1,694 t) of coal and 266 long tons (270 t) of oil. The ships had a range of 6,700 nautical miles (12,400 km; 7,700 mi) at a cruising speed of 10 knots (19 km/h; 12 mph).

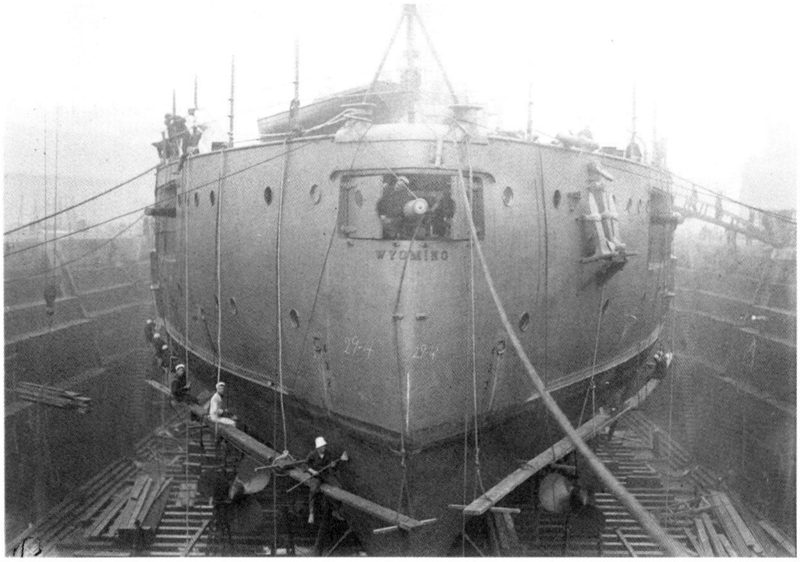

Stern view of *Wyoming*. Note the 5-inch casemate gun right above the ship's name. The *Wyoming*-class was the fourth American dreadnought design, but only an incremental improvement over the preceding *Florida*-class, and the last American battleships to use 12-inch guns.

Wyoming moored in the Philadelphia Navy Yard for "Navy Day" on October 27, 1923. October 27 was the birthday of 26th President Theodore Roosevelt (served 1901–9), who was a promoter of sea power. Note the massive crane in the background that was used to lift heavy armor plates or gun barrels aboard. (U.S. National Archives)

Arkansas and *Wyoming* were about 20 percent larger than their predecessors. This allowed the installation of a sixth gun turret, which increased the number of gun barrels to twelve. However, due to lack of space, some ammunition chambers were located very close to the boiler rooms leading to increased powder temperatures.

Armament

The main battery consisted of 12 12-inch/50 caliber Mark 7 Mod 0 guns in six twin-gun turrets. They were all placed on the centerline, with two of them in a superfiring pair forward. The other four turrets were placed aft of the superstructure in two superfiring pairs. The *Wyomings* were the only American battleships to receive the modified Mark 7 gun, which had a higher muzzle velocity (and thus higher striking velocity) than the previous Mark 5. The 12-inch guns fired an 870 lb (395 kg) shell with a 353 lb (160 kg) propellant charge producing a muzzle velocity of 2,900 ft/s (880 m/s), thus enabling the projectile to penetrate 12.3 inches (310 mm) of contemporary face-hardened armor, compared to 10.8 inches (270 mm) for the Mark 5. At a rate of 2 to 3 rounds per minute, the range was 23,900 yards (21,900 m) at 15° elevation.

The placement of the secondary battery was problematic as the experience with casemates on the main deck had shown. They were heavily drenched with seawater even in moderate seas, thus rendering them practically unusable. While placing the 5-inch (127 mm) guns in the superstructure would have added a significant amount of top weight; installing them in the forecastle (bow) would have stressed the ship's structure where the forecastle stepped down towards the main deck. The solution was a full-length forecastle allowing the casemates to be moved 4 feet (1.2 m) higher in the hull. The 16 5-inch (127 mm)/51 caliber guns were mounted in these casemates along the side of the hull. They fired a 50 lb (23 kg) shell with a charge of 24.5 lb (11.1 kg). As was standard at the time, the *Wyomings* were fitted with a two submerged 21-inch (533 mm) torpedo tubes, with one on each side in the hull. They were equipped with the Mark III Bliss-Leavitt torpedo carrying a 218 lb (99 kg) warhead. This weapon had a range of 4,000 yards (3,700 m) at a speed of up to 26.5 knots (30.5 mph; 49.1 km/h).

Protection

The *Wyoming*'s armor protection was strengthened compared to earlier battleship designs. Measuring 8 feet (2.4 m) in height, the main armor belt had a thickness of 11 inches (280 mm) along the central portion of the ship protecting the ammunition magazines and machinery spaces (armored citadel). The belt tapered to 5 inches (127 mm) toward the stern and on the bottom edge it was reduced to 9 inches (230 mm). While the

Front view of *Wyoming*'s armored conning tower, which was designed to survive hits from enemy shells. It housed observation and range-finding equipment.

belt's forward end was connected with an 11-inch-thick transverse bulkhead with the forward-most main gun barbette, the belt's aft end was connected with a bulkhead 9 inches thick.

The main armor deck over the ammunition magazines and machinery consisted of 2.5 inches (64 mm) of special-treatment steel (STS), reduced to 1.5 inches (38 mm) in less critical areas (berthing, storage rooms). The conning tower had a 3-inch (76 mm)-thick roof and 11.5-inch (292 mm)-thick sides. The main gun turrets were protected by 3-inch-thick roofs and 12-inch (305 mm) faces. The main gun barbettes had a thickness of up to 11 inches.

The battle of Tsushima during the Russo-Japanese War three years earlier had demonstrated the risk of a destroyed exhaust system: Russian battleships had had their funnel uptakes damaged, ducting the boiler smoke into the ship rather than out through the funnels. As a result, the *Wyomings* received longitudinal armored bulkheads inboard of the casemate battery designed to protect the funnel uptakes. The designers also emphasized the need for an improved underwater protection scheme. As a result, the ships were built with a torpedo bulkhead; this was the first time this feature was incorporated in an American battleship design.

Operational History

After entering service in 1912, the *Wyomings* were assigned to the Atlantic Fleet. Two years later, they supported the occupation of Veracruz during the Mexican Revolution. In 1917, during World War I, *Wyoming*, along with other American battleships, reinforced the Royal Navy's Grand Fleet and was stationed in Scapa Flow. *Arkansas*,

Wyoming passing through the Panama Canal in 1919.

after training gun crews for the expanding wartime fleet, joined its sister ship the following year. Although both ships did not see combat during the conflict, they were present when the German High Seas Fleet surrendered in Scapa Flow in November 1918.

The *Wyomings* underwent significant modifications throughout their operational lives. As aircraft increasingly became a threat, they were fitted with several 3-inch (76 mm)/50 caliber antiaircraft guns. To become less vulnerable against aerial attacks, deck armor was increased to 3.5 inches (89 mm). The roof protection of the conning tower and the gun turrets was also improved.

The 1922 Washington Naval Treaty strictly controlled and governed which modifications could be made to existing ships. While displacement could only be increased by 3,000 long tons (3,000 t), no improvements were allowed to the main armament. However, the treaty permitted upgrades to aerial and underwater defense as well to propulsion systems.

The *Wyomings* were fitted with anti-torpedo bulges, improving their underwater resistance, and providing additional fuel oil storage capacity. Their rear lattice (cage) main mast was replaced by a short tripod mast carrying searchlights and radio antennas. Some secondary guns were relocated higher in the ship, improving their workability in heavy seas. The torpedo tubes were removed as they had proven impractical. The *Wyomings* were converted to completely oil-fired boilers with the boilers trunked into a single funnel. This was much more efficient than the coal-fired arrangement, allowing a significantly greater range of 11,000 nautical miles (12,660 mi; 20,370 km).

In accordance with the 1930 London Naval Treaty, which followed the 1922 Washington Treaty, *Wyoming* was to be demilitarized and converted into a training ship in 1931, which required the removal of her anti-torpedo bulges, side armor and half of her 12-inch main armament. Over the next 10 years, the ship conducted training cruises for midshipmen and cadets.

Arkansas remained in active service with the battle fleet. As escort for troop convoys, it supported the peaceful occupation of Iceland in July 1941, a protective measure to prevent the island from falling into enemy hands as a base for German merchant raiders, including U-boats. A few months later, *Wyoming* was reassigned as a gunnery exercise ship training up to 35,000 gun crews until the end of the war and. In 1944, the ship was modernized. In the process, the three remaining 12-inch gun turrets were removed and replaced by 5-inch/38 caliber guns. New fire-control radars were also installed, allowing *Wyoming* (now *AG-17*) to train antiaircraft gunners with the modern weaponry they would use in combat.

Wyoming in its final configuration with its forward lattice (cage) removed, underway in the Atlantic in April 1945.

Arkansas in its final configuration off the American East Coast in April 1944.

Arkansas, together with other Allied warships, fires its 12-inch guns at German positions, while supporting the Omaha Beach landings at Normandy on D-Day, June 6, 1944.

Modifications to *Arkansas* were kept to a minimum. During World War II, it received a new forward tripod foremast and bridgework, as well as an increasingly powerful antiaircraft armament. By 1945, the ship carried 36 40 mm Bofors in nine quadruple mounts and 28 20 mm Oerlikons. The number of 3-inch guns had been increased to ten.

After escorting convoys to the battlefields in North Africa, *Arkansas* supported the Allied invasion of Normandy (Operation *Overlord*) along the battleship *Texas* in June 1944, bombarding German positions at Omaha Beach, before shelling Cherbourg later that month. Its next shore bombardment mission came with Operation *Dragoon*, the subsequent landings in southern France in August 1944. After transferring to the Pacific, *Arkansas*'s accurate guns shelled Japanese positions on Iwo Jima in February 1945 and on Okinawa in April.

After the end of the war in September 1945, the aging battleship joined Operation *Magic Carpet*, the repatriation of American troops who had fought in the Pacific. The following year, *Arkansas* was chosen as one of the target ships for the atomic bomb tests, named Operation *Crossroads* at Bikini Atoll. After surviving the first explosion, an airdropped bomb named *Able*, *Arkansas* was eventually sunk by the force of the second test, *Baker*, an unprecedented underwater detonation. *Wyoming* remained in service until August 1947 and was sold for scrap in October.

Wyoming's ship bell on display at the National Museum of the U.S. Navy, Washington D.C.

Wyoming-class General Characteristics (as built)

Class	*Wyoming*
Name	*Wyoming* (BB-32) *Arkansas* (BB-33)
Shipyard	William Cramp & Sons, Philadelphia (BB-32) New York Shipbuilding Corporation, Camden (BB-33)
Commissioning	September 25, 1912 (BB-32) September 17, 1912 (BB-33)
Displacement (normal) Displacement (full)	26,000 long tons (26,417 t) 27,243 long tons (27,680 t)
Length (overall)	562 ft (171)
Beam	93 ft 3 in (28.42 m)
Draft (max)	29 ft 7 in (9.02 m)
Propulsion	4 × steam turbines (28,000 shp / 20,880 kW)
Maximum speed	ca. 21 kn (39 km/h)
Range	8,000 nmi (9,210 km) at 10 kn
Complement	1,063
Armament	12 × 12-in (305 mm)/50 cal. Mark 7 21 × 5-in (127 mm)/51 cal. 2 × 21-in (533 mm) torpedo tubes Various AA guns
Fate	Sold for scrap, 1947 (BB-32) Sunk as target (Operation *Crossroads*), July 25, 1946 (BB-33)

3
The Next Step—The Super-dreadnoughts

Within five years of *Dreadnought*'s completion, armed with 10 12-inch (305 mm) guns, it was succeeded by a new generation of more powerful "super-dreadnoughts." The British *Orion*-class, armed with 10 13.5-inch (343 mm) guns, was considered the first of these, with a displacement increased by 25 percent and a broadside firepower that had doubled in weight. What made them "super" was the introduction of the heavier 13.5-inch gun caliber, and the placement of the entire main armament on the centerline, with some turrets superfiring over others.

Soon after the completion of the first British super-dreadnoughts, other naval powers followed suit. The American *New York*-class, laid down in 1911, carried 10 14-inch (356 mm) guns in response to the British 13.5-inch guns.

The battleship *New York* (BB-34) leads *Nevada* (BB-36) and *Oklahoma* (BB-37) during maneuvers, 1932. All three ships had been modernized shortly before, as can be seen from the new tripod masts with their observation devices. These masts had replaced the lattice masts.

"Crossing the T" was a naval warfare tactic, in which a line of warships crossed in front of a line of enemy ships, allowing the crossing line to bring all their guns to bear while receiving fire from only the forward guns of the enemy.

The Japanese *Fusō*-class, laid down in 1912, followed by the *Ise*-class in 1914, both carried 12 14-inch (356 mm) guns. The subsequent two ships of the *Nagato*-class, ordered in 1917, were the first dreadnoughts armed with eight 16.1-inch (410 mm) guns, making them de facto the most powerful warships in the world. The French super-dreadnoughts of the *Bretagne*-class were armed with 10 13.4-inch (340 mm) guns. When the Brazilian Navy ordered dreadnoughts, this sparked an arms race in South America, with Argentina and Chile each ordering two super-dreadnoughts from the United States and Great Britain, respectively. While other navies began adopting larger calibers, the Imperial German Navy relied on its highly effective 12-inch (305 mm) guns until 1913, when it laid down the *Bayern*-class, armed with eight 15-inch (381 mm) guns in four twin turrets.

The U.S. Navy's "standard type battleships", beginning with the *Nevada*-class, were designed with long-range engagements and plunging fire in mind; the first of these was laid down in 1912, four years before the battle of Jutland taught the dangers of long-range fire to European navies. An important feature of these battleships was the "all or nothing" armor scheme.

New York-class

The 1908 Newport Naval Conference led to the conclusion that future American warships should be armed with larger guns as a response to the increasing caliber of foreign battleships, notably the 13.5-inch (343 mm) artillery of the British *Orion*-class, and the equally powerful 12-inch (305 mm) artillery of the German *Helgoland*-class. There had already been a debate whether the two *Floridas* should carry a larger caliber than their 12-inch guns. In March 1909, U.S. Congress finally approved the construction of two *Design 601* battleships armed with six 12-inch guns, known as the *Wyoming*-class. At the same time, *Design 502* with 10 14-inch guns, also considered at some point for the *Wyomings*, eventually became the basis for the subsequent *New York*-class, consisting of

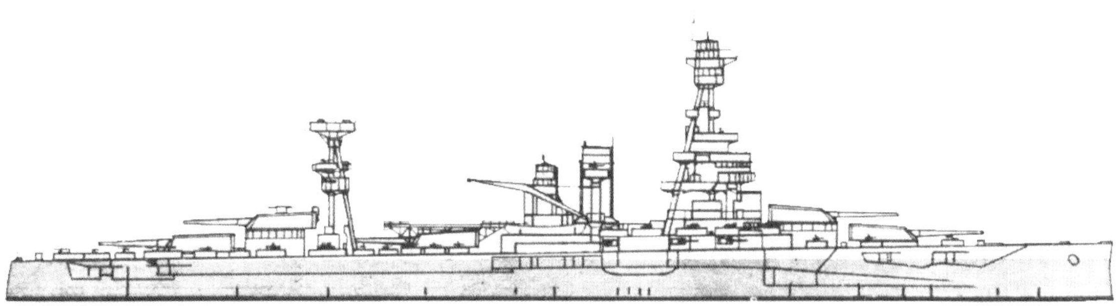

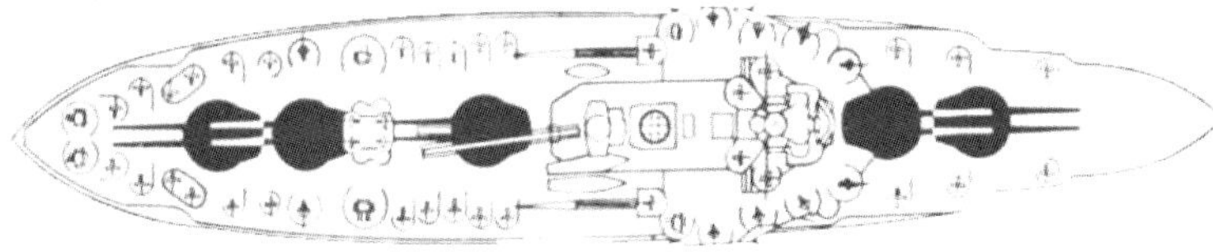

A biplane flies over the U.S.S. *New York* (BB-34) in 1918. The battleship is still in its original configuration without its own aircraft catapult, which was installed in the 1920s. The *New York*-class was the fifth of 11 separate classes planned by the U.S. Navy between 1906 and 1919, a total of 29 battleships and six battlecruisers.

New York (BB-34) and *Texas* (BB-35). Both ships had a standard displacement of 27,000 long tons (27,433 t) and a full-load displacement of 28,367 long tons (28,822 t). After undergoing significant changes and additions in armor and armament over the years, *New York* increased its displacement to 29,340 long tons (29,810 t) standard and 34,000 long tons (35,000 t) full load by 1943, while *Texas* displaced 29,500 long tons (30,000 t) standard and 32,000 long tons (33,000 t) at full load by 1945.

Armament

The main battery consisted of 10 14-inch/45 caliber guns, arranged in five twin-gun turrets. The *New Yorks* were the last American battleships built with a turret mounted amidships. Designed to fire 1,400 lb (640 kg) AP projectiles, these guns proved to have remarkable accuracy. The propellant charge consisted of four silk bags of smokeless powder, each weighing 105 lb (48 kg). At a 15° angle, the guns could fire a projectile out to 23,000 yards (21,000 m). Each gun with its breech had a weight of 142,492 lb (64,633 kg).

For defense against destroyers and torpedo boats, the *New Yorks* carried 21 5-inch (127 mm)/51 caliber guns, with 10 one each side with one at the stern. A 24.5 lb (11.1 kg) charge of smokeless powder gave a 50 lb (23 kg) projectile a velocity of 3,150 ft/s (960 m/s). The range was 15,850 yards (14,500 m) at the maximum elevation of 20°. The rate of fire was 8 to 9 rounds per minute. The accuracy of the guns was poor, especially in rough seas, as they were placed near the ends of the ship and below the main deck, and thus exposed to the waves and spray. Therefore, the number of 5-inch guns was eventually reduced to six.

The *New Yorks* were not designed with antiaircraft (AA) defense in mind, and as naval aviation made significant particularly progress during World War I, this was considered a serious weakness. As a result, both ships received several 3-inch (76 mm)/50 caliber AA guns. Their maximum range was 14,500 yards (13,300 m) at 45° elevation, while their ceiling was 27,400 feet (8,400 m) at 85° elevation.

In 1937, eight 1.1-inch (28 mm)/75 caliber AA guns in two quadruple mounts were installed to reinforce the existing antiaircraft defense. However, the attack on Pearl Harbor had brutally demonstrated that prewar AA weaponry was totally inadequate to defend ships against modern aircraft. Consequently, the *New Yorks* were extensively refitted with large amounts of light antiaircraft guns at the expense of the 1.1-inch quad mounts, which were replaced by 24 Bofors 40-mm guns in six quadruple mounts (later increased to 40 guns) and 42 Oerlikon 20 mm single mount guns. The 3-inch AA gun armament was increased to 10 guns.

Crewmembers posing for a photo on *Texas*'s forward 14-inch gun turrets, 1918. The original range was 23,000 yards, which was increased to 34,300 yards by increasing the gun barrels' elevation during modernization.

The modernized *New York* together with the new carrier U.S.S. *Enterprise* (CV-6) at Naval Base Norfolk, Virginia, 1938. The image symbolizes the U.S. Navy's mindset, as its leadership relied on modernized battleships on the one hand while developing aircraft carriers on the other.

While the preceding *Wyomings* were built with two torpedo tubes, the *New Yorks* were fitted with four as advances in torpedo performance had increased the prominence of this weapon. While two were placed at the bow on either side, the other two were at the stern on either side. The torpedo rooms held 12 Bliss-Leavitt Mark 3 torpedoes and 12 naval defense mines in total. During a 1925–26 refit, all torpedo tubes were removed.

Protection

The armor suite strongly resembled the design of the *Wyomings* with just minor improvements. They were protected by a 12-inch (305 mm) side armor belt tapering to 10 inches (254 mm). The *New Yorks* were the first to feature an armored central plotting room below decks. However, although enclosed in a thin box of splinter armor, it was located on top of the armored deck, which was 2 inches (51 mm) thick. The main gun turret's armor was 14 inches on the face, 4 inches (102 mm) on the top, 2 inches on the sides and 8 inches (203 mm) on the rear. Their barbettes had a thickness between 10 and 12 inches. The massive conning tower was protected by 12 inches of armor on the sides and 4 inches on their tops.

Propulsion

The *New Yorks* were built with two dual-acting triple expansion reciprocating steam engines. Their 28,100 shp (20,954 kW) allowed a top speed of 21 knots (24 mph; 39 km/h). Steam was provided by 14 Babcock & Wilcox coal-fired boilers.

Initially, various design proposals suggested a 14-percent increase in power to 32,000 shp (24,000 kW) over *Wyoming*'s 28,000 shp (21,000 kW). However, it was discovered that the reciprocating engine's greater propulsive efficiency allowed a reduction in power, so that only 28,100 hp was needed to achieve the required 21 knots. While they were the last American battleship powered by coal, the succeeding *Nevada*-class was conceived with fuel oil in mind. Designed to carry 2,850 long tons (2,900 t) of coal, the *New Yorks* had a range of up to 7,060 nautical miles (8,120 mi; 13,080 km) at a cruising speed of 10 knots (12 mph; 19 km/h).

U.S.S. *Texas*'s navigation bridge with various devices such as machine telegraphs and voice tubes, 1919.

Operational History

After entering service, both ships participated in the occupation of Veracruz, Mexico, for several months in 1914. During World War I, they supported the Royal Navy conducting blockade duty and escorting transatlantic convoys which brought food to Great Britain. While *Texas* was the first American warship to fire on a German ship during a convoy mission in 1917, *New York* twice came into contact with German U-boats and is believed to have (accidentally) sunk one.

By the mid-1920s, the *New Yorks* were considered obsolete. While several other aging capital ships were either scrapped or converted to training ships, *New York* and *Texas* were chosen for modernization. In accordance with the 1922 Washington Naval Treaty, both ships received modifications to increase their speed and improve their protection against aircraft and underwater attacks, thus adding an additional 3,000 long tons (3,000 t) to their displacement. Each ship's beam was widened by fitting new anti-torpedo bulges, though these made maneuvering harder at low speeds. Therefore, the *New Yorks* rolled badly, thus reducing their gunfire accuracy in rough seas.

Both ships were converted to carry fuel oil with a capacity of 5,200 long tons (5,300 t). Each received six new Bureau Express oil-fired boilers replacing the 14 older coal-fired boilers with no loss of power. The twin funnels were trunked into one, aft of the forward superstructure. Tripod masts replaced the lattice (cage) masts, with the forward tripod carrying a control tower on its top. A tower built amidships contained additional fire-control devices to back up the foremast system. A new aircraft catapult was placed on top of turret No. 3, and cranes were installed on either side of the funnel for aircraft and boat handling.

U.S.S. *Texas* during a presidential naval review in Hampton Roads, Virginia, June 1927.

Battleships *Texas* (BB-35) and *New York* (BB-34) on the Hudson River, New York, lighting up the night sky with their powerful searchlights in search of imaginary aerial attackers, May 3, 1939.

U.S.S. *New York* (BB-34)

Following the outbreak of World War II in September 1939, the battleship participated in the Neutrality Patrol escorting convoys between New York and Iceland. As the United States was still neutral at this point, it established a combined air and naval patrol along the American Atlantic coast, including the Caribbean. Ships, operating under the Neutrality Patrol, also escorted British ships and reported the sighting of German surface vessels and

A rare color photo depicts U.S.S. *New York* arriving at New York City from the Pacific following the end of World War II, October 1945. In its active career, the ship received various modernization including sea planes, a capable antiaircraft armament, and effective radar systems.

New York was eventually sunk as a target, off Hawaii, on July 8, 1948.

submarines. This proximity between British and American ships led to exchanges of strikes with German naval forces before the United States officially entered the war.

In November 1942, *New York* saw action during Operation *Torch*, the Allied invasion of North Africa, bombarding shore batteries threatening the amphibious landings. After escorting convoys and training crews, the ship was transferred to the Pacific Fleet late in the war. In February 1945, *New York* supported the landings on Iwo Jima, followed by the invasion of Okinawa in April. During the fighting, it was lightly damaged by a Japanese kamikaze aircraft. In 1946 the aging battleship was used as one of the target ships during the Operation *Crossroads* atomic bomb tests at Bikini Atoll. After surviving the two blasts, the damaged, radioactive ship was studied for its effects, before being sunk as a target in Hawaiian waters in 1948.

The keel-up *New York* just before sinking below the waves.

U.S.S. *Texas* (BB-35)

Just like its sister ship, *Texas* participated in the Neutrality Patrol, supported Allied landings in North Africa, and escorted convoys to North African and European ports throughout 1943. On June 6, 1944, it supported Operation *Overlord*, the Allied invasion of the Normandy beaches in France. With its powerful and accurate artillery, *Texas* shelled German fortifications and strongholds on or near the beaches, thus helping the invading forces to create a beachhead. In July its guns supported Operation *Dragoon*, the Allied invasion of southern France. After a major overhaul, *Texas* was transferred to the Pacific, where it provided fire support for the invasions of Iwo Jima in February 1945 and Okinawa two months later. Shortly after the war's end, the obsolete battleship was decommissioned and moved to San Jacinto State Park, Texas, and converted into a museum ship. *Texas* is the only surviving dreadnought-type battleship in the world and for this reason it represents a special engineering museum for capital ships from the World War I era.

Texas in 1943, having received numerous 20 and 40 mm antiaircraft guns during World War II.

In its long active career, *Texas* also served as a technological testbed as it was the first American battleship to mount antiaircraft guns and use directors and range-keepers to control fire.

Texas is the only preserved dreadnought-type battleship in the world. The Japanese *Mikasa* is the world's only surviving pre-dreadnought battleship.

In 1948, *Texas* became the first permanent battleship memorial museum in the United States. U.S.S. *Oregon* (BB-3) was displayed as a floating museum in Portland, Oregon, from 1925 to 1941, but was scrapped in 1956.

In 2022 *Texas* was moved to a dry dock in Galveston, Texas, to undergo an extensive repair project to preserve it for future generations.

New York-class General Characteristics (as built)

Class	*New York*
Name	*New York* (BB-33) *Texas* (BB-34)
Shipyard	New York Navy Yard (BB-33) Newport News Shipbuilding Company (BB-34)
Commissioning	May 15, 1914 (BB-33) March 12, 1914 (BB-34)
Displacement (normal) Displacement (full)	27,000 long tons (27,433 t) 28,367 long tons (28,822 t)
Length (overall)	573 ft (175 m)
Beam	95 ft 2.5 in (29.02 m)
Draft (max)	29 ft 7 in (9.02 m)
Propulsion	2 × triple expansion steam engines (28,100 shp / 20,954 kW)
Maximum speed	ca. 21 kn (39 km/h)
Range	7,060 nmi (13,080 km) at 10 kn
Complement	1,042
Armament	10 × 14-in (356 mm)/45 cal. Mark 7 21 × 5-in (127 mm)/51 cal. 2 × 21-in (533 mm) torpedo tubes Various AA guns
Fate	Sunk as target, July 8, 1948 (BB-34) Preserved as museum ship (BB-35)

Nevada-class

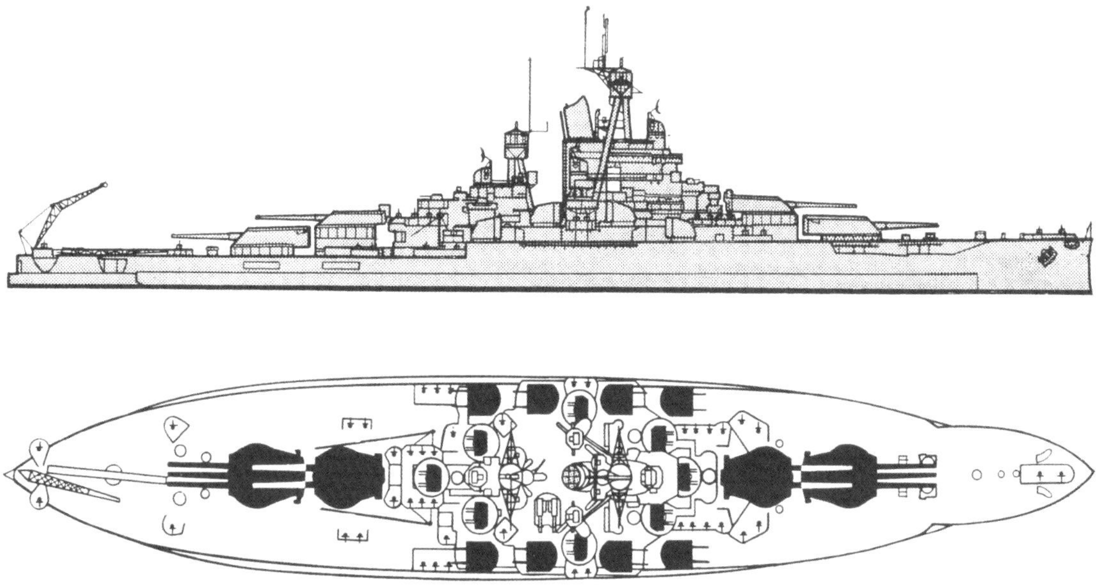

U.S.S. *Oklahoma* (BB-37) shortly before its launch in March 1914, at New York Shipbuilding Company, Camden, New Jersey.

Ms. Lorena J. Cruce, daughter of the Governor of Oklahoma, christens U.S.S. *Oklahoma* on March 23, 1914, before the ship slides into its element.

"All or nothing" armor

Devised with the knowledge that engagement ranges between battle fleets were growing greater as main battery calibers increased, the "all or nothing" concept moved away from previous designs that used heavy, medium, and light armor. The new system envisioned that, at long ranges, ships would be attacked with only AP projectiles, stoppable only by heavy armor. Medium or light armor would only serve to detonate the shells. This concept involved heavily armoring only the vital areas of a ship while the rest received no armor, thus providing "either total (best possible) or negligible protection." Compared to previous armoring schemes, "all or nothing" ships had thicker armor covering a smaller proportion of the hull. The arrangement was made watertight creating an armored raft that contained enough reserve buoyancy to keep the ship afloat even if the unarmored ends were completely flooded. The U.S. Navy introduced this concept in its "standard-type" battleships, starting with the *Nevada*-class, followed by other navies.

U.S.S. *Nevada* (BB-36) on preliminary trials in 1915. It was the first to adopt "the all or nothing" armor. The two *Nevadas* also introduced three-gun turrets and oil-fired water-tube boilers to the American battle fleet.

Standard-type Battleship

The standard-type battleship was a series of 12 American battleships spanning five classes (*Nevada, Pennsylvania, New Mexico, Tennessee, Colorado*), ordered between 1911 and 1916 and commissioned between 1916 and 1923. These were considered super-dreadnoughts, with the ships of the final two classes incorporating many lessons from the battle of Jutland, the largest engagement between British and German dreadnoughts and pre-dreadnoughts in history. The standard-type battleships received numerous structural standardizations to facilitate future maneuvering of the fleet. This also included the conversion to oil-fired boilers and the all-or-nothing armor scheme. The 12 ships formed the U.S. Navy's main battle line in the interwar period, while several of the 10 earlier dreadnoughts were either scrapped or relegated to secondary duties like training or target practice. The Washington Naval Treaty of 1922 had limited the total number and size of battleships and required the cancelation of some ships under construction, so new battleships were not built until the late 1930s.

The *Nevada*-class was conceived during strong political opposition to the constant growth in size (and associated increase in cost) of new battleships being built, which had accelerated with the development of the dreadnought-type. In the early 1900s, the U.S. Navy had embarked on a program to build two new battleships per year, which had been approved by President Theodore Roosevelt. In 1904, however, Congress began to disapprove Navy requests, as it considered them too costly, thus sometimes permitting only one new ship per year, and occasionally no ship at all. Roosevelt's successor, William H. Taft, had little success in changing the decisionmakers' minds in Congress but was at least able to secure two new ships for Fiscal Year 1912, *Nevada* (BB-36) and *Oklahoma* (BB-37). Woodrow Wilson, who was elected president that year, was against what he considered excessive naval spending. As a result, Joseph Daniels, his Secretary of the Navy, blocked the General Board's proposals for larger and thus more expensive battleships, but allowing for two (somewhat smaller) ships per year, resulting in the standard-type battleships of which the two *Nevadas* were the first.

Initial designs based on the *New Yorks* had been prepared by the Navy's Bureau of Construction and Repair (C&R), responsible for supervising the design, construction, maintenance, and repair of ships, in May 1910. The General Board, not comfortable with the installation of five and six twin-gun turrets on earlier dreadnoughts, required the *Nevadas* to be built with four triple-gun turrets boasting a main battery of 12 14-inch (356 mm) guns, two more than on the preceding *New Yorks*, but with four turrets instead of five. To comply, an arrangement like that on contemporary British battlecruisers was used. Thus, two guns were to be placed in the ship's centerline in front of the superstructure and two behind it. This arrangement made the installation of the gun barbettes with their ammunition and powder elevators inside the armored citadel easier, thus saving weight. Additional requirements included a minimum speed of 21 knots, an 11-inch belt armor, a secondary armament of 17 5-inch (127 mm) guns, four torpedo tubes and an "all or nothing" armor scheme, protecting only vital parts of the ship.

A series of studies was made with speeds of 20 knots (23 mi; 37 km/h), 20.5 knots (23.6 mi; 38 km/h), and 21 knots, a main armament of eight to 12 guns, and an armor belt with thicknesses of 11 inches (280 mm) and 14 inches (356 mm). C&R noted that the armor deck would considerably strengthen the hull but pointed out that the 11-inch belt would be insufficient to resist the latest foreign main guns. In 1910, Congress authorized two ships (BB-36 and BB-37) for Fiscal Year 1912 but limited their size to 27,000 long tons; this was too low for C&R's proposals, thus necessitating a redesign. By this time, the first generation of American dreadnoughts had entered service, so operational experiences could be incorporated into the redesign.

Eventually, the Board selected a 10-gun and 20.5 knot design, which had a 14-inch belt that tapered at the top and bottom edge to save weight. An issue was the triple turret, which was the design's linchpin as the weight savings made the heavier belt possible and it corrected design weaknesses present in the earlier battleship classes featuring five or six turrets. As the U.S. Navy had never built a three-gun turret, there were concerns that a single hit could disable all three gun barrels, and that three holes in the turret face would weaken the armor scheme too much.

However, Secretary of the Navy Daniels approved the finalized *Nevada*-class design without a completed and tested turret design. This decision was considered risky as the design might not have been successful. An experimental gun turret, completed in summer 1912, however, proved the concept to be functional. As the finalized design adopted a 10-gun main armament, only two of the four turrets were triple mounts, one forward and one aft, with twin-gun turrets superfiring over them.

Armament

The *Nevada*'s main battery consisted of 10 14-inch/45 caliber Mark 3 guns mounted in two twin and two triple turrets. To keep the latter as compact and light as possible, they had all three barrels supported by two trunnions, requiring all three guns to be elevated as a unit. Both twin turrets were fitted with armored rangefinders placed on top of their roofs. The 14-inch guns fired a 1,400 lb (635 kg) AP shell at a muzzle velocity of 2,600 feet per second (790 m/s). At a maximum elevation of 15°, the range was up to 21,140 yards (19,330 m). During test-firing, the triple turret revealed excessive dispersion caused by interference between the projectiles while in flight. The solution was to fire each gun individually, separated by a tenth of a second apiece.

To defend themselves against destroyers and torpedo boats, the *Nevadas* were armed with 21 5-inch (127 mm)/51 caliber Mark 8 guns in individual mounts. Twelve were installed in casemates in the forecastle deck, six on either side of the hull, and another six were placed in casemates toward the stern at main deck level. One 5-inch gun was located directly at the stern of the ship. At 45° elevation, this weapon fired a 50 lb (23 kg) shell up to 20,142 yards (18,418 m). At 15°, the maximum range was 14,050 yards (12,850 m). As the operational experience with earlier battleships had already proven, these guns became extremely wet, thus making them often unusable. In addition, both ships received several 3-inch (76 mm)/50 caliber antiaircraft guns. Their maximum range was 14,500 yards (13,300 m) at 45° elevation, while their ceiling was 27,400 feet (8,400 m) at 85° elevation.

Crewmen exercising with one of *Nevada*'s 5-inch casemate guns, circa 1921.

Like virtually all battleships of the period, the *Nevadas* received a pair of 21-inch (533 mm) torpedo tubes submerged below the waterline, one on each broadside. They were equipped with Mark 8 Bliss-Leavitt torpedoes carrying a 321 lb (146 kg) warhead. This weapon had a range of 12,500 yards (11,400 m) at a speed of up to 27 knots (50 km/h; 31 mph).

Protection

The *Nevada*'s side armor belt had a thickness of 13.5 inches (343 mm) in the central section protecting the vital parts (magazines and engine spaces). It had a total height of 17 feet 4.6 inches (5 m), of which 8 feet 6 inches (2.59 m) was below the hull's waterline. To save weight, the belt tapered to 8 inches (203 mm) at its bottom edge. This idea relied on the assumption that enemy projectiles that fell short and passed through the water would be slowed down significantly by the water's resistance, thus reducing their ability to penetrate thick armor plating. On either end of the belt, a transverse bulkhead, 8 to 13 inches thick, connected both sides, thus forming an armored citadel. As the bow and stern were considered not vital, they were left unarmored.

The 3 inch (76 mm) armor deck was connected to the top of the belt. It consisted of three layers of STS over the armored citadel and 6.25 inches (159 mm) over the propeller shafts. One deck below was another 1.5 inch (38 mm) thick armor layer designed to absorb splinters from shells and bombs that detonated when they hit the upper deck.

Resting on 13-inch barbettes, the main turrets were heavily armored; the triple turret faces had a thickness of 18 inches (457 mm), with 10 inch (254 mm) sides and 5 inch (127 mm) roofs. The twin turrets were slightly thinner, with 16 inch (406 mm) faces and 9 inch (229 mm) sides. Both turret types had 9-inch-thick rear sides. The conning tower's armor consisted of 16-inch-thick sides and an 8-inch roof, with the latter made of STS. The uptakes from the boilers to the funnel were protected by a conical mantlet up to 13 inches (330 mm) thick.

Propulsion

Operational experience with preceding battleships resulted in the decision to build the *Nevadas* exclusively with oil-fired boilers. These provided several advantages, including the ability to refuel at sea, a considerable reduction in boiler room crews, more compact boiler rooms and greater fuel efficiency. Moreover, the smaller boiler rooms shortened the length of armor necessary to protect the vital spaces such as the engines and magazines, thus saving weight. *Nevada* was the first American battleship to be built with reduction-geared cruising turbines. These could be clutched into the high-pressure turbines to improve fuel economy at low speeds. Steam was provided by 12 oil-fired Yarrow water-tube boilers. *Nevada*'s engines were rated at 26,500 shp (19,800 kW). Despite its designed top speed of 20.5 knots, the ship reached 20.9 knots (24.1 mph; 38.7 km/h) from 26,291 shp (19,605 kW) on speed trials. *Oklahoma*, on the other hand, received two vertical triple-expansion engines and 12 oil-fired Babcock & Wilcox boilers. As this propulsion system was prone to excessive vibration, the Navy considered a conversion to diesel engines in 1925, but their weight made this idea unfeasible. Rated at 24,800 shp (18,500 kW), *Oklahoma* reached 20.5 knots. The designed endurance of both ships was 8,000 nautical miles (9,200 mi; 15,000 km) at a cruising speed of 10 knots (12 mph; 19 km/h) but fell by about 1,500 nautical miles under service conditions.

Operational History

The *Nevadas* deployed to Ireland in 1918 to escort convoys but saw no action. After the war, they were transferred to the Pacific Fleet, where they spent most of the 1920s and 1930s. During this period, they conducted training operations and made several long-distance cruises, including to Australia and New Zealand in 1925 and *Oklahoma*'s voyage to Europe in 1936. As tensions with Japan began to rise in the late 1930s over the latter's

U.S.S. *Oklahoma* (BB-37) during its modernization at the Puget Sound Navy Yard, Bremerton, Washington, in April 1931. The tripod masts were fitted with platforms for .50 caliber antiaircraft machine guns, fire-control devices, and searchlights. Its sister ship *Nevada* (BB-36) is visible in the background.

The modernized *Oklahoma* transiting the Panama Canal, in October 1936, during its deployment to rescue American refugees in Spain during the civil war there.

waging of the Second Sino-Japanese War, the United States began to prepare for the increasingly likely prospect of war. In 1940, the Pacific Fleet was transferred from its homeport, San Pedro, California, to Pearl Harbor, Hawaii, to deter further aggression.

In 1919, both ships were fitted with launch platforms for aircraft on their superfiring turrets. These proved to be problematic as they prevented the guns from being fired without damaging the platforms. In addition, they limited the gun barrels' ability to fully elevate and depress. The *Nevadas* were considerably modernized between 1927 and 1930. While both ships were fitted with six more efficient Bureau Express boilers, *Nevada* received new turbines from the (not commissioned) battleship *North Dakota*. While the designed speed remained virtually the same, power output dropped slightly to 25,000 shp (19,000 kW). The fuel capacity for both ships was also increased, to 3,148 long tons (3,199 t) normally and 6,274 long tons (6,375 t) under wartime conditions, thus increasing the range to 15,700 nautical miles (18,100 mi; 29,100 km) at 10 knots and about 6,000 nautical miles at 15 knots.

The re-boilering saved a significant amount of weight that was used to reinforce the deck armor from 3 to 5 inches (127 mm). The main gun turrets were modified to allow an elevation of up to 30°, increasing their maximum range to 34,300 yards (31,400 m). Besides receiving eight .50 caliber (13 mm) Browning machine guns, the existing eight 3-inch antiaircraft guns were replaced with eight 5-inch/25 caliber guns. Both ships were fitted with torpedo bulges, increasing their beam to 107 feet 11 inches (32.89 m), while their torpedo tubes were removed. Their lattice masts were replaced with more robust tripod masts; they received a pair of aircraft catapults, one installed on the fantail, the other atop the rear superfiring turret. The modifications increased the *Nevada*'s displacement to 30,500 long tons (31,000 t) as designed and a maximum of 33,901 long tons (34,445 t) at full load.

Nevada in dry dock at the Pearl Harbor Navy Yard, Hawaii, circa 1935. Note men painting the hull from stages rigged over the side, and the outline of the port side anti-torpedo blister where it merges with her forward hull. The blisters were added to improve the ship's underwater protection against torpedoes and mines.

The attack on Pearl Harbor as seen from a Japanese aircraft. Ships are, from lower left to right: U.S.S. *Nevada* (BB-36) with flag raised at stern; U.S.S. *Arizona* (BB-39) with rear ship U.S.S. *Vestal* (AR-4) outboard; U.S.S. *Tennessee* (BB-43) with U.S.S. *West Virginia* (BB-48) outboard; U.S.S. *Maryland* (BB-46) with U.S.S. *Oklahoma* (BB-37) outboard; fleet oiler U.S.S. *Neosho* (AO-23) and U.S.S. *California* (BB-44). *West Virginia*, *Oklahoma*, and *California* have been torpedoed, as marked by ripples and spreading oil, and the first two are listing to port. Torpedo drop splashes and running tracks are visible at left and center.

On December 7, 1941, some 350 aircraft launched from six Japanese aircraft carriers in two waves attacked the American fleet moored in Pearl Harbor. The battleship *Oklahoma* was struck by aerial torpedoes and quickly began to capsize before receiving additional torpedo hits. When the ship rolled over, its massive superstructure and masts prevented it from fully inverting, thus coming to rest on its port side in the shallow harbor.

The crew suffered heavy casualties, with 429 officers and enlisted men killed or missing. Many men were trapped inside the capsized hull. Rescue efforts began immediately and continued into the night, in several cases succeeding to evacuate men trapped inside. Julio DeCastro, a Hawaiian civilian shipyard worker, was able to organize a team that saved more than 30 men. This was a particularly tricky and dangerous operation as cutting open the hull released trapped air, thus raising the water levels around the entombed sailors, while cutting in the wrong sections could ignite stored fuel. It is likely that some survivors could not be located or reached in time.

Oklahoma was too seriously damaged to return to service. As a result, the wreck was righted in 1943 and partially dismantled before being sold for scrap. While being towed from Pearl Harbor to San Francisco May 1947, the once-proud battleship slipped its towing line and sank.

Hit by torpedoes, *Oklahoma* capsized (view from aft). The battleship U.S.S. *Maryland* (BB-46) is visible at right.

Cardboard model of *Oklahoma* showing the individual compartments to give the salvage experts a sufficient overview of the interior spaces for the planned salvage operations.

Located aft of the battleship *Arizona* during the attack, *Nevada* was not moored alongside another battleship off Ford Island and was therefore able to maneuver, unlike the other battleships present. It was struck by a single torpedo, but was able to get underway, the only battleship to do so during the attack. The ship received several bomb hits as it moved through the harbor trying to reach the open sea. As the crew feared that *Nevada* might be sunk in the channel that connected Pearl Harbor with the ocean, thus blocking the port entrance, it was eventually decided to beach the ship at a place called Hospital Point. It suffered relatively minor casualties, with about 60 men killed and more than 100 wounded.

After being refloated in February 1942, *Nevada* entered dry dock for temporary repairs at Pearl Harbor so that it could sail to the Puget Sound Navy Yard, Washington, for major repairs and modernization. Here, the tripod mainmast and armored conning tower were removed to save weight and make space for a large bridge structure. The ship also received a new secondary battery consisting of 16 5-inch /38 caliber Mark 12 dual-purpose guns (against surface and aerial targets) in eight twin-gun mounts and Mark 37 fire-control directors. These guns fired a 55.18 lb (25.03 kg) shell to a maximum range of 17,392 yards (15,903 m) or a maximum altitude of 37,200 feet (11,300 m) at an elevation of 45°. The light antiaircraft armament was also replaced. *Nevada* now boasted 36 Bofors 40-mm (1.6-inch) guns in nine quadruple mounts and 38 Oerlikon 20 mm (0.79-inch) cannons in single mounts.

Removal of 5-inch projectiles during the salvage operations.

Aerial view of *Oklahoma*'s salvage operations toward shore with ship in 90° position, March 1943.

After returning to service in 1943, *Nevada* primarily supported amphibious operations including the recapture of the Aleutian Islands in the North Pacific in spring. During the Normandy landings in June 1944, the ship shelled German positions as the Allied soldiers fought inland, followed by similar shore bombardment operations against other ports in occupied France, including Cherbourg. In August, it supported Operation *Dragoon*, the invasion of southern France, which included damaging the French battleship *Strasbourg*, then under German control.

In early 1945, *Nevada* joined several other battleships for an intensive bombardment of Iwo Jima in the Pacific for several days before U.S. Marines went ashore in February. The ship's last combat mission was fire support during the subsequent invasion of Okinawa in spring 1945.

Close view from forward with *Oklahoma* in about 68° position, March 1943.

After it was righted, *Oklahoma*'s holes were closed and the ship was refloated.

Obsolete and worn out after nearly three decades of service when World War II ended, *Nevada* was allocated to the fleet of target ships in Operation *Crossroads* at Bikini Atoll. The target fleet included several other battleships, including the captured Japanese *Nagato*. *Nevada* was used as the aiming point for the first test, an airdropped bomb named *Able* on July 1, 1946, as the U.S. Navy deemed it to be the most resilient of the battleships. The bomb missed the target and inflicted minimal damage. The subsequent test, an underwater blast named *Baker*, took place on July 24, which also failed to sink *Nevada*. The contaminated ship was towed to Pearl Harbor for further examinations and experiments before it was finally sunk off Hawaii in conventional weapon tests in 1948.

U.S.S. *Oklahoma* survivor George Brown (with National Park Service employee Eileen Martinez) visiting the U.S.S. *Oklahoma* Memorial located on Ford Island, Pearl Harbor. His quote about the sinking of his ship can read on top of the memorial plaque.

Nevada beached and burning on December 7, 1941 at Hospital Point after receiving torpedo and bomb hits. The harbor Tugboat *Hoga* (YT-146) is alongside its port bow, helping to fight fires on the battleship's forecastle.

Nevada-class General Characteristics (as built)

Class	*Nevada*
Name	*Nevada* (BB-36) Oklahoma (BB-37)
Shipyard	Fore River Shipyard, Quincy, Massachusetts (BB-36) New York Shipbuilding Corporation (BB-37)
Commissioning	March 11, 1916 (BB-36) May 2, 1916 (BB-37)
Displacement (normal) Displacement (full)	27,500 long tons (27,900 t) 28,400 long tons (28,900 t)
Length (overall)	583 ft (178 m)
Beam	95 ft 2.5 in (29.0 m)
Draft (max)	28 ft 6 in (8.7 m)
Propulsion	*Nevada*: 2 × steam turbines (26,500 shp / 19,800 kW) *Oklahoma*: 2 × triple expansion steam engines (24,800 shp / 18,500 kW)
Maximum speed	ca. 21 kn (39 km/h)
Range	8,000 nmi (14,816 km) at 10 kn
Complement	864
Armament	10 × 14-in (356 mm)/45 cal. 21 × 5-in (127 mm)/51 cal. 2 × 21-in (533 mm) torpedo tubes Various AA guns
Fate	Sunk as target, July 31, 1948 (BB-36) Hulk sank under tow, May 17, 1947 (BB-37)

Hole in *Nevada*'s port side caused by a Japanese Type 91 aerial torpedo. The view runs from about frame 37 at left to about frame 44 at right. *Nevada*'s side armor is visible inside the hole's upper section.

Nevada after its overhaul and modernization following the attack on Pearl Harbor. The ship's silhouette has significantly changed, to now resemble the new *South Dakota*-class. Note the new 5-inch gun turrets on both sides of the superstructure.

Boy Scout Troop 948 from Long Beach, California, marching alongside the replica of U.S.S. *Nevada* at the 48th Annual City of Torrance Armed Forces' Day Parade in 2007.

Pennsylvania-class

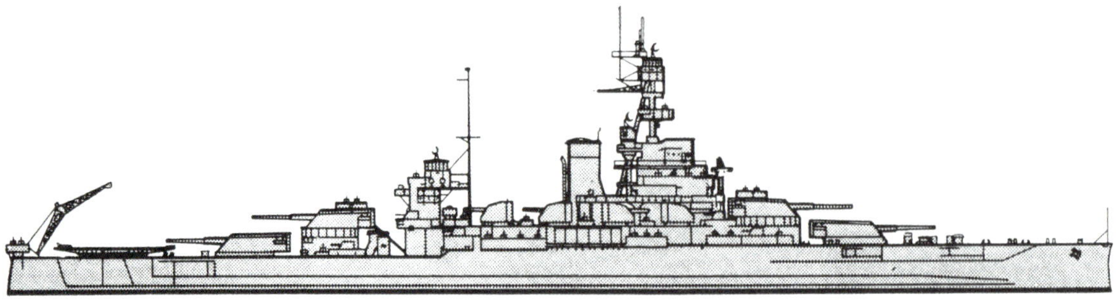

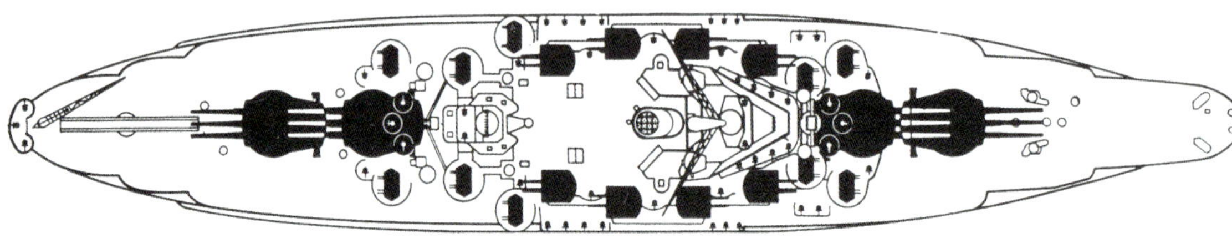

The *Nevada*-class, commissioned in 1916, represented a leap forward from previous American and some contemporary foreign battleship designs. They were the first to employ the "all or nothing" armor scheme and the first of the "standard-type" battleships. In 1911, the General Board's request for the next class of two ships for Fiscal Year 1913 included the implementation of the recent innovations incorporated in the *Nevadas*. The main requirements were a main battery of 12 14-inch guns in triple turrets, a secondary battery of 22 5-inch (127 mm) guns, an armor protection scheme equivalent to that of the *Nevadas* and a top speed of 21 knots (24 mph; 39 km/h).

U.S.S. *Pennsylvania* (BB-38) in its original configuration on the East River, New York City, 1919. The Brooklyn Bridge is in the background.

The first sketch created by C&R featured a rather long ship of about 625 feet (191.5 m) and 30,000 long tons (30,481 t) displacement with a 12.5-inch (320 mm) armor belt, which was actually thinner than the *Nevadas*'. As this protection was considered unsatisfactory, C&R prepared various proposals in 1912. These included designs with reciprocating engines or turbines, different belts ranging from 13.5 to 15 inches (343 to 381 mm) and turret barbettes up to 14 inches thick. While some gave up half a knot of speed in favor of armor, one design called for four triple turrets and was 1,200 tons lighter than the preceding class. The question of whether to install twin or triple turrets was also still up for debate, as the *Nevadas* had not been completed yet. Consequently, the Bureau of Ordnance wanted to wait for the test results conduced with *Nevada*'s guns before choosing 14- or 16-inch guns.

In 1912, the General Board finally chose the design with about 30,000 long tons (30,481 t), a length of 600 feet (183 m) 12 14-inch guns and an armor belt of up to 13.5 inches, thus meeting all requirements for the two ships of the future *Pennsylvania*-class, *Pennsylvania* (BB-38) and *Arizona* (BB-39).

Armament

The *Pennsylvanias* were armed with 12 14-inch/45 caliber guns in triple-gun turrets, numbered from I to IV from front to rear. These could not elevate independently. At a maximum elevation of 15°, the guns had a range of 21,140 yards (19,330 m). The rate of fire was between 1.25–1.75 rounds per minute. Each ship could carry 100 projectiles for each gun (1,200 in total).

For the defense against torpedo attacks from destroyers and torpedo boats, the ships received 22 5-inch (127 mm)/51 caliber guns, which had also been installed in the preceding *Nevadas*. They were mounted in individual casemates in the sides of the hull, thus being vulnerable to spray. At 15° elevation, their maximum range was 14,050 yards (12,850 m); at 45°, it was up to 20,142 yards (18,418 m). Each gun had a supply of up to 230 rounds of ammunition (5,060 in total). Four 3-inch (76 mm)/50 caliber AA guns were installed for air defense. Their maximum range was 14,500 yards (13,300 m) at 45° elevation, while their ceiling was 27,400 feet (8,400 m) at 85° elevation. The ships were also fitted with two submerged 21-inch (533 mm) torpedo tubes carrying 24 Bliss-Leavitt Mark 3 torpedoes.

Protection

Like the *Nevadas*, the *Pennsylvanias* featured an "all-or-nothing" armor scheme protecting only the most vital parts of the battleships. The side belt, which was made of Krupp armor and developed in Germany, had a thickness of 13.5 inches (343 mm) covering the machinery spaces and ammunition and powder magazines. It had a total height of 17 feet 6 inches (5.3 m), of which 8 feet 9.75 inches (2.7 m) was below the hull's waterline. To save weight, the belt tapered to 8 inches (203 mm) at its bottom edge. On either end of the belt, a transverse bulkhead, 8 to 13 inches thick, connected both sides, forming the armored citadel. As the bow and stern were not considered vital, they were left unarmored. The triple turret faces had a thickness of 18 inches (457 mm), with 9-to-10-inch (229 to 254 mm) thick sides and 5-inch (127 mm) roofs.

The main armor deck had a thickness of three steel plates totaling 3 inches (76 mm). Over the steering gear it increased to 6.25 inches (159 mm) in two plates. Below the main armor deck was the splinter deck ranging from 1.5 to 2 inches (38 to 51 mm) in thickness, designed to absorb splinters from projectiles that detonated when they hit the upper deck.

The armor of the main guns' barbettes had a thickness between 4.5 and 13 inches (114 and 330 mm). The massive conning tower had 16 inches (406 mm) of armor and an 8-inch-thick roof.

The uptakes from the boilers to the funnel were protected by a conical mantlet up to 15 inches (381 mm) thick. A 3-inch torpedo bulkhead to absorb the impact of torpedoes was installed 9 feet 6 inches (2.9 m) inboard from the ship's side. In addition, the ships were built with a full double bottom for protection against mines.

People admiring U.S.S. *Arizona* (BB-39) during a naval review in New York City, 1918.

Propulsion

The machinery consisted of four direct-drive steam turbine sets with geared cruising turbines (the latter for extended range). While *Pennsylvania* was fitted with Curtis turbines, its sister ship *Arizona* received Parsons turbines. Steam was provided by 12 Babcock & Wilcox water-tube boilers.

Designed to achieve a total of 31,500 shp (23,500 kW), the top speed was 21 knots (24 mph; 39 km/h). The ships could carry up to 2,305 long tons (2,342 t) of fuel oil, thus giving them a range of up to 6,070 nautical miles (6,990 mi; 11,240 km) at a cruising speed of 12 knots (14 mph; 22 km/h). However, with a clean bottom, this could be extended to about 7,585 nautical miles (8,730 mi; 14,050 km). This was the case when the ships came out of the dock freshly cleaned and painted, resulting in lower water resistance.

Operational History

Both ships were commissioned in 1916, one year before the United States entered World War I on the side of the Allies (Entente). In the same year, *Pennsylvania* became the Atlantic Fleet's flagship. Owing to a shortage of fuel oil in Great Britain, only the coal-burning battleships of Battleship Division 9 were sent across the Atlantic to the European theater. As a result, the *Pennsylvanias*, both built with oil-firing boilers, remained in American waters for the duration of the conflict. After the armistice in fall 1918, *Arizona* was sent to Great Britain, while *Pennsylvania* escorted President Woodrow Wilson's transport, *George Washington*, across the Atlantic for the Paris Peace Conference. In 1922, during the interwar period, both ships were transferred to the Pacific Fleet conducting exercises and training duties.

From 1929 to 1931, the *Pennsylvanias* underwent considerable modernization. The elevation of the main batteries was increased from 15° to 30°, thus improving the range to about 34,300 yards (31,400 m). The torpedo tubes were removed, as were the lattice masts, which were replaced with sturdier tripod variants carrying modern fire-control systems.

The number of 5-inch (127 mm) guns was reduced to 12, and the 3-inch antiaircraft guns were replaced with eight 5-inch/25 caliber antiaircraft guns (four per side). These were mounted on the weather deck located

The modernized *Arizona* pitching in heavy seas, 1930s.

above the secondary anti-ship 5-inch guns. The bridges on both ships were enlarged to hold elevated antiaircraft directors. *Pennsylvania*, which had been built as a fleet flagship, received an expanded conning tower. The living space was increased to accommodate about 2,000 crewmembers and Marines as the additional armament required more personal. Both ships were fitted with two catapults for floatplanes.

As more advanced bomber aircraft became an increasing threat, the *Pennsylvanias*, like most American battleships, received a slight upgrade of up to 2 inches (51 mm) in horizontal armor. To increase the protection against torpedoes launched by aircraft or fired by submarines, and mines, bulges were attached to the outside of the hull and a torpedo bulkhead was added to the engine room. The boiler system was replaced entirely with six small-tube boilers and new turbines, allowing the ships to maintain their design speed of about 21 knots (39 km/h; 24 mph), even with the added bulges.

U.S.S. *Pennsylvania* (BB-38)

After their modernization, *Pennsylvania* and *Arizona* joined the Pacific Fleet. After the beginning of World War II in Europe in 1939 and as tensions with Japan increased, both were stationed in Pearl Harbor, Hawaii. During the attack, *Pennsylvania*, in dry dock at the time, was slightly damaged and had 15 men killed,

The wrecked destroyers U.S.S. *Downes* (DD-375) and U.S.S. *Cassin* (DD-372) in Dry Dock No. 1 at the Pearl Harbor Naval Shipyard, soon after Japanese air attack. *Cassin* has capsized against *Downes*. The battleship *Pennsylvania*, only slightly damaged, is astern, occupying the rest of the dry dock.

14 missing, and 38 wounded. Later in December, it left dry dock, departed Pearl Harbor and arrived in San Francisco, where it underwent further repairs. Following gunnery training and maneuvers, the ship received an overhaul at the Mare Island Naval Shipyard, San Francisco. This included a significant improvement of its antiaircraft capabilities, with 40 Bofors 40 mm in quadruple mounts and more than 50 Oerlikon 20 mm single mounts. The older 5-inch/51 caliber anti-ship casemate guns and 5-inch/25 caliber antiaircraft guns were replaced with rapid-firing 5-inch/38-cal guns in eight twin turrets. The tripod mainmast was removed, and its stump replaced with a deckhouse holding the aft main battery director and a new aircraft detection radar.

In February 1943, *Pennsylvania* was sent to support American forces engaged in the Aleutian Islands campaign in the North Pacific. During this time, it was nearly hit by a torpedo from the Japanese submarine *I-31*, which was later sunk. When the American military began reconquering Pacific islands held by the Japanese in 1944, *Pennsylvania* provided shore bombardment during the battles of Makin, Kwajalein, Eniwetok, and Saipan, along with the Palau Islands campaign.

The ship also participated in the invasion of Leyte and the battle of Leyte Gulf, including the last engagement between battleships in history, the battle of Surigao Strait. *Pennsylvania* did not fire any salvos as the Japanese ships were either turned away or destroyed at ranges that were beyond *Pennsylvania*'s obsolete fire-control system but within range of other, more capable, radar-guided American battleships.

Following a last refit in 1945, the ship bombarded Wake Island in August en route to Okinawa, where it was hit near the starboard propeller shaft by an aerial torpedo. This killed 20 men and knocked out three of *Pennsylvania*'s four shafts, causing extensive flooding that nearly sank it. However, the ship was towed into shallow waters, where it received makeshift repairs. On August 13, 1945, its guns fired at a kamikaze suicide aircraft while under tow to Guam for further repairs. After reaching Navy Yard Puget Sound, Washington, in fall 1945, *Pennsylvania* was prepared to participate in Operation *Crossroads*, the atomic tests at Bikini Atoll, in July 1946. After surviving both tests, *Able* and *Baker*, the damaged and radioactive battleship was decommissioned and used for radiological studies. *Pennsylvania* was finally sunk as a target ship off Kwajalein in the Pacific on February 10, 1948.

Two of the ship's 14-inch guns, which had been replaced during the 1945 overhaul, are on display at the Pennsylvania Military Museum situated in Boalsburg.

Pennsylvania in a floating dry dock (Advanced Base Sectional Dock) in the Pacific, 1944. The availability of such floating docks and repair vessels meant that even without ports, the U.S. Navy could repair or at least patch up its ships almost anywhere.

Arizona ablaze immediately following the explosion of its magazines. The photograph is a frame clipped from a color motion picture taken from on board the hospital ship U.S.S. *Solace* (AH-5).

U.S.S. *Arizona* (BB-39)

At the time of the Pearl Harbor attack, *Arizona* was moored at berth F-7, with the repair ship *Vestal* moored alongside. The battleship suffered hits from several bombs and was strafed. At about 8:05 a.m., it took a death blow. A high-altitude bomber dropped a 1,760 lb bomb. The projectile hurtled through the air, reportedly striking near turret No. 2 and penetrating deep into the battleship's innards before exploding near the forward magazine. In a tremendous blast, *Arizona* exploded. In an instant, most of the men aboard were killed, including Rear Admiral Isaac C. Kidd and Captain Franklin Van Valkenburgh, both posthumously awarded the Medal of Honor. The blast from the *Arizona* blew men off the decks of surrounding ships and threw tons of debris, including body parts, all over the harbor. Survivors of the attack also claimed that *Arizona* was hit by one or possibly two torpedoes. In any case, the battleship was utterly devastated from in front of its first turret back into its machinery spaces. Its sides were blown out and the turrets, conning tower, and much of the superstructure dropped several feet into its wrecked hull. This tipped its foremast forward, giving the wreck its distinctive appearance.

Arizona's tipped foremast after the ship has settled on the harbor bottom.

Abandoned at 10:32 a.m., the ship's burning superstructure and canted masts loomed through the smoke that blanketed the harbor. The wreck burned for almost three days. Credit for the hit was officially given to Japanese pilot Tadashi Kusumi from the aircraft carrier *Hiryu*. The blast that destroyed *Arizona* and sank it at its berth alongside of Ford Island consumed the lives of 1,177 men—over half of the casualties suffered by the entire fleet in the attack.

Of all the ships lost or damaged at Pearl Harbor, *Arizona* offered the most pathetic sight. After several assessment dives, it was considered beyond repair and stricken from the naval register. Beginning in 1942, ammunition, machinery, and other equipment were removed for use on other ships or stations. In May 1942, *Arizona*'s toppled foremast was cut away and removed, followed by the mainmast, the stern aircraft crane, and the conning tower. The U.S. Army received gun turrets Nos. 3 and 4 for use as coastal defense guns. By October 1943, the last salvage work was completed, with the ship stripped down to the main deck; none of the graceful superstructure remained.

U.S.S. *Arizona* Memorial

In 1961, *Arizona* was altered once more. To place the present memorial over the ship, a section of the boat deck that rested over the galley amidships was cut away. Initially this had been the area of a flag and platform for ceremonies and visits to the site from 1950 to 1960. This portion was removed to Waipio Point where it remains today.

The U.S.S. *Arizona* Memorial is the final resting place for the majority of the 1,177 sailors and Marines who lost their lives on December 7, 1941. The structure spanning the mid-portion of the sunken battleship was built to honor not only the fallen crew of *Arizona*, but also the members of the armed forces, who died because of the attack on Pearl Harbor. The U.S.S. *Arizona* Memorial is one of America's most revered and sacred sites. It is a place of quiet contemplation, where visitors can reflect on the great sacrifice made by those who gave their lives to defend America's freedom. From the soaring beauty of the memorial to the aching reality of the men entombed in the ship that lies beneath, visitors from around the world experience a pervasive sense of loss with an enormous feeling of gratitude and pride.

The crew of the aircraft carrier U.S.S. *Bennington* (CV-20) spells out the name *Arizona* as the carrier passes by the temporary *Arizona* Memorial on December 7, 1958.

The carrier U.S.S. *John C. Stennis* (CVN-74) renders honors to the *Arizona* Memorial in 2004.

One question still haunts visitors to the U.S.S. *Arizona* Memorial to this day. Why were the dead not removed? Initially, about 105 bodies were removed but because the ship was never raised, the remainder could not be recovered. The priority at that time was salvage of ships that could be repaired, and *Arizona* was not in that category. As a result, the bodies deteriorated to the point of being unidentifiable. Even as late as 1947, requests were made regarding removal of the dead but were rejected. They are considered buried at sea by the U.S. Navy.

Aerial view of the U.S.S. *Arizona* Memorial, which was erected over the sunken ship. Dedicated in 1962, the structure was designed by Austrian architect Alfred Preis.

Pennsylvania-class General Characteristics (as built)

Class	*Pennsylvania*
Name	*Pennsylvania* (BB-38) *Arizona* (BB-39)
Shipyard	Newport News Shipbuilding (BB-38) New York Naval Shipyard (BB-39)
Commissioning	March 12, 1916 (BB-38) October 17, 1916 (BB-39)
Displacement (normal) Displacement (full)	29,158 long tons (29,626 t) 31,917 long tons (32,429 t)
Length (overall)	608 ft (185.3 m)
Beam	97 ft 6 in (29.72 m)
Draft (max)	29 ft 3 in (8.9 m)
Propulsion	4 × steam turbines (31,500 shp / 23,500 kW)
Maximum speed	ca. 21.38 kn (39.6 km/h)
Range	6,070 nmi (11,240 km) at 12 kn
Complement	915
Armament	10 × 14-in (356 mm)/45 cal. 22 × 5-in (127 mm)/51 cal. 2 × 21-in (533 mm) torpedo tubes Various AA guns
Fate	Sunk as target, 10 February, 1948 (BB-38) Sunk in Pearl Harbor, December 7, 1941 (BB-39)

Pearl Harbor survivor Sterling R. Cale takes a moment in the shrine room of the U.S.S. *Arizona* Memorial to honor the 1,177 crewmembers who lost their lives during the sinking of the *Arizona*.

An archaeologist from the National Park Service (NPS) dives into history.

Diving into History—The Wreck of U.S.S. *Arizona* Today

by Daniel J. Lenihan

(All photos by Brett Seymour, NPS SRC—except where indicated)

National Park Service archaeologist Daniel J. Lenihan. (Photo: Daniel J. Lenihan)

Daniel J. Lenihan has dived as a NPS underwater archaeologist since 1972. He founded a team of diving ranger/archaeologists in 1976 that in 1980 became known as the Submerged Cultural Resources Unit (SCRU). In 2000, when he retired, the team was renamed the Submerged Resources Center (SRC). Dan is the author of *Submerged: Adventures of America's Most Elite Underwater Archaeology Team*, in which he describes his many years as a Florida cave diver and chief of SCRU. He has co-authored three novels with actor Gene Hackman.

The U.S.S. *Arizona* rests heavily on the bottom of Pearl Harbor, weighted down by its own history. Seen from the bright white memorial that arches over the once proud battleship, its remains are difficult to comprehend. With the superstructure salvaged during the war and no guns visible in the wreckage, nothing suggests the remains of a great warship. A huge cylindrical barbette on which the third turret once rotated dominates the scene. But few visitors would understand what it was without seeing the film and underwater model the park service shows them before the short boat ride. Once there, they know enough that the experience speaks for itself. It's not just what they see but being there that does it. Corroded steel from 1916 has the odor of yesteryear. It conspires with the harsh scent of oil still leaking from the ship's ruptured bunkers since 1941. It forms a thin rainbow-colored slick that is ever-present and ever moving. This unintended feature of the memorial somehow finds a place in most visitors' memories. Mixed with hushed voices, the slow shuffle of feet and distinctive headgear of park rangers, usually quiet, hands clasped behind their backs, they let *Arizona* speak for itself. No one has to be told that something important to Americans lies here. A thousand sailors, mainly young, eager, impressionable, whose experience of World War II was about 10 minutes long.

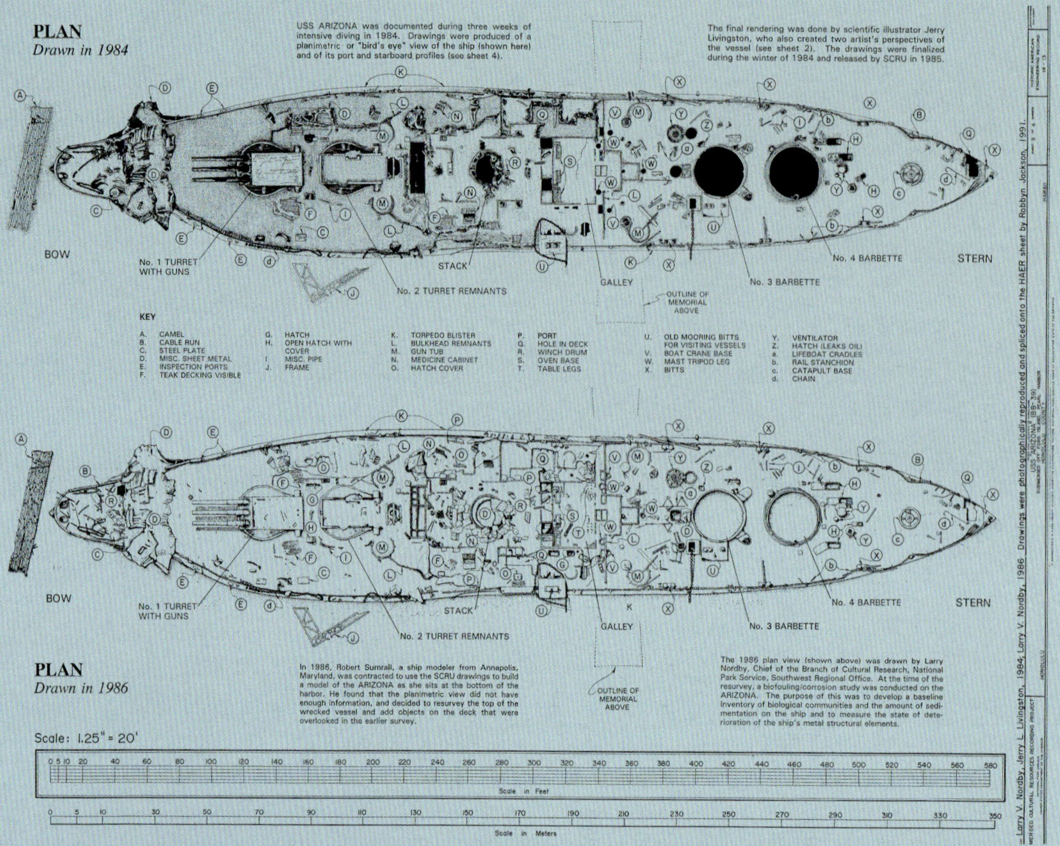

I was first shown the ship in 1982 by Gary Cummins, the memorial superintendent. Gary was deeply wedded to historic preservation and had ulterior motives for serving as my rubber-finned tour guide. He found himself the steward of a major American shrine he couldn't see—and he wanted help. As chief of the National Park Service's underwater archaeology team, I was supposed to provide such help to park managers.

Although a large white memorial spans the site, it doesn't touch the ship; the only knowledge its builders needed was the ship's footprint on the bottom so they could avoid it. There were as-built plans of the ship but no maps or renderings of it since the attack. The only photographs were of the ship under way, of it being destroyed, and a few of the 1943 salvage efforts. Postcards sold in the visitor center provided a modern aerial perspective of the ship with the memorial straddling it, but those too were deceiving. The postcards gave you a good sense of the lay of the wreck and its size. But gaping round holes left in the deck where the turrets had been salvaged reinforced common belief that the ship's 14-inch guns had all been moved to shore batteries during the war.

The new custom-built ROV capable of capturing 3D footage in use at the *Arizona* wreck site.

The massive 14-inch barrels of gun turret No. 1. When NPS archaeologists first dove the *Arizona* in the 1980s they were surprised that this turret was still in place. Gun turrets No. 3 and No. 4 were completely removed and converted into coastal artillery batteries, while only the barrels of No. 2 were removed, with the turret itself still in place at the wreck site.

There was a stunning lack of facts about the remains of the vessel, which would have been unthinkable if the *Arizona* were on land.

Problems of the sort Gary was facing were the stock-in-trade of the SCRU team, as my park service underwater archaeologists are called. The Submerged Cultural Resources Unit existed to help park superintendents extend their management skills to the underwater environment. Gary knew that he had the undocumented remains of a corroding battleship under his charge; that it contained a couple hundred thousand gallons of oil; and that some of that oil was leaking out and forming a rainbow slick on the surface. But he didn't know much more than that. By the following summer, the SCRU team was on its way to Pearl Harbor. During our first dives to assess the ship in 1983, we swam right into the muzzles of the giant guns that weren't there. As we found in dramatic form during our first day of diving, the huge No. 1 turret is intact and in place. It can't be seen from aerial images because the forward deck has collapsed and fallen deeper. Light can't penetrate the murky water to the new level of the turret; so, neither can sight.

Arizona's intact bow. The two NPS archaeologists give an idea of the ship's enormous size.

We soon found there were many things on the ship that defied conventional notions and there was much to be learned. Discoveries we made each day as we mapped the ship attracted considerable attention from naval historians and the public. The *Arizona* is an incomparable touchstone to World War II. No diver stays detached for long when working on that ship. Our professional interest in measuring and mapping and recording in photography, was soon overshadowed by a personal one. By chance, just as we began our research, the dive industry had a technological breakthrough. A way was found to replace the hopelessly awkward black-and-white

VideoRay, a remotely operated vehicle (ROV), explores the Marine Division's secretary office.

video systems with newly marketed color home video cameras in underwater housings. As we began our 1983 efforts, I took a video camera down and documented what we were finding on each dive. The effect on us and on Honolulu was electric. At the end of each work session, I would hand the tape cassette to a local network cameraman who dubbed the day's findings for Hawaii television. Each night, the three network affiliates aired selections from our tape. As park service researchers we work for the public and it was rewarding to see the fruits of our labor shared each evening on our hotel's TV set.

Hatches looming open, porthole covers with air from 1941 trapped inside, bomb holes, live ordnance, personal artifacts—the tapes grew more compelling each day. This vicarious visual return to the war was surpassed only by the intensity of each diver's experience. For all of them, park service and navy, they were undertaking a journey into themselves as much as to the remains of a ship on the harbor bottom. They were swimming through an iconic moment in their nation's history and they knew it. Over a 10-day operation we learned what would and wouldn't work in mapping a battleship longer than two football fields, in 5 to 7 feet of visibility. When we returned for the main project in 1984, we were ready. Pearl Harbor basks in a sea breeze most days, zephyrs that keep the heat down and the flags high. Much of my memory of the time I spent working on the *Arizona* includes a steady sound in the background. It's the flapping of flags and pennants—"Old Glory" from the memorial, where it is still affixed to the remains of the ship's mast, and the familiar red and white of our diver-down flag. It's nice to have the familiar about you while dealing with the alien—and the texture and scent of the water around the ship was definitely alien. The odor of seawater mixed with the unmistakable aftertaste of fuel in the air expelled from our regulators. "Bunker C" is standard for a ship of this period. It oozes black, moving along the overheads at a glacial pace until it can take off toward air and light in little buoyant globules.

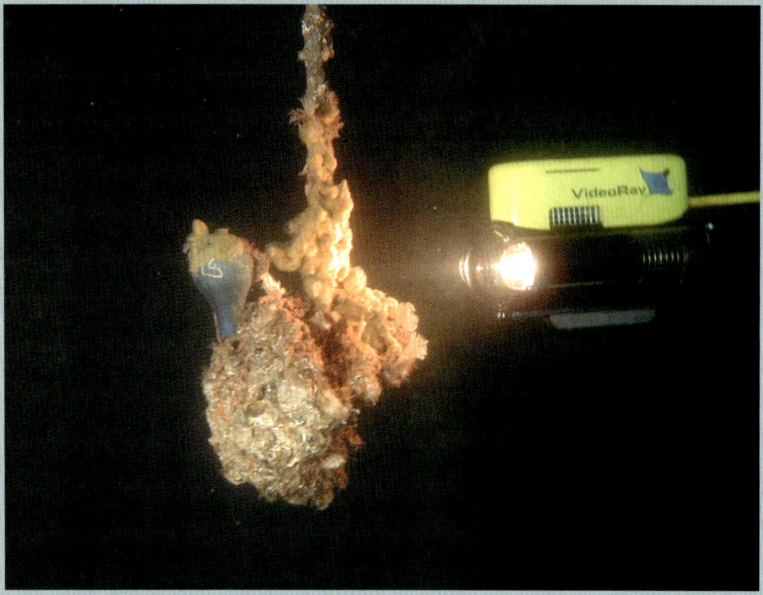

VideoRay explores a chandelier in the cabin of Rear Admiral Isaac C. Kidd, the Commander of Battleship Division I, with U.S.S. *Arizona* being his flagship. He died on board during the attack.

Sunlight touches the sunken *Arizona.*

The *Arizona* envelops those who dive on her. You must hug the deck or some recognizable structure or get lost. Because of the limited visibility, objects take form slowly as you swim toward them. They appear first as suggestions of a recognizable shape, then snap suddenly into a confirmation or denial of one's first impression. Regardless of the outcome, one is always surprised. Even the mundane, such as shoes, medicine bottles, chain, tile, all seem somehow special in this resting place. Strafing holes in the deck are stark and dramatic, signatures of death from above. Slivers of teak decking, intermingled with torn steel, surround larger holes made by AP bombs. The bomb-entrance holes seem small and unfathomable. Did gravity really force them through multiple steel decks? Did a conventional explosion really convert this grand symbol of American will and might into a giant's discarded toy? The sailors are really still in there? Eventually, one's thoughts always return to the men, many of them really only boys. We know 1,177 of them perished here and have become the soul of the *Arizona*. In the end, the ship is just a ship. We glorify the feel of steel and broken artifacts, but it's the broken bodies of those boys 17, 18, 19 years old, frozen forever at those ages that tug at us when we swim by. They didn't even have the chance to be good or bad; their war lasted a little less than 10 minutes. We honor our sailors and tentatively even nod to their attackers. I've seen some survivors of Pearl Harbor embrace their former enemies while others turn away. For the latter, the passing years have healed no wounds. Or maybe they feel it's not their place to forgive their shipmates' killers. Some wounds may be borne in peace yet never forgiven.

The two-year project that started with my snorkel-tour of the ship with Gary ended up involving us intimately with the *Arizona* for a quarter century. My sons accompanied me to Oahu in baby strollers when we laid the first survey lines. Years later, the older dived the site as a member of the Submerged Resources Center, as the SCRU team was renamed. He made those dives just months before he watched the World Trade Center disintegrate on morning TV—the analogy was not lost on him. Now, both my sons are old enough themselves to serve and die. I know I would never forgive their attackers, but then, one shouldn't bemoan a warrior's fate. This ship has been a great

After more than eight decades under water, the teakwood deck remains intact. Teakwood has the advantage that it does not become slippery when wet on the high seas.

Encounter with a seahorse. Over the years, *Arizona* has become the home to various sea creatures.

teacher for me. As a diver, I've seen many things through glass masks in very strange places. I guess all of us see through masks of some sort or another. But, my take on life, death, and calls-to-arms were all influenced by the time I served on the *Arizona*—yes, in a peculiar way I like to think I served on her. Later than most, but also a lot longer. I've seen changes in the ship as the years have passed: survivor reunions at the 50th and 60th commemorations of the *Arizona*'s sinking; personal reunions of shipmates with their ship as their urns were carried down by National Park Service or Navy divers—some I carried down myself. I've seen fellow travelers swell with triumph, collapse in desolation, and rise again—but since my first dives on the *Arizona* I have had a place to return for renewal. It's almost like the lost sailors have gotten used to me and provide silent counsel. I anticipate their company each dive I make and, on each dive, I salute them.

View of the starboard side showing one of the foundation rings for the 5-inch deck guns.

The U.S.S. *Arizona* Memorial in rainy weather. This photograph was taken from the ship's stern.

New Mexico-class

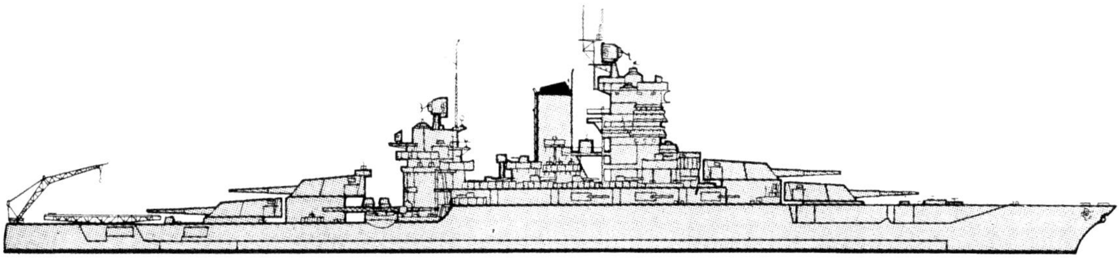

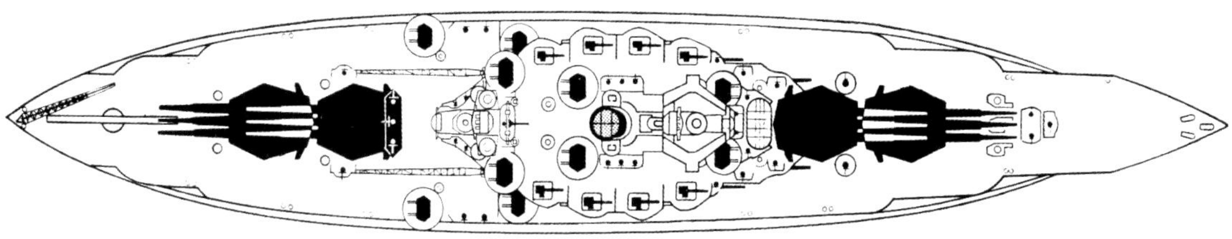

When foreign naval powers introduced the 15-inch (381 mm) caliber shortly before World War I, the U.S. Navy began developing 16-inch (406 mm) guns and evaluated various proposals for ships armed with this powerful weapon. The first sketch envisioned a 10-gun ship with five twin turrets and a secondary battery of 6-inch (152 mm) guns instead of 5-inch (127 mm) weapons including improved armor compared to previous battleships. Another proposal suggested a smaller version with eight 16-inch guns, followed by a 14-inch (356 mm) gun design.

Before the evaluation process of the 16-inch guns had been completed, Rear Admiral Joseph Strauss, Chief of the Bureau of Ordnance (BuOrd), expressed his doubts about the usefulness of these guns. In his opinion,

U.S.S. *New Mexico* (BB-40) in its original configuration. The *New Mexicos* were in most respects copies of the preceding *Pennsylvanias*, carrying over the same 14-inch (356 mm) guns, but increased to 50 caliber. However, they incorporated several other improvements, including a better arrangement of the secondary battery, a clipper bow that improved seakeeping, and an experimental turboelectric propulsion system.

the 14-inch gun was capable of penetrating heavy armor as effectively as the 16-inch guns at the battle distances expected at the time. In addition, a ship armed with 12 14-inch guns had a greater chance of hitting the target than a ship armed with only eight 16-inch guns.

The General Board, the advisory institution of the U.S. Navy, agreed and assigned the designers to work on the 14-inch battleship. In 1913, they presented two versions. The first was a 35,500-long-ton (36,100 t) version with a secondary battery of 20 6-inch guns, while the second incorporated 22 5-inch guns with weight savings in the thickness of the barbette and belt armor and reduced fuel capacity.

The General Board was in favor of the first proposal, arguing that the heavier armor was needed to withstand the hits from the latest foreign 15-inch guns. In addition, a stronger secondary battery was considered necessary to defend against torpedo attacks from destroyers at long range. In early 1914, Secretary of the Navy Josephus Daniels rejected the design due to its higher cost and directed the Navy to accept a slightly improved version of the previous *Pennsylvanias*.

As earlier U.S. battleships were too "wet" forward, the new class was designed with a "clipper bow" reducing the tendency to ship water in heavy seas. In addition, most of the secondary guns were moved a deck higher and further aft, as experience with existing ships had revealed that casemate-mounted guns in the forecastle deck were virtually useless in rough seas. Various weight savings made it possible to strengthen the main deck and the transverse bulkhead at both ends of the armor belt (armored citadel). Moreover, the BuOrd proposed a newly developed longer version of the existing 14-inch gun (50 caliber), promising a higher muzzle velocity, which allowed projectiles to penetrate an additional 2 inches (51 mm) of armor at up to 10,000 yards (9,100 m). When Secretary Daniels approved these changes, it was the birth of the future *New Mexico*-class, consisting of *New Mexico* (BB-40), *Mississippi* (BB-41), and *Idaho* (BB-42).

Crewmen loading 14-inch shells aboard *New Mexico* before the invasion of Guam in 1944.

Armament

The *New Mexicos* carried a main battery of 12 14-inch (356 mm)/50 caliber Mark 4 guns in four turrets with three guns each. These were placed on the centerline, in two superfiring pairs forward and aft of the superstructure. Unlike earlier American battleships fitted with triple turrets, these new mounts were true three-gun turrets: each barrel could be elevated independently. At a muzzle velocity of up to 2,800 feet per second (850 m/s) and 30° elevation, they could fire a 1,400 lb (640 kg) shell up to 36,800 yards (33,600 m). The rate of fire was about 1 salvo per minute. Each gun had a supply of 100 shells (1,200 in total).

The secondary battery consisted of 14 5-inch (127 mm)/51 caliber Mark 8 guns, virtually identical to that on the *Pennsylvanias*, and were installed in casemates in the superstructure amidships. Firing a

50 lb (23 kg) shell at a rate of 8 to 9 rounds per minute, they had a muzzle velocity of 3,150 ft/s (960 m/s). At 45° elevation, the range was up to 20,142 yards (18,418 m). The secondary battery was completed by four antiaircraft 3-inch (76 mm)/50 caliber guns in high-angle mounts. At a rate of 20 rounds per minute (or more), they fired a 13 lb (5.9 kg) shell at a velocity of 2,700 ft/s (820 m/s). Their maximum range was 14,500 yards (13,300 m) at 45° elevation, while their ceiling was 27,400 feet (8,400 m) at 85° elevation.

All three ships were also fitted with two 21-inch (533 mm) torpedo tubes, mounted submerged in the hull, one on each broadside. Each tube was supplied with six Bliss-Leavitt Mark VII torpedoes, armed with a 321 lb (146 kg) warhead. This weapon had a range of up to 12,500 yards (11,400 m) at a speed of up to 27 knots (31 mph; 50 km/h).

Protection

Like the two preceding classes, the *New Mexicos* were built with the "all or nothing" principle. This reserved armor protection only for the vital sections, thus creating an armored citadel that had enough reserve buoyancy to keep the ship afloat even if its unarmored portions were flooded.

The main side armor belt had a thickness of 8 to 13.5 inches (203 to 343 mm), with the thickest section protecting the machinery spaces and magazines. The transverse bulkheads connecting both ends of the belt had the same thickness.

The *New Mexicos* had two armored decks: the first (main deck) consisted of two layers of STS, each 1.75 inches (44.5 mm) thick, totaling 3.5 inches (89 mm) with a reinforcement over the steering compartment further aft. The lower armor deck also consisted of two STS layers, with the first 1 inch (25 mm) thick and the second 2 inches (51 mm) thick, totaling 3 inches (76 mm). The massive gun turrets of the 14-inch main battery had 18-inch (457 mm) thick faces, with 10-inch (254 mm) thick sides, 9-inch (229 mm) rears and 5-inch (127 mm) roofs. Their barbettes had a thickness of up to 13 inches (330 mm). The conning tower had 16-inch (406 mm) thick sides.

Innovative Propulsion

Standard propulsion for warships at the time was based on steam turbines driving propeller shafts. While they operated most efficiently at high speed, the propellers generated their greatest thrust at relatively low speed. The Bureau of Steam Engineering (BuEng) recommended the relatively new system of turbo-electric transmission using turbines to generate electric power that in turn powered electric motors driving the screws.

In addition, it offered various advantages over traditional direct-drive systems, including greater fuel economy and smaller machinery, thus saving weight. The motors could be mounted further to the stern by using flexible electric cables instead of the bulky steam pipes (that would connect the boilers with the turbines). This reduced vibration and weight by shortening the propeller shafts. In addition, the turbines would only need to spin in one direction, thus allowing a simpler machinery without reverse gears. Switching between forward and reverse was done by simply reversing the electrical polarity of the motors. It was also advantageous to operate all four propellers if one of the turbogenerators failed. While this propulsion system was efficient, robust, and reliable, it was not easy to maintain and service. The engines also required special ventilation measures to remove heat and keep out the salty air. Even with elaborate insulation measures, protection from moisture or flooding due to battle damage or other causes remained problematic. Moreover, in the event of damage, there was a risk of high voltage to the crew. As this was an unproven technology, only *New Mexico* was built with the turbo-electric system, while its sister ships, *Mississippi* and *Idaho*, received traditional direct-drive systems.

All three ships were fitted with four Curtis turbines each. Steam was provided by nine oil-fired Babcock & Wilcox boilers. *New Mexico*'s turbines powered electrical motors driving the screw propellers. The system was rated at 27,500 shaft horsepower (20,500 kW). *Mississippi* and *Idaho*, built with traditional direct-drive propulsion, were rated at 32,000 shp (24,000 kW). The maximum speed of all three ships was 21 knots (24 mph; 39 km/h). The fuel oil storage capacity for heating the boilers was 1,467 long tons (1,491 t), though additional spaces in the hull could be used to increase this to 2,200 long tons (2,200 t). This allowed a range of up to 8,000 nautical miles (9,200 mi; 15,000 km) at a cruising of speed of 10 knots (12 mph; 19 km/h).

Fleet Problems

During the 1920s, the U.S. Navy conducted various major naval exercises known as *Fleet Problems*, (including a naval exercise simulating the defense of the Panama Canal). During one of these maneuvers, *Mississippi* sank the obsolete pre-dreadnought battleship *Iowa*, converted into a target ship. *Mississippi* achieved this by using aircraft to spot its shots at long range. This was the first time this had been accomplished in the U.S. Navy. The *Fleet Problems* usually took place once a year providing the basis for American naval operations and further planning in the event of war in the Pacific. The experience gained from these exercises showed that the standard-type battleships, which included the *New Mexicos*, were too slow to operate with aircraft carriers. This awareness later led to the development of the "fast battleships" in the 1930s.

Aircraft

As early as 1921, the first American battleships received aircraft catapults to operate floatplanes for aerial reconnaissance as well as fire observation and direction. The *New Mexicos* first carried Hanriot HD.2s and then Vought UO-1s, which were replaced by various other models including the Vought O2U Corsair, the Curtiss SOC Seagull, and Vought OS2U Kingfisher.

Modernization and Operational History

Like many other American battleships, the three *New Mexicos* were heavily modernized in the early 1930s. Their main deck armor was reinforced with additional 2 inches (51 mm) of special treatment steel, thus increasing the total thickness from 3.5 inches (89 mm) to 5.5 inches (140-mm). To improve the resistance against torpedoes, a second torpedo bulkhead was installed outboard of the original one, and anti-torpedo bulges were added to

The modernized U.S.S. *Idaho* (BB-42) during the mid-1930s. Note the massive superstructure, which visually set the *New Mexicos* apart from other modernized battleships.

the hull. Both lattice (cage) masts were replaced by a heavy tower bridge and a light pole mast. *Idaho* was fitted out as a flagship, which included the installation of a flag bridge for an admiral and his staff. The main battery turrets were modified to allow an elevation to 30°, thus extending the range of the guns from 25,000 to up to 36,800 yards (33,600 m).

While two 5-inch guns were removed, eight 5-inch/25 caliber antiaircraft guns were installed. The *New Mexicos* received an overhaul of their propulsion systems, which included new Westinghouse turbines and six BuEng boilers. Rated at about 40,000 shp (30,000 kW), the new power plant increased the top speed to 22 knots (25 mph; 41 km/h), despite the displacement increase to 33,420 long tons (33,960 t) standard and 36,157 long tons (36,737 t) full load, which resulted from the new bridge, the additional armor plating, and the bulges.

During the Neutrality Patrols protecting American shipping caught in the battle of the Atlantic during the earlier stages of World War II, the *New Mexicos* were transferred from the Pacific to the Atlantic Fleet. Their task was to reinforce the patrols in May of 1941 escorting convoys between the United States and Iceland, though they saw no action with German U-boats.

As the Japanese air strike on Pearl Harbor had shown, battleships had demonstrated their extreme vulnerability to air strikes. The *New Mexicos*, in service in the Atlantic at the time of the attack, immediately received improved antiaircraft armament including 1.1-inch (28 mm) antiaircraft guns and fire-control radars.

Immediately after the attack, the three battleships were assigned to the Pacific Fleet to reinforce its battleship strength. After arriving in California in January 1942, they spent the next several months patrolling the American West Coast and escorting convoys in the area. In fall of 1942, *New Mexico* and *Mississippi* received two quadruple Bofors 40 mm AA guns and several 20 mm Oerlikon AA guns, while *Idaho* was fitted gradually with 10 quadruple Bofors and more than 40 Oerlikons. Later in the war, all three ships were equipped with new fire-control radars and new 5-inch guns, as well as additional antiaircraft guns. Between May and July 1943, the *New Mexicos* participated in the Aleutian Islands campaign in the North Pacific, shelling the Japanese-held islands of Attu and Kiska as part of the reconquest of the archipelago.

U.S.S. *Mississippi* (BB-41) docked in Dry Dock No. 4 at Puget Sound Naval Shipyard, 1940. Though the *New Mexico*'s turbo-electric propulsion system was effective, and it was repeated in the follow-on *Tennessee*-class, the U.S. Navy ultimately decided that it was too heavy and occupied too much space in the hull, and later ships reverted to traditional turbine propulsion.

New Mexico's 5-inch guns prepare to fire during the bombardment of Saipan, June 1944. Note the time-fuze setters on the left side of each gun mount, each holding three "fixed" rounds of ammunition.

When the Gilbert and Marshall Islands campaign began in November of that year, all three ships, along with other warships, provided fire support to the U.S. Marines, who successfully invaded various Japanese-held islands including Tarawa, Kwajalein, and Eniwetok.

While *New Mexico* and *Idaho* participated in the Mariana and Palau Islands campaign in the Central Pacific beginning in June 1944, *Mississippi* underwent an overhaul during the first part of the operations. Both ships bombarded Japanese positions on Saipan, Tinian, and Guam as part of the amphibious landings that took place on each island. *New Mexico* and *Idaho* covered the invasion fleet from Japanese attacks while the Fast Carrier Task Force decisively defeated the Japanese aircraft carrier force during the battle of the Philippine Sea later in June 1944.

In October, *Mississippi* supported the invasion of Leyte providing fire support. This operation prompted the Japanese to launch Operation *Shō-Gō I*. This was a major naval counterattack leading the battle of Leyte Gulf in October, a complex battle that involved various actions, resulting in the destruction of the remnants of the Imperial Japanese Navy as a threat. *Mississippi* participated in the battle of Surigao Strait during the night of October 24/25, which was one component of the battle. During the engagement, the overwhelming American fleet destroyed the Japanese ships (Southern Force) including two older battleships, *Yamashiro* and *Fusō*. *Mississippi*, still fitted with old radars, had difficulty in finding a target in the darkness and fired only one salvo in the last battleship-to-battleship action in history.

In January 1945, *New Mexico* and *Mississippi* supported the invasion of Lingayen Gulf on the island of Luzon, Philippines. During the battle both ships were struck by kamikaze suicide aircraft but remained in action until February when they departed for Pearl Harbor for repairs. By that time, *Idaho* took part in the battle of Iwo Jima, shelling the island extensively before the Marines went ashore and continued to provide fire support during the landing.

All three sister ships were reunited to support the invasion of Okinawa in May 1945, the last major invasion of Japanese-held territory. As Okinawa was the last bastion before the homeland, and with Japan's desperate military situation continuing to deteriorate, Japanese pilots began to launch kamikaze attacks in large numbers. While *New Mexico* and *Mississippi* were both struck, *Idaho* was damaged by a near miss. *New Mexico* was also hit by a bomb. All three ships were repaired in time to participate in the occupation of Japan after the surrender in August 1945.

U.S.S. *Idaho* bombarding Okinawa with its 14-inch main battery guns, April 1945, as part of the preparation to invade the island. The artillery of the old battleships proved very precise.

Since the postwar navy was considerably downsized for cost reasons and only modern ships remained, *New Mexico* and *Idaho*, both obsolete, were decommissioned as early as 1946 and scrapped the following year. *Mississippi*, however, survived the postwar draw-down through conversion into a gunnery training and evaluation ship replacing the older battleship *Wyoming*. With the new hull number *EAG-128* to designate its status as an auxiliary vessel, *Mississippi* was reconstructed from November 1945 through April 1948. The new armament included a variety of different weapons. It then served as the flagship of the Operational Test and Evaluation Force. At the dawn of the missile age, the *Mississippi* helped test and evaluate antiaircraft missiles before being decommissioned and sold for scrap in 1956. By that time, the old battleship had served its country for nearly 39 years.

New Mexico-class General Characteristics (as built)

Class	*New Mexico*
Name	*New Mexico* (BB-40) *Mississippi* (BB-41) *Idaho* (BB-42)
Shipyard	New York Naval Shipyard (BB-40) Newport News Shipbuilding (BB-41) New York Shipbuilding Corporation, Camden (BB-42)
Commissioning	May 29, 1918 (BB-40) December 18, 1918 (BB-41) March 24, 1919 (BB-42)
Displacement (normal) Displacement (full)	32,000 long tons (32,514 t) 33,000 long tons (33,530 t)
Length (overall)	624 ft (190 m)
Beam	97 ft 5 in (29.7 m)
Draft (max)	30 ft (9.1 m)
Propulsion	4 × steam turbines / turbo-electric (BB-40) (32,000 shp / 24,000 kW)
Maximum speed	ca. 21 kn (39 km/h)
Range	8,000 nmi (15,000 km) at 10 kn
Complement	1,081
Armament	12 × 14-in (356 mm)/50 cal. 14 × 5-in (127 mm)/51 cal. 2 × 21-in (533 mm) torpedo tubes Various AA guns
Fate	Broken up at Newark, 1947 (BB-40 and BB-42) Broken up at Baltimore, 1956 (BB-41)

Tennessee-class

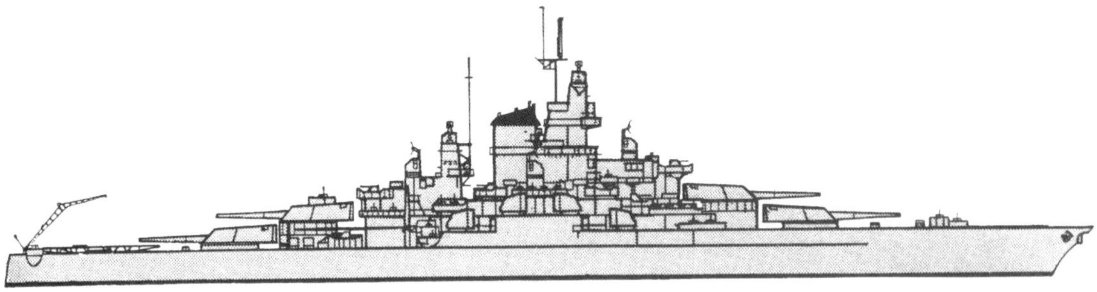

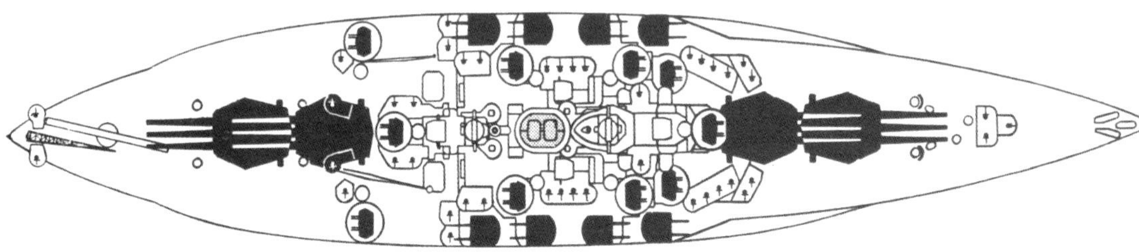

By the time war broke out in 1914, European navies had begun introducing capital ships armed with 15-inch (381 mm) guns: Great Britain with the *Queen Elizabeth*-class and eventually Germany with the *Bayern*-class. In addition, Europeans began to develop longer-ranged torpedoes that could reach well into the expected battle distances of the day, 10,000 to 14,000 yards (9,100 to 12,800 m). At the same time, design work on the future *Tennessee*-class, initially known as "Battleship 1916" and based on the preceding *New Mexico*-class, had begun in the United States. Consequently, the General Board proposed a battleship that departed from the standard-type battleship series, which incorporated relatively minor incremental improvements, particularly in terms of armor and underwater protection against the latest European 15-inch guns, torpedoes, and mines. However, Secretary of the Navy Josephus Daniels overrode the General Board and ordered that the new battleships be based on the *New Mexico*-class, with only minor changes.

U.S.S. *California* (BB-44) steaming at maximum speed of 21 knots, circa 1921. The *Tennessee*-class was essentially a repeat of the preceding *New Mexico*-class, with the primary improvements being a significantly strengthened underwater protection system, and increased elevation of the 14-inch main guns for longer ranges.

One of *Tennessee*'s (BB-43) lattice (cage) masts with the ship's bell. The ocean liner in the background is the *Leviathan*, the former German *Vaterland* seized by the United States in World War I.

To ensure the ship could survive an underwater explosion, the designers incorporated four torpedo bulkheads, thus creating four voids. Of these, the inner pair would be filled with either water or fuel oil, absorbing the pressure and gas of the explosion. Two ships, *Tennessee* (BB-43) and *California* (BB-44), were authorized in 1915, while design work was still in progress. Testing of the torpedo bulkhead system was not completed until February 1916. In the meantime, work had already begun on the design of the succeeding class ("Battleship 1917"), which became the *Colorado*-class, which was essentially a copy of *Tennessee* with 16-inch (406 mm) guns.

Propulsion

Like its predecessor, the new design was built with turbo-electric propulsion: eight oil-fired Babcock & Wilcox water-tube boilers generated steam powering two Westinghouse turbo-electric generators (turbines). They in turn operated electric motors that drove four 3-bladed screws. The two turbines were placed in separate watertight compartments, with four boilers apiece; each boiler had its own watertight room, with two boilers located on either side of the turbines. The electric motors were arranged in three rooms: a larger, central room for the two motors driving the inboard shafts, and one for each outboard shaft on either side.

Control board in one of *Tennessee*'s engine rooms, 1921. Dials and gauges on this board show what all engines are doing at all times.

Rated at 28,600 shp (21,300 kW), the propulsion system allowed a top speed of 21 knots (24 mph; 39 km/h). During speed trials, *Tennessee* was able to reach 21.38 knots (24.6 mph; 39.6 km/h) from 29,609 shp (22,079 kW). The fuel oil storage capacity for heating the

One of the fire rooms aboard the *Tennessee*-class. Powered by turbo-electric drive, eight oil-fired Babcock & Wilcox water-tube boilers generated steam powering two Westinghouse turbo-electric generators that in turn provided power for four electric motors that drove four screws. The turbines were in separate watertight compartments.

boilers was 1,900 long tons (1,930 t), though additional spaces in the hull could be used to increase this to 4,656 long tons (4,731 t). This allowed a range of 8,000 nautical miles (9,200 mi; 15,000 km) at a cruising speed of 10 knots (12 mph; 19 km/h). With full emergency oil, the range could be doubled, to about 20,500 nautical miles (23,600 mi; 38,000 km).

Armament

The main battery consisted of 12 14-inch (356 mm)/50 caliber Mark IV guns in four triple turrets. These were arranged on the centerline in superfiring pairs forward and aft of the superstructure. The mounts allowed each gun barrel to be elevated independently. Unlike the preceding *New Mexicos*, the *Tennessees* were laid down after the battle of Jutland, which had taken place in mid-1916 and proven the value of long-range plunging fire. Consequently, the main battery turrets were modified while still under construction, thus allowing an improved elevation to 30°, resulting in a maximum range of up to 35,100 yards (32,100 m) with the standard 1,500 lb (680 kg) AP shell (capable of penetrating ship armor). This was fired with a muzzle velocity of 2,625 feet per second (800 m/s). When firing the lighter 1,275 lb (578 kg) HC shell (against unarmored targets and for shore bombardment), the muzzle velocity increased to 2,825 feet per second (861 m/s) resulting in a greater range of 36,650 yards (33,510 m). The rate of fire was about 1.75 rounds per minute.

The secondary battery consisted of 14 5-inch (127 mm)/51 caliber Mark 8 guns, identical to the ones mounted on the *New Mexicos*. Ten were installed in casemates in the superstructure amidships, one deck (01 level) above the main deck. The remaining four 5-inch guns were installed in open pivot mounts on the 02 deck. The early antiaircraft defense consisted of four 3-inch (76 mm)/50 caliber guns located on the 02 deck. During the 1920s, both ships underwent a series of minor alterations to their secondary and antiaircraft armament, which included the installation of .50 caliber machine guns.

As it was standard at the time, both ships were fitted with two 21-inch (533 mm) torpedo tubes for the Bliss-Leavitt Mark VII torpedoes. Carrying a 321 lb (146 kg) warhead, they had a range of up to 12,500 yards (11,400 m) at a speed of up to 27 knots (31 mph; 50 km/h).

Protection

The *Tennessees* were built with a side armor belt, which was 8 to 13.5 inches (203 to 343 mm) thick and about 18 feet (5.5 m) high, half of which was above the waterline. This belt extended from the most forward to the aftmost barbette, thus covering the ammunition magazines and propulsion machinery spaces inside the armored citadel. Both ends of the belt were covered by armored 13.5-inch-thick transverse bulkheads. The main armor deck had a strength of up to 3.5 inches (89 mm). It was connected to the top of the side belt, running between the two transverse armor bulkheads. A second armor deck, 2.5 inches (64 mm) thick, was

Stern view of U.S.S. *California* (BB-44) in 1924. The ship has been fitted with an aircraft catapult at the stern. Note the "range clock" on the lattice mast. The "range clocks" are not rangefinders, but range displays, used alongside deflection marks on turrets to indicate to other friendly ships the direction and range of what the ship's aiming at.

installed below the main deck. Further aft, where it provided the only horizontal protection, it increased to a strength of 5 inches. Over the bow section, the lower armor deck was increased to 3 inches.

The gun turrets of the main battery were armored with 18-inch (457 mm) thick faces, 10-inch (254 mm) thick sides, 9-inch (229 mm) rears and 5-inch (127 mm) roofs. A layer of teak wood was used to cushion the structures from shell hits during battle. The turrets' barbettes had a thickness of up to 13 inches (330 mm). The conning tower had 16-inch (406 mm) thick sides and a 6-inch (152 mm) roof. The armored coamings for the funnel uptakes had a strength of up to 9 inches (229 mm).

Aircraft

In the 1920s, both ships were equipped with aircraft-handling equipment. While *Tennessee* received an aircraft catapult on the fantail, *California*'s catapult was installed on the aft gun turret. Up to three Vought UO-1 floatplanes were used for aerial reconnaissance and fire observation and direction. By the 1930s, each ship had catapults on both the aft turret and fantail.

Operational History

While both ships served in the Pacific Fleet during the interwar years, *California* operated as its flagship. In the 1920s and 1930s, they participated in various naval exercises, including the annual *Fleet Problems*. Highlights of this period were cruises around the Americas and a goodwill visit to Australia and New Zealand in 1925. While in Long Beach, California, both ships sent crewmembers ashore to provide relief after the 1933 earthquake there.

In 1940, the American Battle Fleet was moved from California to Pearl Harbor, Hawaii, to deter further Japanese aggression. As the situation deteriorated into a war-like crisis, the *Fleet Problems* exercise for 1941 and the planned modernization of the *Tennessees* were canceled as the U.S. Navy decided to keep the fleet at a high state of readiness. Nevertheless, when the Japanese carrier aircraft attacked Pearl Harbor, the U.S. Navy taken completely by surprise. Moored along Battleship Row with other battleships on that December 7, both ships were unprepared for the air strike. *Tennessee*, moored inboard of the battleship *West Virginia* and thus protected from aerial torpedo attacks, emerged relatively unscathed. However, it was trapped by the sunken battleships around it, and fires from other ships warped some of its hull plates. *California*, the southernmost ship moored along Battleship Row was an easier target. Hit by several torpedoes and bombs, it suffered severe internal and uncontrollable flooding, causing it to sink on an even keel.

The crew abandoning the damaged *California* as burning oil drifts down on the ship, at about 10 a.m. on December 7, 1941, shortly after the end of the air attack. The capsized hull of *Oklahoma* is visible at the right.

On December 20, 1941, after being freed from its mooring place at Battleship Row, *Tennessee* was able to sail under its own power to the Puget Sound Navy Yard, Washington, for repairs and modernization.

Over the next several months, workers and divers patched the hull and pumped out the water, finally refloating the ship on March 25, 1942. On April 5, an accidental explosion occurred, most likely the result of a mixture of fuel oil vapor and hydrogen sulfide gas. The force of the explosion dislodged the patch that had covered the forward hole in the hull and damaged several watertight doors, thus causing serious flooding. After repatching the hull and pumping the water out again, *California* was dry-docked in Pearl Harbor for initial repairs on April 9. In mid-June, the ship was taken to Puget Sound to be rebuilt and modernized.

By mid-1942, *Tennessee* had returned to service with an upgraded light antiaircraft battery but saw no active operations due to fuel shortage in the Pacific at the time. The Navy decided that the ship should be rebuilt to the same design as *California*, so it returned to Puget Sound.

Both ships received modern air-search radars as well as fire-control radars for their main and secondary guns. The mixed battery of 51 caliber and 25 caliber 5-inch (127 mm) guns was replaced by a uniform battery of 16 5-inch/38 caliber guns in eight twin mounts. The light antiaircraft armament now consisted of 10 quadruple

Struck by torpedoes (and later by bombs), *California* sank into the shallow waters of Pearl Harbor. The ship had been prepared for inspection at the time of the attack, so the watertight doors and many portholes had all been opened. The crew was still in the process of closing the doors when the torpedoes struck and flooding began.

U.S.S. *Tennessee* underway in Puget Sound, Washington, in May 1943, after its extensive modernization, which included the installation of modern 5-inch and antiaircraft guns, radar systems and electronics. The rebuilt superstructure now resembled the new *South Dakota*-class.

40 mm Bofors guns and 43 20 mm Oerlikons, all in single mounts. These alterations required doubling the crew, to a total of up to 114 officers and 2,129 enlisted men.

To strengthen their resistance to underwater damage, the *Tennessees* received anti-torpedo bulges and an improvement of their internal compartmentalization. The superstructures were completely revised, thus altering the ships' silhouettes. The aft funnels were removed, with the associated boilers being trunked into an enlarged forward funnel. The foremasts were replaced by tower masts, housing the bridge and the main battery director.

To improve resistance to air attack, the horizontal protection was considerably strengthened by adding 3 inches of STS to the deck over the ammunition magazines, while 2 inches (51 mm) of STS was added elsewhere.

As *Tennessee* was completed first, the rebuilt battleship returned to service in May 1943, just in time to participate in the Aleutian Islands campaign providing naval fire support. During the upcoming island-hopping campaign in the Pacific, the battleship conducted preparatory bombardments to destroy Japanese defensive positions and support Navy and Army ground forces as they fought their way ashore, suppressing Japanese defenders and targeting defensive strongholds. Beginning with the battle of Tarawa in November 1943, *Tennessee* took part in the Gilbert and Marshall Islands campaign, followed by the battles of Kwajalein and Eniwetok in early 1944.

As *California* returned to service in time for the Mariana and Palau Islands campaign in mid-1944, both ships bombarded Japanese positions on Saipan, Tinian, and Guam. While en route to Peleliu, the last target in the campaign, the two ships collided, preventing *California* from participating in the battle of Peleliu, though *Tennessee* remained operational.

Both ships joined the Philippines campaign that began with the invasion of Leyte in October 1944. The *Tennessees* supported the landing operations, which prompted the Japanese to launch Operation *Shō-Gō I*, a major naval counterattack resulting in the battle of Leyte Gulf on October 23–26. On the night of October 24/25, both ships participated in one component of the complex battle, the action of Surigao Strait. There, ships of the U.S. Seventh Fleet destroyed the Japanese Southern Force. *Tennessee* and *California* fired only briefly during this engagement, as a miscommunication between their commanders almost caused another collision. This threw both ships out of firing position during the last battleship-to-battleship action in history.

In January 1945, during the battle of Lingayen Gulf (Philippines), *California* was hit by a kamikaze aircraft. The ship was only slightly damaged, but its crew lost more than 50 men, with more than 150 wounded. When it returned to Puget Sound for repairs, its sister ship *Tennessee* participated in the landings at Iwo Jima in February, providing fire support.

In April 1945, *Tennessee* joined the Allied invasion of Okinawa. While shelling the island, the Allied fleet was exposed to heavy kamikaze attacks. *Tennessee* was hit by a suicide aircraft on April 12 that did little damage but killed more than 20 of its crew with more than 100 wounded. After being repaired at Ulithi Atoll in the Caroline Islands, the battleship returned to the final stages of the fighting off Okinawa in June, now joined by its sister ship *California*.

Both ships were then transferred to Task Force 95 patrolling the East China Sea, with *Tennessee* becoming the flagship of its commander, Vice Admiral Jesse B. Oldendorf. Both ships supported the initial occupation of Japan in September 1945 before returning to the United States later that month.

After being decommissioned in 1947 and assigned to the Atlantic Reserve Fleet, based in Philadelphia, the *Tennessees* were struck from the Naval Vessel Register in March 1959, sold for scrap, and eventually broken up.

Tennessee-class General Characteristics (as built)

Class	*Tennessee*
Name	*Tennessee* (BB-43) *California* (BB-44)
Shipyard	New York Naval Shipyard (BB-43) Mare Island Naval Shipyard, Vallejo (BB-44)
Commissioning	June 3, 1920 (BB-43) August 10, 1921 (BB-44)
Displacement (normal) Displacement (full)	32,300 long tons (32,818 t) 33,190 long tons (33,723 t)
Length (overall)	624 ft (190.2 m)
Beam	97 ft 5 in (29.7 m)
Draft (max)	30 ft 2 in (9.2 m)
Propulsion	2 × steam turbines / turbo-electric (32,000 shp / 24,000 kW)
Maximum speed	ca. 21 kn (39 km/h)
Range	8,000 nmi (15,000 km) at 10 kn
Complement	1,083
Armament	12 × 14-in (356 mm)/50 cal. 14 × 5-in (127 mm)/51 cal. 2 × 21-in (533 mm) torpedo tubes Various AA guns
Fate	Sold for scrap, 1959 (BB-43 and BB-44)

Colorado-class

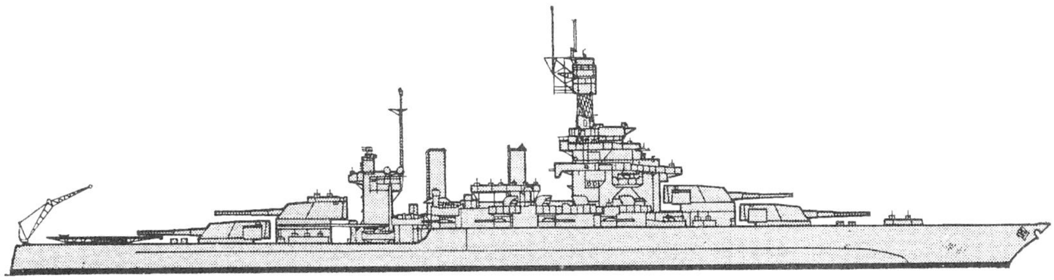

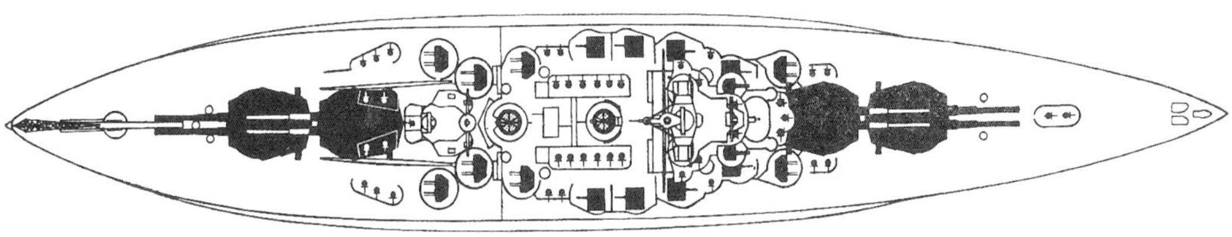

U.S.S. *Colorado* (BB-45) in the final stage of construction, 1921.

The 14-inch (356 mm) gun dominated American battleship design between 1913 and 1916 as the 12-inch (305 mm) gun had done from 1908 to 1910. However, as early as of 1911, the General Board proposed the construction of battleships armed with 16-inch guns. The caliber upgrade promised twice the muzzle energy of the 12-inch gun in service at the time, and 50 percent more than the 14-inch gun then being introduced. After its approval in 1912, the weapon was successfully test-fired two years later.

When it became apparent that the naval powers Great Britain, Japan, Germany, and Italy might adopt the 15- and 16-inch calibers, the General Board considered canceling the *Pennsylvania*-class, then under construction, in favor of an upgunned design. However, such a move would have meant an increase of about 8,000 tons in displacement per ship, twice as much as the step from the *Nevadas* to the *Pennsylvanias*. The debate continued for the following three years. During that period, Secretary of the Navy

Josephus Daniels balked at the potential cost increases and instead ordered that the design features of the standard-type battleship be retained. Eventually, he approved the "Battleship 1917" design by allowing a 16-inch (406 mm) main battery. This became the *Colorado*-class, which was essentially a copy of the preceding *Tennessee-class* with more powerful guns. However, this was the only major authorized alteration.

Likewise, the *Tennessees* were the results of modifications to the preceding *New Mexicos*. This pattern would continue in the *South Dakota*-class battleships and the *Lexington*-class battlecruisers (both eventually canceled because of the 1922 Washington Naval Treaty) as the U.S. Navy continued to standardize the designs of its capital ships. This was largely the result, in part, of the Navy's experience gained during World War I, when more than 250 destroyers and some 450 submarine hunters had to be built quickly to fight German U-boats in the Atlantic.

This was achieved by a process resembling assembly-line production principles, sticking to one basic design per class with a maximum amount of standardization. Since the 1916 Naval Act specified the construction of up to 16 battleships and six battlecruisers, production had to be streamlined to save time, labor, and resources. Also for this reason, American battleships were standardized as much as possible, and design improvements were incorporated whenever practicable and wherever applicable. Although the final design had already been finalized before the keel of the first *Colorado* was laid in 1917, the concept for the underwater protection against torpedoes, mines, and projectiles (that fell short of the ship but traveled through the water to hit it underneath the waterline) could not be completed in time. An effective protection system could only be determined by tests in caissons; these would eventually demonstrate that a series of compartments divided between being filled with liquid and being left empty would be an effective defense against torpedoes. The selected shipyards were therefore required to allow possible changes to the design even three months after the start of construction.

The new class was to consist of four ships: *Colorado* (BB-45), *Maryland* (BB-46), *Washington* (BB-47), and *West Virginia* (BB-48). Keel laying took place between 1917 and 1920. However, the Washington Naval Treaty, adopted a short time later, limited the number of battleships to be built in the future. Therefore, construction of the 75.9-percent completed battleship of the same name, *Washington*, was discontinued in 1922. On November 26, 1924, it was sunk as a gunnery target by the battleships *New York* and *Texas*.

Propulsion

The *Colorados* were built with a modified and more fuel-efficient variant of the turbo-electric drive, which already had been installed in the *Tennessees*. Each of the four propellers was powered by a 7,375 hp (5,424 kW) electric motor, powered by two turbogenerators (turbines). Steam was provided by eight oil-fired Babcock & Wilcox water-tube boilers. The combined power of the four electric motors was rated at about 28,900 electrical horsepower (ehp), allowing a top speed of 21 knots (24 mph; 39 km/h). With a maximum fuel oil storage capacity of 4,570 tons, the maximum range was at least 8,000 nautical miles (9,200 mi; 15,000 km) at a cruising speed of 10 knots (12 mph; 19 km/h).

Armament

The *Colorados* were the first American battleships armed with eight 16-inch (406 mm)/45 caliber Mark 1 guns. At a muzzle velocity of 2,600 ft/s (792 m/s) and a rate of up to 1.5 rounds per minute, this weapon fired a 2,110 lb (960 kg) AP shell to a range of 34,300 yards (31,400 m) at a maximum gun barrel elevation of 30°. The guns were arranged on the centerline in superfiring pairs forward and aft of the superstructure.

The *Colorados* were originally built with 14 5-inch (127 mm)/51 caliber Mark 15 guns to defend against destroyer attacks. At a muzzle velocity of 3,150 ft/s (960 m/s) and a rate of up to 7 rounds per minute, this

Colorado during the 1920s. Boasting eight 16-inch guns, the three *Colorados* were the most powerful American battleships until the *North Carolina*-class entered service on the eve of World War II.

weapon fired a 50 lb (23 kg) projectile to a maximum range of 15,850 yards (14,500 m) at 20° elevation. The guns were placed in unarmored casemates on the main deck, one deck higher than in previous classes, thus allowing them to be operated in heavy seas as well.

The antiaircraft defense initially consisted of four 3-inch (76 mm)/23 caliber guns, followed by an additional one. In the late 1920s, all these guns were replaced with 5-inch (127 mm)/25 caliber guns. This weapon was the U.S. Navy's first gun designed specifically for antiaircraft defense. It fired a 54 lb (24 kg) projectile at a muzzle velocity of 2,155 ft/s (657 m/s) at a rate of up 20 rounds per minute. The maximum range was up to 14,500 yards (13,300 m) at an elevation of 45°, with the ceiling up to 27,400 feet (8,400 m) at 85°. The torpedo armament consisted of two (eventually removed) submerged 21-inch tubes.

Protection and Torpedo Tubes

Built with the "all or nothing" armor scheme, introduced in the *Nevadas* and applied to all standard battleships, the armor protection of the *Colorado*-class was virtually identical to the preceding *Tennessees*. The only significant difference was the increased thickness of the armor belt near vital spaces to up 16 inches (406 mm) tapering to 8 inches (203 mm) below the waterline. The upper armor deck was 3.5 inches (89 mm) thick, while the lower deck armor measured between 1.5 and 2.25 inches (38 and 57 mm). While the main guns were protected by 18-inch (457 mm) thick faces, the barbettes were to up to 13 inches thick. The conning tower had a maximum thickness of 11.5 inches (292 mm).

Colorado in New York in 1932. Its 16-inch (406 mm)/45 caliber Mark 1 gun was based on a bored-out and relined 13-inch (330 mm) Mark 2 gun, with the promise of up to 50 percent more the muzzle energy of the 14-inch caliber. The *Colorados* were the last American battleships to enter service for nearly two decades and the final ones armed with twin-gun turrets.

Launch of *Washington* (BB-47) on September 1, 1921. *Nomen est omen?* The ship was over 75 percent complete completed when it was canceled under the terms of the 1922 Washington Naval Treaty.

Aircraft

In the 1920s, each of the *Colorados* received two catapults for seaplanes for aerial reconnaissance and fire observation and direction. One catapult was mounted at the stern, with full traverse (and an operating crane for recovery behind it) and another fixed, located on the upper aft turret (No. 3). From 1924 Curtiss VE-7 floatplanes were used, followed by the Vought UO-1, and then by the O3U Corsair. Later floatplanes included the Vought OS2U Kingfisher and the Curtiss SC Seahawk.

Operational History

Commissioned between 1921 and 1923, the three *Colorados* participated in various training and fleet exercises. In the summer of 1937, *Colorado*'s aircraft participated in the extensive but futile search for aviation pioneer Amelia Earhart, who had disappeared in the Pacific during her attempt to fly around the world. *Maryland* made a goodwill voyage to Australia and New Zealand in 1925 and transported President-elect Herbert Hoover on the Pacific leg of his tour of Latin America three years later.

While older battleship classes received various modifications in the late 1920s, the modernization of the newer so-called "Big Five"—the two *Tennessees* and three *Colorados*—was not a priority. Nevertheless, in 1931, initial plans were drawn up based on experience with the modernized *New Mexicos*. As with this and preceding classes, the U.S. Navy found it possible to exploit previously discovered loopholes in the 1922 Washington Naval Treaty that, in effect, allowed both antiaircraft and underwater defenses to be strengthened at will, fire control to be improved, but not, for example, existing ships to be upgunned. Inside the hull, anything could be done to increase protection and even speed and range, as long as the thickness of the main armor belt was not changed.

Possible modifications included increased deck and gun turret armor, improved ammunition hoists, modern fire-control systems, and new main battery projectiles. As this modernization resulted in a notable increase in weight, the installation of new machinery was necessary to maintain the 21-knot top speed. To save costs, it was proposed to recondition the engines rather than replacing them, which would

A salvo from the battleship *New York* strikes the *Washington* (BB-47) on its starboard side while being used as a target off Virginia Capes, Virginia, November 26, 1924. The battleship *Texas* is in the background.

mean an acceptable loss of up to 1 knot in speed. However, the weight increase was also a cause for concern, as it also increased the draught, which meant that a considerable part of the side armor belt would be submerged. Even without new heavy fittings, the ships suffered from overweight in service, as they always operated with an emergency storage of oil, for increased range. Therefore, the fitting of anti-torpedo bulges not only provided the chance to improve underwater protection but also increase buoyancy. While several cost-saving modernization variations were discussed, the worsening Great Depression of the 1930s shelved all plans.

After the outbreak of World War II in Europe in 1939, the U.S. Navy began to apply lessons learned by the British as their combat experience had shown the vulnerability of warships fitted with insufficient antiaircraft batteries. Consequently, the U.S. began to increase their own ships' defenses against air attacks. The existing 5-inch (127 mm)/51 caliber guns (defense against destroyers) and 5-inch/25 calibers (defense against aircraft) were both primarily replaced by more capable 5-inch/38 dual-purpose guns. Although there were plans to also equip the ships with a powerful battery of 40-mm and 20-mm AA guns, there were major concerns about the weight increase and the long shipyard layover with regards to a possible imminent American entry into the war.

However, the fitting of anti-torpedo bulges was approved for the "Big Five" because they not only strengthened underwater protection but also improved buoyancy. Only two of the ships, *Colorado* and *Maryland*, were fitted with the bulges, as this took place before the Japanese attack on Pearl Harbor on December 7, 1941. However, the air strike initially prevented the refits planned later for *West Virginia* and the two *Tennessees*, as these ships were hit during the attack. While *Maryland*, also present in Pearl Harbor, was not struck badly, its sister ship *West Virginia* was severely damaged and needed a major refit. *Colorado* was not hit as it was in the shipyard at Puget Sound, Washington.

During the air strike, *West Virginia* was on the outboard side of *Tennessee*. Japanese bombers hit it with two 16-inch (410 mm) AP naval shells that had been converted into bombs. The first struck the port side penetrating the superstructure deck, causing explosions of the ammunition stored in the casemates below. The second bomb hit and penetrated the rear superfiring turret roof but failed to explode.

Torpedo bombers struck *West Virginia* with several torpedoes on its port side. One hit aft, disabling the rudder, at least three struck the hull below the belt armor, and at least one hit the belt, damaging several armor plates. These torpedoes opened two large holes in the hull; at least one passed through the holes after the ship began to list and exploded inside.

With the torpedo hits causing serious damage, *West Virginia* avoided capsizing only through prompt damage control efforts

Sailors in a motor launch rescue a survivor from the water alongside *West Virginia* (BB-48), which was sunk by torpedoes. U.S.S. *Tennessee* (BB-43) is visible behind *West Virginia*.

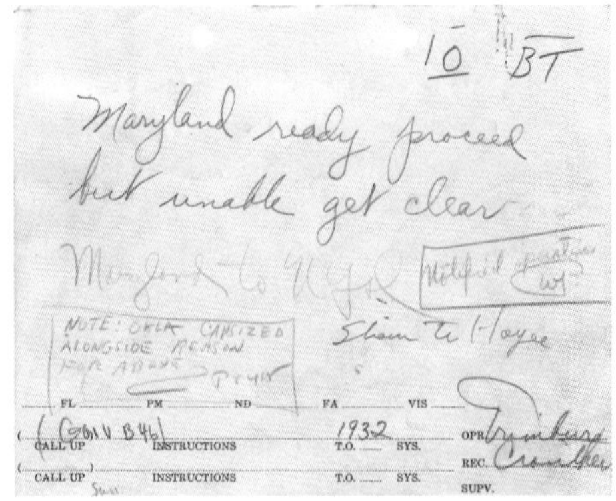

10 BT

Maryland ready proceed but unable get clear

NOTE: OKLA CAPSIZED ALONGSIDE REASON FOR ABOVE

FL PM ND FA VIS

CALL UP INSTRUCTIONS 1932 T.O. SYS. OPR.

CALL UP INSTRUCTIONS T.O. SYS. REC.

SUPV.

Maryland (BB-46, left) was moored inboard of *Oklahoma*, and thus protected from the torpedo attacks. However, it was hit by two AP bombs. Despite the resulting flooding, the ship remained afloat.

Message from *Maryland* that it cannot move because of the *Oklahoma* capsized next to it.

initiated by Lieutenant Claude V. Ricketts. The ship's commanding officer, Captain Mervyn S. Bennion, was mortally wounded by bomb fragments from a hit on *Tennessee*. However, he was awarded the Medal of Honor posthumously for remaining aboard and assisting in its defense until dying from his wounds. Doris Miller, a mess attendant second-class, was ordered to man an antiaircraft gun. Although he never had operated such a weapon before, he was credited with downing at least two Japanese aircraft. Miller was the first Afro-American to be awarded the Navy Cross, the highest decoration for valor presented by the U.S. Navy, and the second highest in the United States after the Medal of Honor. As *West Virginia* slowly sank on an even keel, fuel oil leaking from *Arizona* caught fire and engulfed it in flames, which was also fed by its own leaking fuel oil. The fires were eventually extinguished the next day. More than 100 crewmembers lost their lives in the attack.

Maryland was moored inboard of *Oklahoma*, and thus protected from the initial torpedo attack. When the torpedo hits caused the latter to roll over quickly, many of its survivors climbed aboard *Maryland* to assist its antiaircraft defenses. The ship was hit by two AP bombs detonating low on its hull. The first struck the

Aerial view of Battleship Row after the attack. In upper left is the sunken *California*. Diagonally, from left center to lower right are *Maryland*, lightly damaged, with the capsized *Oklahoma* outboard; a barge is alongside *Oklahoma*, supporting rescue efforts; *Tennessee*, lightly damaged, with the sunken *West Virginia* outboard; *Arizona*, sunk, with its hull shattered by the explosion of the magazines below the two forward turrets.

Tennessee, at left, alongside the sunken *West Virginia*, photographed from the capsized hull of *Oklahoma* on December 10, 1941, three days after the attack.

forecastle, leaving a hole about 12 feet by 20 feet (3.7 m by 6.1 m). The second bomb exploded after entering the hull at Frame 10. Despite causing flooding, the ship remained afloat. Four crewmembers were killed in the attack. Shortly after the attack, the damaged ship entered Puget Sound Navy Yard for repairs. Over the course of the next two months, it was repaired, overhauled, and fitted with new 5-inch (127 mm)/38 caliber dual purpose guns. *Maryland* was sent back into action in June 1942.

After patching over the two torpedo holes and pumping the hull dry, *West Virginia* was refloated in May 1942. The subsequent inspection in dry dock revealed that the ship had been hit by seven torpedoes, not five as had been initially believed. While carrying out temporary repairs to make the ship seaworthy, shipyard workers discovered the remains of more than 60 men who had been trapped below decks when *West Virginia* sank. Some had survived for several days in air bubbles, but their oxygen and emergency rations ran out long before the ship was refloated. After completing repairs, it got underway for the Puget Sound Navy Yard in Bremerton, Washington, for a radical reconstruction lasting until summer 1944. This included anti-torpedo bulges and a completely revised superstructure. With the second funnel removed, its boilers were trunked into an enlarged forward funnel. The foremast was replaced with a tower mast housing the bridge. *West Virginia* received air-search radar and fire-control radars for its 16-inch main battery and secondary guns. The latter

The reconstructed *West Virginia* in 1944. The superstructure, arrangement of antiaircraft guns, and fire-control systems now closely resembled those of the new *North Carolina*- and *South Dakota*-classes.

were replaced by 16 5-inch/38 caliber guns in eight twin mounts. The light antiaircraft armament now consisted of 10 quadruple 40-mm Bofors guns and 43 20-mm Oerlikons.

Colorado and *Maryland*

As *Colorado* and *Maryland* were urgently needed in the war theater and with many of the existing battleships badly damaged at Pearl Harbor, neither ship received a major refit until 1944, although minor additions and removals were made periodically. Throughout the war, they saw their antiaircraft battery upgraded constantly. This included the addition of 40-mm Bofors guns, most of them in quads, 20-mm Oerlikons and several .50 caliber machine guns.

Beginning with 1944, a second overhaul of antiaircraft defense was made as the U.S. Navy considered 20-mm shells too light to stop Japanese kamikaze aircraft. Each ship eventually carried some 40 quad 40-mm and up to 50 20-mm guns. In the same year, *Colorado* and *Maryland* received major refits. This included the removal of their cage masts in favor of tower masts and new radar. During repairs after a kamikaze hit, *Maryland* received some improvements. While eight 5-inch/38 dual-purpose guns were added, the conning tower was removed and replaced with a very light STS structure to compensate for the additional weight of the new 5-inch guns.

During the upcoming island-hopping campaign in the Pacific, *Colorado* and *Maryland* conducted preparatory bombardments destroying Japanese defensive positions and supporting landing operations by suppressing Japanese defenders. Both ships participated in the Gilbert and Marshall Islands campaign, the Mariana and Palau Islands campaign, the Philippines campaign, and the battle of Okinawa. In summer 1944, *West Virginia* rejoined the Pacific Fleet for combat operations on the eve of the Philippines campaign. This

West Virginia in floating dry dock, off Aessi Island, New Hebrides, November 1944. The battleship was docked for upkeep and repair to propellers damaged when it touched bottom off Leyte in October.

also resulted in the battle of Surigao Strait on October 24–25, 1944, the last battleship-to-battleship action in history, during which *Maryland* and *West Virginia* were present. Here, the latter was able to hit the Japanese battleship *Yamashiro* with its first salvo—in the dark—at 22,800 yards (20,800 m) using its sophisticated Mark 8 fire-control radar. In February 1945, *West Virginia* participated in the battle of Iwo Jima, followed by its last combat operations during the battle of Okinawa. Following the end of the war, the three *Colorados* participated in Operation *Magic Carpet*, the repatriation of American soldiers. Decommissioned in 1947, all three ships were eventually sold for scrap in 1959.

Colorado-class General Characteristics (as built)

Class	*Colorado*
Name	*Colorado* (BB-45) *Maryland* (BB-46) *Washington* (BB-47) *West Virginia* (BB-48)
Shipyard	New York Shipbuilding Corporation, Camden (BB-45 and BB-47) Newport News Shipbuilding Company (BB-46 and BB-48)
Commissioning	August 30, 1923 (BB-45) July 21, 1921 (BB-46) Canceled (BB-47) December 1, 1923 (BB-48)
Displacement (normal) Displacement (full)	32,600 long tons (33,100 t) 33,590 long tons (34,130 t)
Length (overall)	624 ft 3 in (190.27 m)
Beam	97 ft 4 in (29.67 m)
Draft (max)	30 ft 6 in (9.3 m)
Propulsion	2 × steam turbines / turbo-electric (28,900 shp / 21,600 kW)
Maximum speed	ca. 21 kn (39 km/h)
Range	8,000 nmi (15,000 km) at 10 kn
Complement	1,080
Armament	8 × 16-in (406 mm)/45 cal. Mark 1 12 or 14 × 5-in (127 mm)/51 cal. 2 × 21-in (533 mm) torpedo tubes Various AA guns
Fate	Sold for scrap, 1959 (BB-45, BB-46 and BB-48) Sunk as target, November 25, 1924 (BB-47)

South Dakota-class

Prior to World War I, the U.S. Navy had been inadequately funded by Congress as the latter had not implemented the General Board's recommendation to build two battleships per year. In addition, President Woodrow Wilson and his Secretary of the Navy Josephus Daniels considered additional expenditures on capital ships as not worthwhile. However, the outbreak of the war in 1914 led to a change in thinking. While the General Board now demanded the construction of four battleships in 1916, the Committee on Naval Affairs disagreed and favored modifying the existing program after the experience of the war. However, the sinking of the American passenger ship *Lusitania* by a German U-boat, the belief that a victorious Germany with its powerful fleet might become a threat to American shipping and its coastlines, as well as Japanese expansion in Asia made the United States and its Navy look weak in the public eye. While Wilson reconsidered his opinion, the General Board argued that the Navy should be the equal to the strongest fleet in the world, that of the British, not just to the most likely enemy, Imperial Germany, with the second strongest fleet. Therefore, the General Board demanded the construction of 10 battleships over five years, together with battlecruisers and smaller warships.

The first *South Dakota*-class was a group of six battleships laid down in 1920 but scrapped before completion due to the regulations of the 1922 Washington Naval Treaty. The ships were designed for a speed of 23 knots to keep up with the increasing speeds of British and Japanese battleships.

The General Board's five-year program was compressed into three years, with four ships in fiscal year 1917 and three in each of the following years. While the first four ships (the *Colorados*) featured only minor modifications over the preceding *Tennessees* (expect their increased 16-inch caliber), the changed attitude towards the value of battleships enabled the General Board to propose more powerful and more expensive ships for the future. Consequently, it requested a main armament of 12 16-inch (406 mm) guns and a top

South Dakota (BB-49) under construction at the New York Naval Shipyard in 1922. This view is from the ship's bow looking aft. The size was limited by the possibility of passing through the Panama Canal. This was a fundamental part of the U.S. Navy's strategy as it saved weeks of time when warships had to transfer from the Atlantic to the Pacific or vice versa.

speed higher than the 21 knots to keep up with fast foreign designs such as the Japanese *Nagato*- and British *Queen Elizabeth*-classes. After comparing various proposals and conducting gunnery trials with triple turrets used by *Pennsylvania* the Bureau of Construction and Repair (C&R) chose four triple-gun turrets for the new *South Dakota*-class, which were based on an enlarged version of the *Colorados* with an estimated displacement of 42,000 long tons (43,000 t). The General Board selected the newly developed 16-inch/50 caliber Mark 2 gun rather than the older 45 caliber Mark 1 as the former was significantly more powerful with only a minimal increase in weight. In late 1916, Daniels approved these preliminary characteristics. Despite its larger displacement, the *South Dakota*'s design strongly resembled the standard-type battleship, thus representing the ultimate development of the standard-type battleships that characterized the *Nevada*- through *Colorado*-classes.

Propulsion

Turbo-electric propulsion, which had already been adopted with the earlier *New Mexicos*, was continued in the *South Dakotas*. Two turbogenerators powered four electric motors, each driving one propeller shaft, rated at 15,000 shp (11,200 kW). Steam for the generators was generated by 12 water-tube boilers. With a total of 60,000 shp (45,000 kW), the *South Dakota*'s designed top speed was 23 knots (42.6 km/h). Their fuel oil storage capacity allowed a designed range of 8,000 nautical miles (9,200 mi; 15,000 km) at a cruising speed of 10 knots (12 mph; 19 km/h).

Armament

The main battery consisted of 12 16-inch (406 mm)/50 caliber Mark 2 guns in four triple-gun turrets. At a rate of two rounds per minute, this weapon fired the same 2,100 lb (953 kg) shell as the older 45 caliber Mark 1 of the *Colorados*. At a barrel elevation of 46° and a muzzle velocity of 2,650 feet per second (810 m/s), the maximum range was up to 45,100 yards (41,200 m).

Unlike their predecessors, which were armed with 5-inch guns, the *South Dakotas* were designed with a secondary armament consisting of 16 6-inch/53 caliber Mark 12 guns. Twelve of these were to be placed in unarmored casemates on the side of the superstructure and the remaining four guns abreast the forward superstructure. At a barrel elevation of 20° and a muzzle velocity of 3,000 feet per second (910 m/s), this gun could fire a 105-lb (48-kg) projectile at a maximum range of 21,000 yards (19,000 m) at a rate of up to 7 rounds per minute.

The *South Dakota*'s antiaircraft defense was to consist of four 3-inch (76 mm)/50 caliber guns in single mounts amidships. At a velocity of 2,700 feet per second (820 m/s), this weapon could fire a 13 lb (5.9 kg) projectile at a maximum range of 14,590 yards (13,340 m) at a rate of up to 15 rounds per minute. The ships were also to be fitted with two 21-inch (533 mm) underwater torpedo tubes.

Protection

The armor belt had a thickness of 13.5 inches (343 mm) tapering to 8 inches (203 mm) below the waterline. Extending between the fore and aft turret barbettes, it protected the magazines and propulsion machinery. The front and rear ends of the belt were closed by transverse bulkheads 8 to 13.5 inches (203 to 343 mm) thick, forming an armored citadel. The main armor over the armored belt consisted of two layers of steel, each 1.75 inches (44.5 mm) thick: one was made of nickel steel (NS), the other of special treatment steel (STS).

Below the armor deck was the splinter deck made of up to 1.25 inches (32 mm) of STS. It was designed to absorb splinters from shells that burst on the main deck. The faces of the main gun turrets had armor of 18 inches (457 mm), with up to 10-inch (254 mm) thick sides and a roof 5 inches thick. The barbettes were protected by up to 13.5 inches of armor. The massive conning tower had 16-inch (406 mm) thick sides and an 8-inch (203 mm) roof.

The underwater protection against torpedoes and mines strongly resembled that of the preceding *Colorados*. It was five layers deep with watertight compartments, separated by three 0.75-inch (19 mm) thick torpedo bulkheads, extending from the splinter deck to the ship's bottom and between the transverse bulkheads. While the outermost compartment was empty, the three middle ones were used as fuel oil tanks; the innermost one was also empty.

Fate

After the approval of the *South Dakotas* in 1917, their construction was postponed, thus enabling the U.S. Navy to examine the results of the battle of Jutland, fought between British and German capital ships in mid-1916, and incorporate helpful findings into the design. Keel laying was delayed even until 1920 (after the end of the war) because in the interim, priority was given to the completion of destroyers and other small warships, which were urgently needed to fight German U-boats in the North Atlantic.

Since the 1922 Washington Naval Treaty limited the total tonnage allowed to the U.S. Navy for battleships and the size of individual ships to 35,000 long tons (36,000 t), construction of all six *South Dakotas* was discontinued that same year. Their unfinished hulls were broken up shortly thereafter. While the guns were transferred to the U.S. Army to be used as coastal-defense guns, the boilers and armor were used to modernize older battleships, as permitted by the treaty.

South Dakota-class General Characteristics (as planned)

Class	*South Dakota*
Name	*South Dakota* (BB-49) *Indiana* (BB-50) *Montana* (BB-51) *North Carolina* (BB-52) *Iowa* (BB-53) *Massachusetts* (BB-54)
Shipyard	New York Naval Shipyard (BB-49 and BB-50) Mare Island Naval Shipyard, Vallejo (BB-51) Norfolk Naval Shipyard, Virginia (BB-52) Newport News Shipbuilding Company (BB-53) Fore River Shipyard (BB-54)
Commissioning	Canceled
Displacement (normal) Displacement (full)	43,200 long tons (43,900 t) 47,000 long tons (47,800 t)
Length (overall)	684 ft (208.5 m)
Beam	106 ft (32.3 m)
Draft (max)	33 ft (10.1 m)
Propulsion	4 × steam turbines / turbo-electric (60,000 shp / 45,000 kW)
Maximum speed	23 kn (43 km/h)
Range	8,000 nmi (15,000 km) at 10 kn
Complement	1,616
Armament	12 × 16-in (406 mm)/50 cal. Mark 2 16 × 6-in (152 mm)/53 cal. 2 × 21-in (533 mm) torpedo tubes Various AA guns
Fate	Sold for scrap, 1923 (BB-50: scrapped on slipway)

4

The Interwar Period—A Dawn for New Battleships

Although the end of World War I had largely halted battleship construction, a new naval arms race commenced as soon as "peace broke out." American and Japanese ambitions to expand their fleets sparked the postwar naval arms race in the Pacific. Japan's naval buildup was inspired by the doctrine of Admiral Satō Tetsutarō who advocated that Japan's security could only be guaranteed by a powerful navy. Therefore, Japan should have the means of defeating the naval power representing the greatest hypothetical threat.

After the Russo-Japanese War of 1904–5, Japan's military focus shifted from Russia towards the United States, which was now considered that primary hypothetical threat to Japan's future security. On the other hand, America, determined to create a navy "second to none," watched Japan's naval buildup and its territorial expansion in the Pacific with growing concern, in particular after Japanese forces had seized some of Germany's colonies during World War I, thus becoming a potential rival to American interests in the Asia-Pacific Region.

As a result, the United States Naval Appropriations Act of 1916 authorized the construction of more than 150 new warships, including 10 battleships and six battlecruisers. This building program began slowly, in part because American naval architects wanted to incorporate as many lessons as possible from Jutland in their new designs. For the first time, and with Germany after its defeat in World War I no longer being a first-rank sea power, America was threatening Great Britain's naval supremacy. Although the building program was never fulfilled entirely, the U.S. Navy's three new battleships of the *Colorado*-class, laid down in 1917–20, and the battlecruisers of the *Lexington*-class, capable of 33 knots (two ships laid down in 1920–21) outgunned the British *Queen Elizabeth*-class and *Admiral*-class by mounting 16-inch (406 mm) guns.

Across the Pacific, the Imperial Japanese Navy—in response to the U.S. Navy's plan to build an additional 10 battleships and six battlecruisers—received authorization for its ambitious "Eight-Eight Fleet Program" in 1917, which called for a future fleet of eight modern battleships and

American warships (Victory Fleet) in the Hudson River near New York following the end of World War I in late 1918. U.S.S. *New York* (BB-34) is probably in the foreground, while its sister ship U.S.S. *Texas* (BB-35) is in the background.

eight battlecruisers. This included the two new battleships of the *Nagato*-class, laid down in 1917–18, armed with eight 16.1-inch (409 mm) guns, thus boasting equal firepower as their American rivals of the *Colorado*-class.

In 1919, American President Woodrow Wilson, in response to Japan's "Eight-Eight Fleet Program," proposed a further expansion of the U.S. Navy in addition to the 1916 program by asking for another 10 battleships (beginning with the six vessels of the *South Dakota*-class in 1920) and six battlecruisers. In response to Wilson's proposal, Japan's parliament finally authorized the construction of four additional fast battleships of the *Kii*-class, armed with 16.1-inch guns and capable of 30 knots, to be followed by four slower battleships (Nos. 13–16 or *Number 13*-class), which were to carry eight 18-inch (457 mm) guns. This would have resulted in a fleet of 24 capital ships.

Great Britain, although one of the victors of World War I, was financially exhausted after four years of fighting, and faced the risk of slipping behind the United States and Japan in terms of naval strength. With only one postwar ship, the battlecruiser *Hood*, completed, the British Admiralty outlined a future fleet consisting of more than 30 battleships and eight battlecruisers. The 1921 British Naval Estimates included the construction of four battlecruisers of the G3-class, armed with nine 16-inch guns and capable of 32 knots, and four battleships of the *N3*-class, with nine 18-inch guns, with another four to follow the subsequent year. To avoid the crippling expense of a naval arms race, the major naval powers met at a conference 1921.

The Washington Naval Treaty of 1922

With the emerging naval arms race unwelcomed by the American public, who wanted to resume the non-interventionism of the prewar years, Congress disapproved President Wilson's naval expansion plan of 1919. Great Britain, although still possessing the world strongest navy, could barely afford an arms race similar to that against Germany before 1914. When the British planned a conference about the strategic situation in the Asia-

The 1922 Washington Naval Treaty strictly stipulated the demolition of many battleships to reduce existing battle fleets.

Pacific Region, the newly elected U.S. government under President Warren G. Harding "beat" the British to it by inviting the leading powers to the Washington Naval Conference during November 1921, thus also satisfying domestic demands for global disarmament talks.

Based on the American proposal, this treaty limited the number and size of capital warships each major naval power was allowed to possess. The tonnage limits resulted in a strength ratio of approximately 5:5:3:1.75:1.75 for Great Britain, the United States, Japan, France, and Italy, respectively. The treaty also detailed individual ships to be retained by each navy, thus allowing the United States to complete two more ships of the *Colorado*-class, armed with 16-inch guns, and Great Britain, as a means of compensation, to build the two battleships of the *Nelson*-class, carrying the same caliber.

Washington Naval Treaty tonnage limitations (in long tons)		
Nation	Capital ships	Aircraft carriers
British Empire	525,000 tons	135,000 tons
United States	525,000 tons	135,000 tons
Empire of Japan	315,000 tons	81,000 tons
France	175,000 tons	60,000 tons
Italy	175,000 tons	60,000 tons

This ratio required Great Britain to accept parity with the United States and to abandon its alliance with Japan, as American delegates had made it clear that they would not sign the treaty unless the British ended their "partnership" with the Japanese. Moreover, the Royal Navy would no longer be able to maintain adequate fleets in the North Sea, the Mediterranean, and the Far East simultaneously, thus provoking strong criticism from various parts of the navy. However, the British government was under immense to agree to the American

British warships during a naval exercise in the 1930s. A *Nelson*-class battleship, launched in 1925, is in the foreground, while the others are modernized World War I-era vessels of the *Queen Elizabeth*- and *Revenge*-classes. The *Nelsons* were the first battleships built to comply with the limitations of the Washington Treaty. The need to limit displacement resulted in reducing the armor weight. Therefore, the 16-inch gun turrets were all mounted in front of the superstructure to shorten the armored citadel.

The Washington Naval Treaty limitations meant that fewer new battleships were launched in 1919–1939 than in 1905–1914.

proposal to avoid another costly arms race, which it would likely lose. Moreover, the risk of an armed conflict with the United States was increasingly regarded as merely theoretical, due to the very few policy differences between both powers.

The treaty laid out a list of ships, including most of the older battleships and battlecruisers and almost all the newer ships under construction, which were to be scrapped, sunk, or rendered ineffective for military use. A limited number of ships could be converted into target or training vessels by removing their armament, armor, and other combat-essential parts. Some ships under construction, including two of the American *Lexington*-class, one of the Japanese *Tosa*-class, and one of the *Amagi*-class, were completed as aircraft carriers. In all, the United States had to scrap 30 existing capital ships, Britain, 23 and Japan, 17.

Moreover, the treaty declared a 10-year "building holiday" (moratorium) during which no new battleships or battlecruisers were to be built. The ships surviving the treaty, including the most modern super-dreadnoughts, formed the bulk of the major naval powers' capital ship strength through the 1920s and 1930s and, with some modernization, during World War II.

At the time of the Washington Naval Conference in 1921, Japan only possessed 55 percent of what capital ships the U.S. had and 18 percent of American GDP, thus foreshadowing that Japan would lose any future arms race against the United States.

The treaty also halted the development of larger ship designs (battleships and battlecruisers) by putting maximum limits on the displacement of ships and their armament, resulting in a 35,000 long tons (35,560 t) standard displacement and guns of no larger than 16-inch caliber. Battleship designs such as the projected British *N3*-class, the (first) American *South Dakota*-class, and the Japanese *Kii*-class—all of which continued the trend to larger and more heavily armed ships—never got off the drawing board. While aircraft carriers were allowed to have a displacement of 27,000 long tons (27,430 t), all other warships were limited to 10,000 long tons (10,160 t) and a maximum gun caliber of 8 inches (203 mm). Initially, some members of the Japanese delegation rejected the 3:5 ratio in relation to the United States and Britain, respectively, as it would reduce Japan to a second-rank naval power compared to the two Anglophone nations. Nevertheless, Japan finally accepted this ratio to avoid a potential arms race with the United States, as the relative

The partly modernized American battle fleet steaming in formation off the California coast during the 1920s. The three leading ships are (in no particular order) most likely *Colorado* (BB-45), *Maryland* (BB-46), and *West Virginia* (BB-48), followed by *Tennessee* (BB-43) and three older battleships.

industrial strength of the two nations would cause Japan to lose such a contest and possibly plunge it into an economic crisis.

The French delegation, which demanded a total capital ships tonnage of 350,000 long tons (355,616 t), slightly over Japan's 315,000 long tons, initially responded negatively to the prospect of reducing it to 175,000 long tons (177,808 t). Finally, several concessions regarding cruisers and submarines helped convince them to agree to that limit on capital ships. The French, however, strongly criticized Italy's demand of parity, as it was, in their opinion, unsubstantiated. Nevertheless, British and American pressure caused them to accept it. Although Italy never attained that parity, it considered the concession of 175,000 long tons an important success over France, Italy's rival in the Mediterranean. The ships constructed under the terms of the Washington Naval Treaty, signed on February 6, 1922, to replace obsolete vessels were labelled "treaty battleships." After the Washington Naval Conference, the term "dreadnought" became less widely used, as with most pre-dreadnought battleships being scrapped or hulked it became less necessary. The treaty was followed by a series of other naval agreements, including the First Geneva Naval Conference (1927), the First London Naval Treaty (1930), the Second Geneva Naval Conference (1932), and finally the Second London Naval Treaty (1936). They all set limits on capital warships as well as on cruisers, destroyers, and submarines.

Rise of Air Power

> *"Sea craft of all kinds, up to and including the most modern battleships, can be destroyed easily by bombs dropped from aircraft, and further, that the most effective means of destruction are bombs. [They] demonstrated beyond a doubt that, given sufficient bombing planes—in short, an adequate air force—aircraft constitute a positive defense of our country against hostile invasion."*
>
> —Brigadier General William "Billy" Mitchell, United States Army Air Service, 1921

When World War I broke out, fixed-wing aircraft had been in use for just a decade. During the conflict, they made a remarkable transition from simply transport and reconnaissance vehicles to fighting machines contributing significantly to the outcome of the war, in particular over the trenches in France and Flanders. During these early pioneer days of flight and aerial warfare, some experts in various countries already anticipated that if an aircraft could drop bombs on a trench, railroad, or fortification, it also could effectively bombard moving and armored objects of the size of warships. Repeated successful aerial attacks on (mostly surfaced) German U-boats

Aerial bombardment of the ex-German battleship *Ostfriesland*, July 1921. A contemporary cartoon in the *Chicago Tribune* described the result of the ship's sinking as seen from both sides. While the pro-battleship partisan observes claimed that the ship was "a stationary, defenseless target, and yet see how long it took the bombing planes to sink it," pro-aircraft partisan observers responded, "Yes, but we DID sink it, didn't we?" (U.S. Air Force)

with bombs eventually led to the mounting of a torpedo under the aircraft's fuselage, thus allowing it to attack ships from a safe distance out of range of the ship's antiaircraft guns. Recognizing the increasing capabilities of aircraft, some military leaders, including British Admiral Percy Scott, predicted as early as 1914 that even heavily armored battleships would soon be made virtually irrelevant by aircraft.

In 1921, the Italian general and airpower theorist Giulio Douhet completed his influential treatise, *The Command of the Air (Il Dominio dell'Aria)*, which foresaw the dominance of air power over warships.

This view was shared by Brigadier General William "Billy" Mitchell, the Assistant Chief of the United States Air Service. An experienced aviator, he had fought as a pilot in France in World War I and was in command of all American air combat forces there when the conflict ended. Billy Mitchell's strong belief in the superiority of airpower went that far that he testified in front of Congress that the American military could construct a thousand bomber aircraft for the cost of one new battleship, and moreover, that a squadron of these could destroy such a battleship. Therefore, the investment in aircraft would mean a more efficient use of the American defense budget. Although this statement antagonized the Navy, Mitchell received permission to turn his theory into results by conducting a series of bombing tests using Army, Marine Corps, and Navy bombers against decommissioned warships, including several former German vessels, which had been handed over to the United States after World War I as war prizes.

However, the U.S. Air Service and the Navy had cross purposes—while the former was determined to demonstrate that airpower could destroy warships, the latter stated that the bombing tests should show how much damage ships could withstand. The "prize" for Mitchell's demonstration of airpower was the ex-German dreadnought battleship *Ostfriesland*, commissioned in 1911, once one of the world's most powerful warships and a veteran of the battle of Jutland. Known for its effective underwater compartmentalization and Krupp armor protection, it was indeed not one of the latest battleships, but still an impressive floating fortress that could take a lot of punishment. Built in an era when there was no aerial threat to capital warships, Mitchell, and other American military leaders as well as domestic and foreign officials were keen to see what would happen to a battleship when ferociously attacked by bombers. Like the ships used in the other tests, *Ostfriesland* was not attacked under "war-time conditions," meaning that it was stationary, defenseless, and without any damage control. By violating some rules of engagement including an agreement that would have allowed navy engineers to examine the effects of various munitions, *Ostfriesland* was sunk after three bombing runs on July 21, 1921. When it rolled over and sank at 12:40, Mitchell had achieved his goal by demonstrating the vulnerability of battleships against aerial attacks. Although the results were widely publicized, sparking great controversy in the American public, they were downplayed in public by General of the Armies, John J. Pershing, who hoped to smooth the relations between the U.S. Army and Navy. The efficacy of the tests remains in debate to this day, as later studies of *Ostfriesland*'s wreck revealed that it had suffered little topside damage from bombs and was sunk by progressive flooding that might have been contained by a well-drilled damage control crew. While battleships remained the backbone of the fleet, the U.S. Navy made headway towards the expansion of its nascent aircraft carrier program. Eventually, the events of World War II would show the effects of modern airpower against even the largest and most modern battleships.

In 1924, Billy Mitchell was sent on an inspection tour to Hawaii and Asia, returning with a report that predicted a future war with Japan, including the attack on Pearl Harbor destroying the American Pacific Fleet stationed there. Mitchell, however, downplayed the value of aircraft carriers in his predicted attack on the Hawaiian Islands, believing they were of little practical use due to their incapability of operating effectively on the high seas or launching enough aircraft at one time to execute a concentrated operation. He believed instead that a surprise attack on Pearl Harbor would be conducted by land-based, long-range aircraft operating

Billy Mitchell was a strong advocate for airpower. (U.S. Air Force)

U.S.S. *Langley* (CV-1), the first American aircraft carrier, at anchor in 1923. Two battleships are in the background. At the time, few experts could have imagined that carrier-based aircraft would destroy numerous battleships less than 20 years later.

from various islands in the Pacific. When Mitchell wrote his report, aircraft carriers were still considered experimental. Until the late 1930s, these ships, along with carrier-based aircraft, made significant progress, thus becoming powerful weapons, which was difficult to conceive in 1924. Although his views on airpower were widely supported in the press, his increasingly combative behavior towards superior army and navy officers eventually resulted in a court martial for insubordination that forced him to retire from the military in 1926. Billy Mitchell died in 1936, five years before Japanese carrier-based aircraft successfully attacked Pearl Harbor.

Upgrading the Battle Fleets

During the 1930s, the United States, Great Britain, Japan, and Italy substantially modernized and upgraded their World War I-era capital ships. New features included increased stability for the optical rangefinder equipment used for fire control, enhanced armor on the decks around the gun turrets for protection against plunging fire and aerial bombing, and additional antiaircraft weapons for self-defense. Several ships received external bulges to improve buoyancy to compensate weight increase caused by additional armor and equipment and provide an improved underwater protection against torpedoes and mines.

The 1930s saw the introduction of early radar devices to supplement optical fire control and reconnaissance. Radar was effective beyond visual range and effective in complete darkness or adverse weather.

With Benito Mussolini becoming Italy's *Il Duce* in Italy in the 1920s, and Adolf Hitler the *Führer* in Germany in the 1930s, Europe's post-World War I order consequently lost its balance of power. Moreover, in the Pacific, the Washington Naval Treaty and its subsequent treaties became one of the factors that contributed to the deterioration of the relationship between the United States and Japan, not least because Japanese ultranationalists considered the 3 to 5 ratio in capital warships as unfair—even though Japan would lose a full-scale naval arms race with the United States.

Armed with eight 16.1-inch guns, the two ships of the *Nagato*-class were de facto the most powerful warships in the world by 1920/21. Both were extensively modernized in the interwar period.

However, Japan, a signatory of the Washington Naval Treaty of 1922 and the First London Naval Treaty of 1930—the latter basically a continuation of the Washington Treaty—withdrew from a second conference in London in January 1936, which was to result in the Second London Naval Treaty with the intention to limit the growth in naval armaments until 1942. Moreover, Italy also declined to sign the treaty, largely because of the controversy over its invasion of Abyssinia (modern-day Ethiopia). As a result, Italy found itself under sanctions from the League of Nations. With the absence of Japan and Italy, it was not possible to reach a worldwide agreement on the quantity and size of warships. The treaty, however, did limit the number of ships, and their maximum size and caliber of the signatory nations, now reduced to the United States, Britain, and France.

Although the Second London Naval Treaty restricted the size of capital ships to 35,000 long tons (35,560 t) standard displacement and an armament of 14-inch (356 mm) guns, it also included a so-called "escalator clause" at the urging of the American delegation. This provision allowed the signatory nations—Great Britain, the United States, and France—to increase the armament from 14-inch to 16-inch guns if Japan

Battleships designed during the 1930s featured thicker and more robust horizontal armor protection against aerial attacks, a large number of antiaircraft guns, and better underwater compartmentalization against mines and torpedoes.

Although the signatory nations of the naval treaties of Washington and London agreed to a displacement of 35,000 long tons (35,560 t), virtually every battleship eventually reached a higher displacement up to 40,000 long tons.

or Italy still refused to sign the Second London Treaty after April 1, 1937. Neither Japan nor Italy signed. In 1938, the three signatory nations agreed on a new displacement limit of 45,000 long tons (47,200 t) for new capital ships. The Second London Naval Treaty, as well as all previous treaties, effectively ended on September 1, 1939 when World War II broke out.

Besides building aircraft carriers, the U.S. Navy had designed the *North Carolina*-class, laid down in 1937–38, and the subsequent *South Dakota*-class, laid down in 1939–40, both capable of 27 knots (32 mph; 52 km/h). The former was designed before the escalator clause was invoked, therefore being intended to displace 35,000 long tons (35,560 t) and carry 14-inch guns. With the U.S. Navy invoking the clause after Japan and Italy had refused to sign the Second London Naval Treaty, both ships were eventually completed with 16-inch guns. The design of the subsequent *Iowa*-class, capable of 33 knots (38.0 mph; 61.1 km/h), of which six were to be built, began in 1938. Ordered the following year, with the Second London Treaty no longer effective, they carried 16-inch guns on a displacement of 45,000 long tons (47,200 t). The decision to build the *Iowa*-class with a larger displacement than its predecessors was influenced by the intelligence gathered on Japanese capital ship building. Although Japan prioritized the construction of aircraft carriers and kept the new construction program secret, the U.S. Navy knew that its potential rival across the Pacific had laid down two gigantic battleships of the *Yamato*-class, *Yamato* and *Musashi*, between 1937 and 1938, followed by a third in 1940, *Shinano*, which was later completed as an aircraft carrier. The fourth and fifth ships were canceled.

The Japanese battleships *Yamato* (depicted here) and *Musashi* were the largest and most powerfully armed battleships ever built. Both were sunk by American carrier-based aircraft.

Turret face plate from a *Yamato*-class battleship. This 25-inch-thick armor plate was penetrated by a U.S. Navy 16-inch shell during post-World War II tests.

North Carolina-class

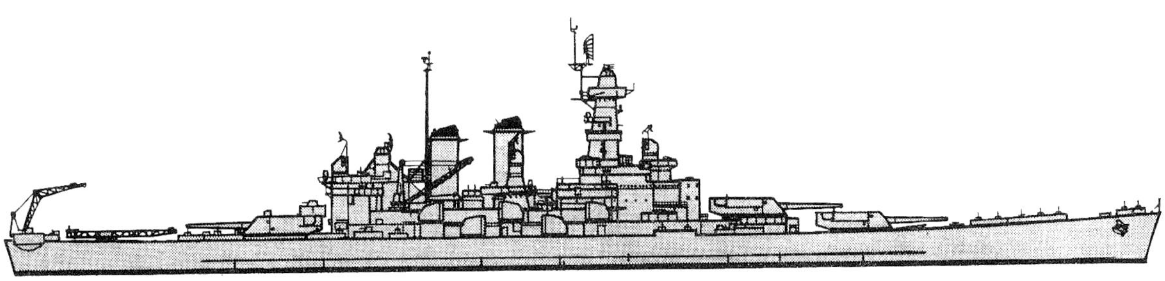

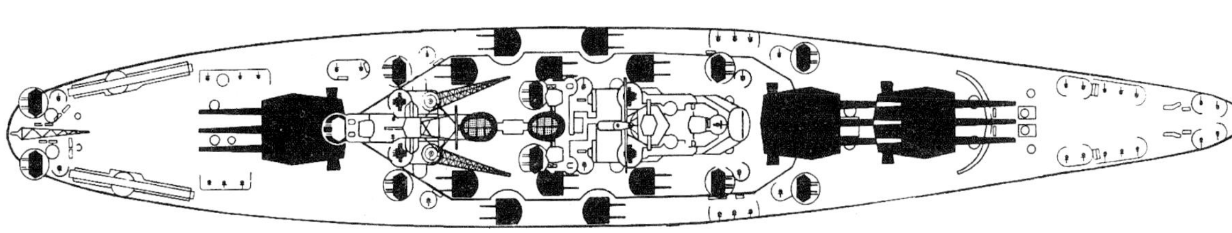

The 1922 Washington Naval Treaty limited all future battleship designs to a standard displacement of 35,000 long tons (35,560 t) and a maximum gun caliber of 16 inches (406 mm). It also stipulated that the five signatory nations—United States, Great Britain, France, Italy, and Japan—could not construct additional capital ships for 10 years and could not replace any vessel that had survived the treaty until it was at least 20 years old. The 1935/36 Second London Naval Treaty retained many of the Washington Treaty's requirements but restricted the gun caliber on new warships to 14 inches (356 mm).

Both treaties had a major impact on the design development of the two ships of the *North Carolina*-class, as evidenced by a long and erratic struggle to find a ship that incorporated everything the U.S. Navy deemed necessary, while not exceeding 35,000 long tons (35,560 t). When the General Board began preparations for a new battleship class in 1935, they received three design studies: Design "A" was a ship displacing 32,150 long tons (32,670 t) armed with nine 14-inch guns in triple turrets, which were all forward of the bridge. The maximum speed was 30 knots, with an armor protection against 14-inch projectiles; Designs "B" and "C" were both over 36,000 long tons (36,580 t), capable of reaching 30.5 knots (35.1 mph; 56.5 km/h) and protected against 14-inch shells. The major difference between these two proposals was the planned main battery, as "B" featured 12 14-inch guns in triple turrets, while "C" had eight 16-inch guns in dual turrets. Design "A" was the only variant that did not exceed the 35,000-long-ton limit set in the 1922 Washington Naval Treaty and reaffirmed in the 1935/36 Second London Naval Treaty.

A model of the *North Carolina*-class (1937) built during the lengthy design development. Models like this are now sought-after collector's items or valuable exhibits in museums.

Although these initial three studies were all "fast" battleships (compared to all previous American battleships), the General Board hesitated to commit to the higher top speeds. As a result, five additional designs ("D"–"H") were produced in September 1935. These featured ships capable of 23–30.5 knots, armed with eight or nine 14- or 16-inch guns, and with a standard displacement between 31,500 and 40,500 long tons (32,000 t and 41,150 t).

While designs "D" and "E" were fast battleships with 16-inch guns and protection against the same caliber, both displaced more than permitted by the Washington Naval Treaty. On the other hand, design "E" was a rather daring idea of a hybrid battleship–aircraft carrier, with three catapults mounted fore and eight 14-inch guns installed aft. In fact, carrier- or land-based aircraft were superior to catapult-launched aircraft, which required floats to land on water because they could not land back on the ship. As a result, this idea was quickly abandoned. Designs "G" and "H" represented slower 23-knot ships armed with nine 14-inch guns. However, the General Board finally favored faster vessels, thus eliminating "G" and "H."

These very different studies demonstrated the various difficulties the designers faced with a displacement limit of 35,000 long tons: They could create a faster ship, capable of 30 knots, requiring a lighter armament and armor protection compared to contemporary foreign battleships. Alternatively, they could sketch a slower vessel armed with heavier guns but fitting effective armor protection against newer and more powerful 16-inch (406 mm) shells would be extremely challenging. In October 1935, the preliminary design section drew up five additional studies ("I"–"M"). All featured 14-inch (356 mm) guns, some of them even in quadruple turrets (like the French *Dunkerque*), various armor thicknesses, and a top speed of 30 knots.

U.S.S. *Washington* (BB-56), the second ship of the *North Carolina*-class, under construction at the Philadelphia Naval Yard, January 1939.

Based on the numerous early studies, at least 35 different final designs were proposed (numbered "I" through "XVI-D") differing significantly in all categories except standard displacement and speeds. While only one ship exceeded 35,000 long tons (35,560 t), all others complied with this limit. The examination of various gun mountings ranged from eight to 12 14-inch guns. "XVI" was one of the final designs proposing a ship capable of 27 knots (50 km/h), 714 feet (218 m) long, and armed with 12 14-inch guns. Finally, a modified version of it was chosen for the two ships of the new *North Carolina*-class, *North Carolina* (BB-55) and *Washington* (BB-56).

Although the Second London Naval Treaty called for a maximum gun caliber of 14 inches, the American signatory was able to enforce the inclusion of a so-called "escalator clause" in this agreement in case any country that had signed the 1922 Washington Naval Treaty refused to adhere to the 14-inch caliber limit. The clause allowed the signatories Britain, the United States and France to raise the gun caliber from 14 to 16 inches in case Japan or Italy refused to agree to the limitation. Japan formally rejected the 14-inch limit in 1937 arguing that it could not accept this unless the number of battleships was also limited, thus urging the United States and the Great Britain to agree to having an equal number of battleships with Japan, but this was a condition that the two countries refused to accept. Fearing that Japan would build so-called super-battleships with 16-inch guns or even more firepower (as it eventually did with the *Yamato*-class), the U.S. Navy invoked the "escalator clause" and modified the *North Carolina* design to incorporate nine 16-inch guns.

The relatively long and erratic design history meant that a fast battleship with nine guns and a top speed of 30 knots, but with good armor protection, was eventually abandoned in favor of a variant that sacrificed both speed and protection for firepower—a combination hitherto unprecedented in American capital ship development.

Washington (shown here) and its sister ship *North Carolina* were the first representatives of a completely new generation of American capital ships, which differed considerably from their predecessors of the early 1920s due to the long break in construction and technological advances. With a top speed of 27–28 knots, this class was significantly faster than any previous American battleship and could operate in formation with fast aircraft carriers with limitations.

Propulsion

During the conception of the *North Carolina*'s power plant, recent innovations in turbine development including high-pressure steam technology were incorporated. Both ships were built with four General Electric geared turbines and eight Babcock & Wilcox three-drum express-type boilers. To reach the required top speed of 27 knots (31 mph; 50 km/h), the power plant was originally designed to generate 115,000 shp (85,755 kW), but new technologies improved this to 121,000 shp (90,000 kW). Despite the additional power, the maximum speed only increased by 1 knot. Various performance-enhancing power plant modifications were incorporated too late in the design process. As a result, the four turbines already installed could not take full advantage of the higher steam pressure and did not achieve the efficiency intended. The power plant was divided into four engine rooms, all located on the centerline. Each room had a turbine and two boilers, without any division between the turbines and the boilers to limit the risk of capsizing in case the ship sustained heavy flooding in the engine rooms.

Based on model basin tests, the *North Carolinas* were designed with a bulbous bow, which was a protruding bulb just below the waterline. It modified the water flow around the hull, which in turn increased speed, range, fuel efficiency, and stability. In addition, the hull had an unusual stern design for the time: the two inboard propulsion shafts were placed in skegs, which were also designed to reduce drag and improve flow conditions for the propellers. Moreover, they reinforced the structural strength of the stern by acting as girders and providing structural continuity for the torpedo bulkheads. However, they also contributed to vibration problems, which were particularly acute near the aft main battery director, thus requiring various modifications. After solving the

Front view of U.S.S. *North Carolina* (BB-55). Commissioned in 1941, it was the first American battleship built after the requirements of the 1922 Washington Naval Treaty.

problem, skews were also incorporated in the hull designs of the subsequent *South Dakota*- and *Iowa*-classes.

When the *North Carolinas* entered service in spring 1941, their top speed was 28 knots (32 mph; 52 km/h). In 1945, after adding other equipment including antiaircraft guns, the speed was reduced to 26.8 knots (30.8 mph; 49.6 km/h). The ships' original range was 17,450 nautical miles (20,080 mi; 32,320 km) at a cruising speed of 15 knots (17 mph; 28 km/h), which was also reduced to 16,320 nautical miles (18,780 mi; 30,220 km) due to the increases in weight.

Armament

The *North Carolinas* (and the subsequent *South Dakotas*) were armed with nine 16-inch/45 caliber Mark 6 guns in three-gun turrets. Each gun barrel could be raised independently. This weapon was an improved variant of the artillery mounted on the *Colorados*. While each gun had a weight of 85.85 long tons (87,230 kg) without its breech, each turret weighed up to 1,437 long tons (1,460 kg). A significant difference from the older gun was the ability to fire a new 2,700 lb (1,200 kg) AP shell. At a muzzle velocity of 2,300 feet per

Stern view of *North Carolina*. As the first battleship of a new era, it received such widespread attention from the American public that it was nicknamed the "Showboat."

Lifting one of *Washington*'s three-gun turrets swung into its armored barbette.

second (700 m/s), the gun could fire up to 2 rounds per minute. The maximum range with the heavy AP shell was 36,900 yards (33,700 m), while the lighter 1,900 lb (860 kg) HC projectile would travel 40,180 yards (37,000 m). The maximum gun barrel elevation was 45°. The number of rounds a gun could fire before it needed to be relined or replaced ("barrel life") was about 395 when using AP shells (2,860 with practice shells). Each turret could train to 150° on either side of the ship, while rotating 4° a second.

The *North Carolinas* received 20 5-inch (127 mm)/38 caliber Mark 12 guns in twin turrets. Originally designed during the 1930s to be used against destroyers, this reliable, robust, and accurate weapon turned out to be so successful that it was installed on numerous American warships during World War II. As an effective dual-purpose gun, it not only proved itself against smaller ships, but also against aerial targets. At a muzzle velocity of 2,600 feet per second (790 m/s) and at a rate of up to 15 rounds per minute, the gun's maximum horizontal range with a 55 lb (25 kg) projectile was 17,392 yards (15,903 m). In the antiaircraft role, it had a ceiling of 37,200 feet (11,300 m) at 85° elevation, which was 10,000 feet (3,050 m) more than that of the older single-purpose 5-inch/25 anti-air gun used on previous battleships. Up to 4,600 rounds could be fired before the barrel needed to be replaced.

As designed, the *North Carolinas* were equipped with an AA battery of four quadruple 1.1-inch (28 mm) autocannons and 12 .50 caliber (12.7 mm) Browning machine guns, but the AA armament was expanded by a growing number of Bofors 40-mm and Oerlikon 20-mm guns. When World War II ended in August 1945, both ships had eight twin 20-mm guns each. *North Carolina* also carried 20 single 20-mm mounts, while *Washington* had 63 single guns and one quadruple 20-mm. In addition, each ship had 15 quadruple 40-mm guns.

Electronics

When entering service, the *North Carolinas* were the first American battleships to be equipped with radar systems. The CXAM air search radar, mounted on top of the tower foremast, had a detection range of up to 70 nautical miles. This was supplemented by the SG surface search radar, whose parabolic antenna was located under the top mast platform of the tower foremast. The SG radar had a detection range of up to 22 nautical miles (41 km) for surface targets and up to 15 nautical miles (28 km) for aerial targets.

From 1943, the CXAM radar was superseded by its improved SK-type successor, which was able to detect an approaching bomber at an altitude of up to 10,000 feet at about 100 nautical miles (185 km). In 1944, the new SK-2 was introduced, which had a 5.2 meter circular antenna that improved the lateral detection field. In 1945, the SP radar was also installed as a backup system, with a detection range of up to 70 nautical miles (130 km) against air targets and 35 nautical miles against surface targets.

For fire control and range-finding, the three 16-inch (406 mm) gun turrets had their own rangefinders. These were supplemented by two Mark 38 fire-control systems on the tower foremast and aft superstructures, which had a rangefinder and a Mark 13 radar antenna. Fire control for the 5-inch (127 mm) secondary guns was provided by four Mark 37 fire-control systems. Two were located forward and aft of the superstructure, two on each side. The installations had a rangefinder as well as a Mark 12 radar system and could track aircraft in level flight up to a speed of 400 knots (460 mph; 740 km/h) and in dive up to a speed of 250 knots (288 mph; 463 km/h). Each of the 40-mm quadruple antiaircraft guns also had their own Mark 57 fire-control unit including a Mark 34 radar.

Although each 16-inch guns turret was built with its individual fire-control and range-finding systems, the primary system was the Mark 38 fire-control system, which was installed on the forward and aft superstructures, consisting of a rangefinder and a Mark 13 radar antenna.

The CXAM air search radar, seen here aboard the carrier U.S.S. *Ranger*.

Aircraft

The North Carolinas had two turnable aircraft catapults on their fantail. These were powered by powder charges to launch the Vought OS2U Kingfisher aircraft, of which each ship carried three. Two were accommodated on the catapults, while the third was placed on the quarterdeck in front of the gun turret. After their water landing, the aircraft were taken back on board by a crane located at the stern.

Protection Scheme

The *North Carolina* design incorporated the "all or nothing" armor scheme, which weighed 41 percent of the total displacement and which first had been adopted by the *Nevada*-class. It consisted of an armored citadel extending from just forward of the first gun turret to just aft of the rear gun turret. The main belt, made of Class A armor, was 12 inches (305 mm) thick amidships, inclined at 15°, and backed by 0.75 inches (19 mm) of STS. This tapered down to 6 inches (152 mm) on the lower edge of the belt.

With regards to the growing threat of air attack by increasingly powerful bombers, the ships were built with three armored decks. While the main deck was 1.45 inches (37 mm) strong, the second and thickest deck consisted of 3.6 inches (91 mm) of Class B armor laminated on 1.4 inches (36 mm) of STS totaling 5 inches (127 mm). The third and thinnest deck was up to 0.75 inches (19 mm) thick. While the first deck was intended to cause delay-fuzed projectiles to detonate, the more resilient second deck below would protect the ships' vital spaces. Finally, the third deck was designed to protect against the projectile's splinters that might have penetrated the second deck. It also served as the upper support for the torpedo bulkheads. The armor thickness of the conning tower ranged from 4.7 inches (373 mm) on the front and rear to 16 inches (406 mm) on both sides; the roof was 7 inches (178 mm) thick.

A U.S. Navy Douglas SBD-5 Dauntless dive bomber on an antisubmarine patrol low over U.S.S. *Washington* en route to the invasion of the Gilbert Islands in the Pacific, November 1943. The carrier in the background is U.S.S. *Lexington* (CV-16). With their massive antiaircraft armament, battleships escorted carriers on their strike missions.

The faces of the massive main gun turrets were 16 inches (406 mm) thick, their sides 9 inches (229 mm), their rear sides 11.8 inches (300 mm), and the roofs 7 inches (178 mm). The thickness of the main turret barbettes ranged from 11.5 inches (292 mm) to 16 inches (406 mm). The 5-inch secondary gun turrets and their ammunition magazines were armored with 1.95-inch (50 mm) STS plates.

The *North Carolina*'s side protection scheme consisted of five compartments divided by torpedo bulkheads and an anti-torpedo bulge covering the length of the armored citadel. While the outer two compartments, the innermost compartment and the bulge would remain empty, the third and fourth compartments would be filled with liquid. The system was reduced in depth at both ends by the forward and rear main gun turrets. In these sections, there was no fifth compartment, but an outer empty compartment and two liquid-filled spaces, backed by another empty compartment. To compensate for the reduced underwater protection system, these sections had additional armor plating up to 3.75 inches (95 mm) thick.

The complete underwater protection system was 18.5 feet (5.64 m) deep. It was designed to withstand warheads of up to 700 lb (318 kg) of TNT. The underwater protection was completed by a 5.75 feet (1.75 m) deep triple bottom. While the liquid-filled bottom layer was 3 feet (0.9 m) thick, the upper 2.75 foot (0.8 m) thick layer was kept empty. The bottom was heavily subdivided to prevent uncontrollable flooding should the upper layer be pierced.

U.S.S. *North Carolina* (BB-55)

Although commissioned in spring 1941, both ships did not join the active fleet due to acute longitudinal vibrations from their propeller shafts. It was only cured after testing different propellers. After its shakedown cruise, *North Carolina* joined Task Force 16 escorting the aircraft carrier *Enterprise* (CV-6) during the invasions of Guadalcanal and Tulagi in August 1942, followed by the battle of the Eastern Solomons in August, during which American aircraft sank the Japanese light carrier *Ryūjō*. While shooting down several aircraft, *North Carolina* remained relatively undamaged.

North Carolina off the coast of Japan during the final stage of World War II, July 1945. The carrier U.S.S. *Randolph* (CV-15) is visible in the background.

On September 15, 1942, while protecting the carrier *Saratoga* and supporting American troops fighting on Guadalcanal, torpedoes fired from the Japanese submarine *I-19* hit the carrier *Wasp*, the destroyer *O'Brien*, and *North Carolina*. A 660 lb (300 kg) warhead struck the battleship on its port side 20 feet (6.1 m) below the waterline just behind the first turret, thus creating a 32 feet by 18 feet (9.8 m by 5.5 m) hole, killing five men and causing about 980 long tons (990 t) of water to flood into the ship. This had to be compensated by counter-flooding, which brought in another 480 long tons (490 t) of water in. While *North Carolina* was able to steam at 18 knots (33 km/h; 21 mph), structural damage beneath the first turret rendered it unable to fire unless in absolute need, and the main search radar failed.

As this was the first torpedo hit on a modern American battleship, there was an enormous interest from various Navy officers and bureaus to learn about it. As the torpedo defense system had come close to collapsing near a magazine—one of the most important areas of the ship—some experts saw this as a confirmation that the ship's designers should have made the underwater protection more resilient. As a result, the General Board demanded that the fifth and sixth *Iowa*-class battleships, *Illinois* and *Kentucky*, then under construction, receive a torpedo bulge outside their magazines. However, the Bureau of Ships argued that the system worked as intended, so no changes were made to the *Iowas*.

After its repair in Pearl Harbor, *North Carolina* escorted carrier groups while they covered supply and troop movements in the Solomons and launched strikes against Makin, Tarawa, Kavieng, and New Ireland. In 1944, it joined Task Force 58 supporting carrier-launched strikes on Kwajalein, Namur, Truk, Saipan, Tinian, Guam, Palau, Woleai, and Hollandia.

In late June, *North Carolina* joined the battle of the Philippine Sea (the so-called "Marianas Turkey Shoot"), where several hundred Japanese aircraft were shot down and three carriers sunk at little cost to the American naval forces: 134 aircraft lost, most ditching in the sea after running out of fuel. After providing air cover for various landing operations including Leyte and Luzon (Philippines) and surviving two typhoons, the battleship

View of *North Carolina*'s secondary guns and the two smokestacks.

The mighty No. 3 gun turret as seen from the fantail. (Photo: Joseph Fuller)

provided bombardment support for troops ashore during the invasions of Iwo Jima and Okinawa, while downing several kamikaze aircraft during the latter battle. In July, *North Carolina*, in company with U.S. battleships *Alabama*, *Missouri*, *Wisconsin* and the British HMS *King George V*, shelled the industrial area in Hitachi, Ibaraki, Japan. After the Japanese surrender, members of ship's crew assisted in the country's occupation. *North Carolina* also participated in Operation *Magic Carpet*, the return of American troops to the United States.

In 1947, the ship was decommissioned and moved to the Reserve Fleet. *North Carolina* escaped scrapping when it was sold to the state of North Carolina for $250,000 in 1961 to be preserved in Wilmington as a museum ship.

In 1961, the decommissioned *North Carolina* arrived in Wilmington, North Carolina, to begin its second life as a museum ship. Today, *North Carolina* welcomes thousands of visitors every year, hosts various events and commemorates the citizens of the state who lost their lives in World War II.

North Carolina is one of eight battleships preserved in the United States. Dedicated staff, volunteers and generous donors are doing their part to preserve this historic ship. Visitors can explore nine levels, climb inside gun turrets, marvel at early computers and see where the crew ate, slept, and worked.

U.S.S. *Washington* (BB-56)

In early 1942, *Washington* became the flagship of TF 39 and, along with the aircraft carrier *Wasp*, the cruisers *Wichita* and *Tuscaloosa*, and various smaller ships, sailed to Scapa Flow, Scotland, to bolster the British Home Fleet. Renamed TF 99, they escorted several Arctic convoys, which were carrying vital supplies to the Soviet Union. During one mission, the accompanying British battleship *King George V* accidentally rammed the destroyer

A rare color photo of U.S.S. *Washington*, maneuvering off Oahu, Hawaii, in 1943. Images like these are a valuable resource for ship modelers to recreate the original color scheme of the ship.

Washington's collapsed bow after the collision with the U.S.S. *Indiana* (BB-58) in February 1944.

HMS *Punjabi*, which had maneuvered to avoid a mine, and cut it in two, causing *Punjabi* to sink. Directly behind *King George V*, *Washington* passed through the same stretch of sea receiving light damage to its rangefinders, circuit breakers, three fire-control radars, and the search radars from exploding depth charges. The American ships were then briefly stationed in Iceland as the Allies sought to protect it from a German invasion and use it for their own operations. In the fall, the ship was deployed to the Pacific to protect supply convoys for American forces on Guadalcanal attempting to prevent Japanese control of the island.

In November 1942, when the Japanese made a last attempt to recapture Guadalcanal, the American and Japanese navies had to deploy their battleships to surface combat, mostly due to the exhaustion of their carrier forces. After the battleship *Hiei* was scuttled after being critically damaged by American cruisers and bombers on November 14, *South Dakota* and *Washington*, both armed with nine 16-inch guns and equipped with the latest radar, sank *Hiei*'s sister ship, *Kirishima*, armed with eight 14-inch guns and fitted with inferior radar. Soon after the battle, the Japanese began evacuating Guadalcanal.

After an overhaul and participating in exercises, *Washington* joined Task Group (TG) 53.2 providing additional firepower for the attack on the Gilbert Islands. In late November 1943, the ship first steamed to Makin Island to provide protection for ships operating there, then Ocean Island to prepare to bombard Nauru along with its sister *North Carolina*, all four *South Dakota*-class battleships, and the carriers *Bunker Hill* and *Monterey*.

Before dawn on February 1, 1944, with the cloudy sky still dark, *Washington* collided with the

Washington received a false bow (makeshift bow) in Pearl Harbor and finally a new one in Puget Sound Naval Yard, Washington.

battleship *Indiana*, when the latter left formation to refuel four destroyers. *Washington* gave *Indiana* a glancing blow, scraping down a large aft portion of the latter's starboard side. *Washington*'s fore section was severely damaged, with about 60 feet (18 m) of its bow hanging down into the water. Six men from *Washington* and four from *Indiana* lost their lives. After temporary repairs, the ship received a false bow (makeshift bow) in Pearl Harbor and finally a new one in Puget Sound.

In summer 1944, *Washington* joined Operation *Forager*, the invasion of the Mariana and Palau Islands, serving as a carrier escort, followed by a shore bombardment of Japanese positions on Saipan and Tinian. After participating in the battle of the Philippines, beating off Japanese air attacks, the ship supported troops assaulting Peleliu and Angaur, bombarded Iwo Jima, escorted carriers deploying aircraft raids against Japan, and finally shelled Okinawa in April 1945. When the war ended, *Washington* was receiving an overhaul at Puget Sound Naval Shipyard. It later helped to return American troops home from England (Operation *Magic Carpet*). After only six years of active service, the ships were placed into reserve in 1947 and scrapped 14 years later. Conversion plans to increase the speed of the *North Carolinas* for operations with the fast carriers or the conversion into helicopter carriers proved too complex and costly and were therefore not implemented.

North Carolina-class General Characteristics (as built)

Class	*North Carolina*
Name	*North Carolina* (BB-55) *Washington* (BB-56)
Shipyard	New York Naval Shipyard (BB-55) Philadelphia Naval Shipyard (BB-56)
Commissioning	April 9, 1941 (BB-55) May 15, 1941 (BB-56)
Displacement (normal) Displacement (full)	36,600 long tons (37,200 t) 44,800 long tons (45,500 t)
Length (overall)	728 ft 8.625 in (222.113 m)
Beam	108 ft 3.875 in (33.017 m)
Draft (max)	35 ft 6 in (10.82 m)
Propulsion	4 × steam turbines / turbo-electric (60,000 shp / 45,000 kW)
Maximum speed	28 kn (52 km/h)
Range	17,450 nmi (32,320 km) at 15 knots
Complement	ca. 1,880
Armament	9 × 16-in (406 mm)/45 cal. Mark 6 20 × 5-in (127 mm)/38 cal. Various AA guns
Fate	Preserved as museum ship (BB-55) Sold for scrap, 1961 (BB-56)

South Dakota-class

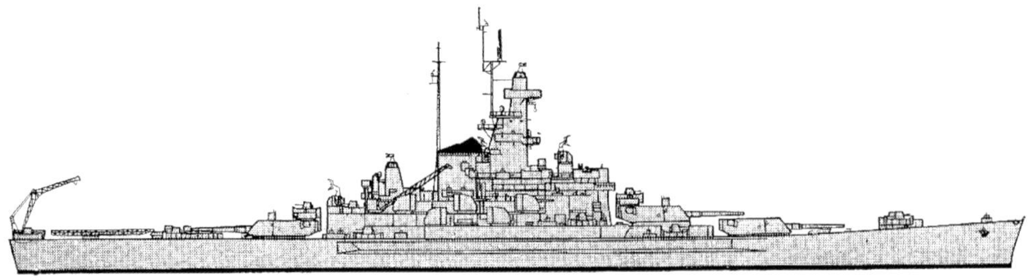

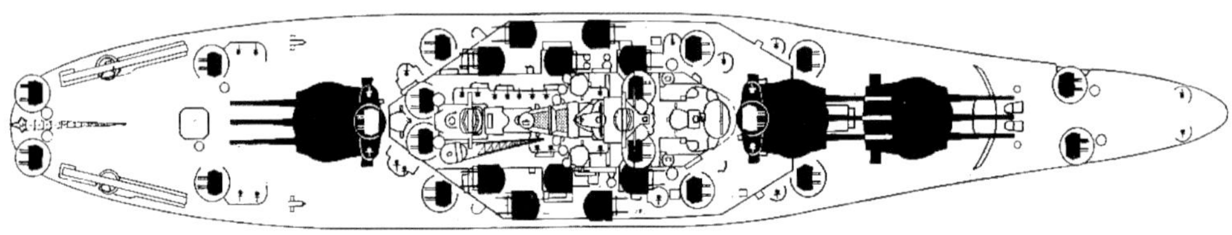

In 1936, after assigning the keel laying of the two *North Carolinas* to Fiscal Year 1937, the U.S. Navy's General Board proposed the construction of two additional identical battleships in fiscal year 1938. However, the Chief of Naval Operations, Admiral William H. Standley, demanded a new design. This meant that the keels could not be laid down by 1938, so the new class was assigned to fiscal year 1939. After formally approving the basic layout for two new 35,000 long ton (35,560 t) ships by the Secretary of the Navy in June 1937 and working out several details, both vessels were ordered in April the following year.

U.S.S. *South Dakota* (BB-57) under construction at the New York Shipbuilding Corporation, April 1940. This view shows the ship's interior amidships, including six major watertight transverse bulkheads and anti-torpedo longitudinal bulkheads along the sides.

The deteriorating international relations in Europe and Asia prompted Congress to authorize two additional battleships of the new *South Dakota*-class, for a total of four. Several weaknesses in the preceding *North Carolinas* were to be fixed. This included an improvement of the underwater protection.

The designers created various proposals including a 23-knot variant armed with nine 16-inch guns in three triple turrets and a 5.9 inch (150 mm) thick deck armor. This would have made the ships widely immune to plunging fire out to 30,000 yards (27,430 m) and several types of aerial bombs. Unlike the preceding *North Carolinas*, the *South Dakotas* were to be designed to resist hits from 16-inch (406 mm) projectiles—the same caliber the ships were to be armed with. This characteristic—proofing a ship against its own armament—was known as "balanced armor." To

South Dakota's superstructure in an advanced stage of construction, January 1942. The circular platforms were mounted for the installation of antiaircraft guns and radar systems.

achieve this, the main armor belt would have to be increased from *North Carolina*'s 12 inches (305 mm) to 15.5 inches (390 mm). However, this would have raised the ship's weight to an excessive level. A solution to this this problem was to incorporate sloped armor. However, it was infeasible in an external belt as it would compromise stability to a dangerous degree.

Instead, an internal armor belt was installed behind the unarmored outer hull plates. However, this concept had several drawbacks. It made construction difficult, and if the armor belt was damaged, the outer armor had to be removed first before repairs to the belt could begin.

Defining the optimal hull size was a challenge: a longer hull usually resulted in a higher top speed but required a longer (and heavier) armor section for protection. For a higher top speed with a shorter hull, more powerful engines were necessary. As the *South Dakotas* were 49 feet (15 m) shorter than the preceding *North Carolinas*, the new class would require a modified power plant to achieve the same top speed.

To escort fast carrier task forces and to counter the Japanese *Nagato*, capable of at least 26 knots (30 mph; 48 km/h), a similar top speed was considered possible if the *North Carolina*'s power plant could be reduced in size enough to fit into the *South Dakota*'s tighter hull. As a result, the propulsion system was arranged as close together as possible, with the boilers placed directly alongside the turbines. By this time, the design process had established a hull length of 666 feet (203 m) between perpendiculars (680 feet overall) incorporating a single internal sloped armor belt. However, various alternatives included longer, faster ships armed with 14-inch guns in triple turrets, slower ships with 14-inch guns in quadruple turrets, improved *North Carolina*-class variants, and a 27 knot (31 mph; 50 km/h) vessel with nine 16-inch guns with a similar layout to the *North Carolinas*.

In late 1937 it was agreed on that the 666-foot design was a compromise, meeting the specified requirements for speed, protection, and the nine 16-inch guns. The eventual emphasis on speed anticipated the development of what would become the *Iowa*-class—the largest, fastest, and last completed by the U.S. Navy.

Propulsion

The *South Dakotas* were fitted with eight Babcock & Wilcox three-drum, express-type boilers that produced a steam pressure of 600 psi (4,100 kPa) at a temperature of 850°F (454°C) driving four geared turbines, one for each propeller shaft, producing at least 130,000 shp (97,000 kW) in total, which gave the ships a top speed of 27.5 knots (31.6 mph; 50.9 km/h). The fuel oil capacity of about 6,600 long tons (6,700 t) provided a range of 15,000 nautical miles (17,000 mi; 28,000 km) at a cruising speed of 15 knots (17 mph; 28 km/h).

Like the *North Carolina*-class, the power plant was divided into four machinery spaces, each containing two boilers and one set of turbines. The machinery spaces did not have longitudinal bulkheads to reduce the risk of asymmetric flooding and capsizing. The ships featured a bulbous bow, triple bottom under the armored citadel, and skegs. These characteristics were shared by all American fast battleships (*North Carolina*, *South*

View under *Indiana*'s hull, looking aft to show all four propellers. This photograph shows the outboard skegs, incorporating the outer propeller shafts, that were a feature of the *South Dakota*-class of battleship. The ship's twin rudders are directly aft of the inboard propellers.

Dakota, *Iowa*). They had four propellers, with the two outboard ones mounted in skegs (inboard on the *North Carolinas*). However, vibrations during service led to different propeller blade arrangements being used during the war. Compared to the *North Carolinas*, the shorter hull form resulted in improved maneuverability.

The *South Dakota*'s 16-inch main battery was identical to the preceding *North Carolinas*.

Armament

The *South Dakotas* carried a main battery of nine 16-inch (406 mm)/45 caliber Mark 6 guns in three three-gun turrets, identical to the *North Carolinas*. The secondary battery with 20 5-inch (127 mm)/38 caliber Mark 12 guns in 10 Mark 28 Mod 0 twin dual-purpose mounts (against air and surface targets) was also identical to that of the preceding class. However, *South Dakota*, the lead ship, was the exception. Built as a fleet flagship, it featured an additional deck on its conning tower for extra command space, so there was no room for 5-inch guns, which meant that the ship had only 16 5-inch in eight twin mounts.

As designed, the *South Dakotas* were equipped with an antiaircraft (AA) battery of 12 1.1-inch (280 mm) autocannons and 12 .50 caliber (12.7 mm) machine guns. Over time, the former were (more or less completely) removed, while the number of the latter was reduced. Instead, as the war progressed and bombers became a serious threat, more than 70 40-mm Bofors AA guns (some in quadruple mounts) and more than 65 20-mm Oerlikon AA guns were added to each ship.

The *South Dakotas* were fitted with more than 70 40-mm AA guns and more than 65 20-mm AA guns.

Electronics

When commissioned in 1942, the *South Dakotas* were equipped with the SC air-search radar, which was eventually replaced by the more capable SK and SK-2 air-search radar. The directors for the main battery were first equipped with the Mark 3 fire-control radar, and shortly later with the Mark 8. This system gave the American battleships a significant advantage over their Japanese counterparts, which for the most part were fitted with optical devices. This was proven when *South Dakota* and *Washington* (*North Carolina*-class) sank the battleship *Kirishima* at night off Guadalcanal in late 1942, as their radars worked more effectively.

The Mark 37 directors for the 5-inch secondary batteries were equipped with the Mark 4 radar, making them very capable against surface targets. Moreover, in combination with proximity fuzes, this system proved its value as an excellent antiaircraft weapon. As it was difficult to hit a moving aircraft with a 5-inch projectile, proximity fuzes were used to automatically detonate a military explosive charge at a defined distance in front of targets (aircraft). The Mark 4 radar was eventually replaced by the Mark 12/22. The *South Dakotas* were able to benefit from the various advances of radar technology during the war. Like the preceding class, they received two catapults and three Vought OS2U Kingfisher floatplanes each.

Protection

Unlike the preceding *North Carolinas*, the *South Dakotas* were better designed to resist hits from 16-inch (406 mm) projectiles, the same caliber the ships were armed with. The side armor's immunity zone—the range of distance at which a hit would not penetrate it—against the 2,240 lb projectile fired by the 16-inch/45 caliber guns of the *Colorados* was 17,700 to 30,900 yards (16.2 to 28.3 km). However, against the new 2,700 lb Mark 8 shell fired from the *South Dakotas*, the immunity zone was smaller as the side armor was only effective at ranges between 20,500 and 26,400 yards (18.7 and 24.1 km).

The 12.2-inch (310 mm) thick armor belt was only slightly thicker than that of the *North Carolinas* (12 inches; 305 mm), while being more sloped (19° compared to 15°). This stronger inclination required an internal belt arrangement to retain an adequate waterline beam for stability and to avoid a loss of speed due to excessive width. Located behind the 1.25-inch (32 mm) STS outer hull plating, the internal armor belt consisted of 12.2-inch (310 mm) thick Class A Krupp cemented (KC) armor mounted on 0.875-inch (22 mm) thick STS plating and was inclined 19° from the vertical. This was equal to 17.3 inches (440-mm) of vertical belt armor when hit by a 16-inch shell over 19,000 yards (17 km).

Stern view of the new battleship U.S.S. *Alabama* (BB-60) in camouflage paint, circa December 1942. Note the crane used to lift the floatplane back on board after its landing in the water.

The armor belt extended to the triple bottom tapering from the 12.2 inches (310 mm) down to 1 inch (25 mm) at the lowest portion at the bottom to protect against the penetration of projectiles that hit the ship's side below the waterline. The ends of the armored citadel, ranging from the first to the third gun turret barbette, were protected by 11.3-inch (287 mm) thick traverse bulkheads.

With regard to the growing threat of air attacks, the horizontal deck protection was made of three layers. While the weather deck (bomb deck) was 1.5 inches (38 mm) strong, the second deck consisted of a 5.75- to 6.05-inches (146 to 154 mm) thick combination of Class B and STS armor. The third and thinnest layer was a 0.625-inch (16 mm) STS splinter deck with 1-inch (25 mm) STS over the magazines.

The faces of the massive main gun turrets were 18 inches (457 mm) thick, their sides 9.5 inches (241 mm), their rear sides 12 inches (305 mm), and the roofs 7.25 inches (184 mm). The thickness of the main turret barbettes ranged from 11.3 inches (287 mm) to 17.3 inches (439 mm). The conning tower was protected by armor up to 16 inches (406 mm) thick.

An internal bulge consisting of four longitudinal torpedo bulkheads formed a multilayered system designed to absorb the enormous energy from an underwater explosion caused by torpedoes or mines equivalent to 700 lb (318 kg) of TNT. The protection scheme was designed for the torpedo bulkheads to deform and absorb the explosion's energy. The armor belt that extended to the triple bottom, where it tapered to 1 inch (25 mm), formed the third torpedo bulkhead. The two outer areas between the hull and the first torpedo bulkhead were filled with water and fuel oil, while the inner space directly in front of the armor belt remained empty and was intended to absorb the explosive energy of torpedoes and mines by disrupting the gas bubble and preventing fragments from entering the ship's innards. The total system depth was 17.9 feet (5.46 m) on each side. The ship had a triple bottom in the citadel area (otherwise double bottom), which was 6 feet (1.82 m) thick.

The designers hoped that extending the armor belt to the triple bottom as one of the torpedo bulkheads would help improve the protection system compared to that of the *North Carolinas*. However, caisson tests in 1939 indicated that the *South Dakota*'s system was *less*, or at best, only partially as, effective. This was due to the armor belt's rigidity causing the force of a detonation to considerably displace the final holding bulkhead inwards despite remaining watertight. This and further tests led to several modifications, including the system's liquid loading scheme: whereas the *North Carolinas*' third and fourth outboard compartments were liquid-filled, the *South Dakotas* had their outer two compartments liquid-filled with fuel oil, while the inner two compartments were void spaces. This was done to reduce the danger of listing after an underwater hit. The system received further reinforcements and refinements in the subsequent *Iowa*-class.

U.S.S. *South Dakota* (BB-57)

Commissioned in March 1942, *South Dakota* was assigned to the Pacific to escort the aircraft carrier *Enterprise* and to prevent any Japanese forces from approaching Guadalcanal. This led to the battle of Santa Cruz in October, where in protecting the carrier, the battleship was credited with downing 26 Japanese aircraft, while being hit by a 500 lb (230 kg) bomb on turret 1. During the fighting the U.S. Navy lost the carrier *Hornet* (CV-8) and one destroyer.

On October 30, 1942, the battleship collided with the destroyer *Mahan*, while the latter was investigating a potential sonar contact to a submarine. After being repaired, *South Dakota* formed Task Force 64 with the battleship *Washington* (*North Carolina*-class) and four destroyers. In the second naval battle of Guadalcanal, the ships intercepted a Japanese bombardment force on the night of November 14/15, damaging the cruisers *Takao* and *Atago* in addition to forcing the battleship *Kirishima* and destroyer *Ayanami* to be scuttled. When a power failure incapacitated *South Dakota*'s defense, it was hit by more than 40 shells causing significant damage, knocking out radio communications, three fire-control radars, and the main radar.

South Dakota (right) and two light cruisers laid up in the Reserve Fleet, Philadelphia 1961. The battleship was broken up the following year.

After being repaired and overhauled in New York, the ship escorted the carrier *Ranger* in North Atlantic operations until mid-April, and then reinforced the British Home Fleet. In the fall of 1943, *South Dakota* supported the invasion during the battle of Tarawa, and, along with five other battleships, shelled Nauru Island in December. In early 1944, it protected carriers providing air support for various amphibious assaults on Kwajalein Atoll, followed by a bombardment of Saipan and Tinian.

South Dakota joined the battle of the Philippine Sea where several hundred Japanese aircraft were shot down and three carriers sunk. However, the ship was hit by a 500 lb bomb (230 kg) on the main deck, killing more than 20 men. For the rest of the war, *South Dakota* operated in the Pacific mostly as a carrier escort. In March and April, it shelled Okinawa, followed by various targets in Japan. In September, *South Dakota* and numerous other warships were present at the surrender of Japan in Tokyo Bay. After just five years of service, the ship was decommissioned in 1947 and scrapped in 1962. *South Dakota* is memorialized at Sioux Falls, South Dakota, where memorabilia and parts are on display within an outline of the main deck. One of the ship's propellers is on display outside the U.S. Navy Museum in Washington, D.C.

U.S.S. *Indiana* (BB-58)

Commissioned in April 1942, *Indiana* conducted its shakedown cruise, and was sent directly to the Solomon Islands, arriving off Guadalcanal in November and providing shore bombardment in support of the U.S. Marines. Here, it replaced its sister ship *South Dakota*, which needed repairs. In November 1943, both battleships supported the invasion of Tarawa.

After participating in the Marshall Islands landings, *Indiana* collided with the battleship *Washington* before dawn on February 1, 1944, when the former left formation to refuel four destroyers. *Washington* gave *Indiana* a glancing

Indiana makes a sharp turn to starboard as a part of its post-refit builder's trials in Puget Sound, Washington, November 1944.

Indiana fires a salvo at the Japan Iron Company's Kamaishi plant, 400 km north of Tokyo, July 14, 1945. A second before, *South Dakota*, from which this photo was taken, fired the initial salvo of the first naval bombardment of the Japanese home islands. The superstructure of *Massachusetts* is visible directly behind *Indiana*. A heavy cruiser is in the left center distance.

blow, scraping a large aft portion of the latter's starboard side, thus damaging the longitudinal bulkheads and flooding several void spaces and fuel tanks. While the starboard outboard propeller and its shaft were damaged, several 40-mm and 20-mm guns were destroyed, as well as the starboard catapult and its floatplane. When *Indiana* suffered a list to starboard, this was corrected by counter-flooding. After temporary repairs at Majuro Lagoon, the ship sailed to Pearl Harbor, where a complete refit took place; this was one of the most extensive repairs that took place there.

During the battle of the Philippine Sea in June 1944, *Indiana* provided antiaircraft support to the carrier fleet. After downing two Japanese aircraft, a third crashed into the ship, disintegrating upon striking the side armor. Some aircraft wreckage was scattered across the fantail but the ship suffered only minor damage.

Indiana participated in the shore bombardment of Iwo Jima, as well as in attacks on the Japanese home islands. During the landings at Okinawa, it provided ground support fire as well as antiaircraft defense against kamikaze aircraft attacking the invasion fleet. Decommissioned in 1947, *Indiana* was eventually scrapped in 1963.

Battleships and heavy cruisers steaming in column off Kamaishi, as seen from *South Dakota*. *Indiana* is the nearest ship, followed by *Massachusetts* and two heavy cruisers.

Indiana's mast, prow, and a pair of antiaircraft guns on display at Memorial Stadium of the Indiana University.

Several parts of the ship have been preserved in the state of Indiana. One of the anchors is on display at the Allen County War Memorial Coliseum in Fort Wayne. The bell is at the Heslar Naval Armory in Indianapolis. The wheel is at Shortridge High School, also in Indianapolis. The main mast, prow, and a pair of antiaircraft guns are on display at the Memorial Stadium of Indiana University.

U.S.S. *Massachusetts* (BB-59)

Commissioned in May 1942, *Massachusetts* crossed the Atlantic in October to participate in Operation *Torch*, the Allied invasion of French North Africa near Casablanca, Morocco. The incomplete French battleship *Jean Bart* was in the harbor, having arrived there in 1940 to escape the German invasion of France. As the French defenders did not surrender to defect to the Free French, the American ships were tasked with neutralizing the primary French coastal batteries, several submarines, and surface ships (including *Jean Bart*) on November 8, 1942. *Massachusetts* hit *Jean Bart* several times, thus disabling its one active 15-inch (381 mm) gun turret. It also sank and damaged several other ships. During this naval battle of Casablanca, *Massachusetts*, which was only slightly damaged by enemy fire, fired almost all its ammunition: 786 shells from the main battery and 221 rounds from its 5-inch guns. The French defenders finally agreed to a ceasefire on November 11.

This allowed *Massachusetts* to supported operations in the South Pacific, including guarding convoy lanes, escorting aircraft carriers, and bombarding Japanese positions on various islands, including Nauru and Kwajalein. In 1944, the battleship protected carriers by providing antiaircraft defense during their attacks against Saipan, Tinian, and Guam, and supported the invasions of the Caroline Islands, Hollandia and Leyte Gulf (Philippines).

During the battle for Leyte Gulf in October, *Massachusetts* protected U.S. carrier task groups attacking Japanese warships. In early 1945, it

Starboard view of superstructure *Massachusetts* (BB-59) during refueling at sea.

The incomplete French battleship *Jean Bart* at Casablanca, Morocco, showing damage from the 16-inch shells fired from U.S.S. *Massachusetts* on November 8.

After U.S.S. *Massachusetts* was turned over to its namesake state in 1965, it became a floating museum at Battleship Cove, Fall River. (Photo: Matthew Bothelo/Shutterstock)

provided antiaircraft cover for airborne raids on Iwo Jima and the Japanese homelands. In March and April, the ship bombarded Okinawa and once again provided antiaircraft defense for Allied ships operating off Okinawa. In July, *Massachusetts* protected carriers attacking Japan before shelling land targets itself. In 1947, just after five years of service, the ship was decommissioned and transferred to the Atlantic Reserve Fleet.

After *Massachusetts* was stricken from the naval register and slated for disposal, former crewmembers lobbied to have it preserved as a museum ship. The *Massachusetts* Memorial Committee eventually raised enough money to purchase the vessel from the U.S. Navy, including through a donation campaign by children in the state. In 1965, the Navy officially transferred the ownership of *Massachusetts* to the state after which the ship was named. In August, it arrived at Battleship Cove in Fall River, Massachusetts.

The museum is also home to other World War II-era vessels including the destroyer U.S.S. *Joseph P. Kennedy Jr.*, the submarine U.S.S. *Lionfish*, two PT boats, as well as the former Cold War-era East German corvette *Hiddensee*, and various other exhibits.

View of the superstructure and forecastle of the battleship. (Photo: Wangkun Jia/Shutterstock)

When the Navy reactivated the *Iowa*-class in the 1980s, parts of the preserved battleships *Massachusetts*, *Alabama* and *North Carolina* were cannibalized to bring the *Iowas* back into service as engine room components were no longer available in the Navy's inventory. Aside from the material removed in the 1980s and the aircraft catapults (previously removed), *Massachusetts* is still largely in its wartime configuration.

U.S.S. *Alabama* (BB-60)

Commissioned in August 1942, *Alabama* was assigned to the British Home Fleet in spring 1943 escorting convoys carrying vital supplies to the Soviet Union. In August, it transferred to the Pacific to join the U.S. Third Fleet during the amphibious invasions of the Gilbert and Marshall Islands, particularly Kwajalein Atoll in January 1944. Here, *Alabama*, its sister ship *South Dakota*, and *North Carolina* shelled the island of Roi-Namur, targeting defensive positions, airfields, and other facilities. For the remainder of the campaign, it patrolled to the north of Kwajalein to guard against a possible Japanese counterattack that did not happen.

During the night of February 21, the ship's 5-inch guns were firing upon by Japanese aircraft. When the ship turned in the direction of the planes to better engage them, the rearmost 5-inch turret was masked behind the turrets amidships. When gunner in the rearmost turret accidentally overrode the safety mechanism—designed to prevent the gun from firing in exactly that circumstance—the gun fired, hitting the 5-inch turret in front of it. This incident killed five men and wounded eleven. A subsequent investigation concluded that the override switch was flawed and therefore prone to accidental activation.

In June 1944, *Alabama* provided antiaircraft defense during the battle of the Philippine Sea and then joined other battleships in providing fire support to the ground troops in the Marianas. In October, the battleship participated in the battle of Leyte Gulf. In May 1945, during the final stages of the Pacific War, *Alabama* provided antiaircraft support to the fast carrier groups launching air strikes against the Japanese main island of Kyushu. After shelling various areas along the Japanese coast, *Alabama*'s last wartime duty was to assist in the landing of occupation forces in Japan, after which it returned to the United States. In 1947, the battleship was decommissioned and placed into the Reserve Fleet in Bremerton, Washington. The ship escaped scrapping when the U.S.S. *Alabama* Battleship Commission acquired it in 1962.

Task Force 50 en route to the Gilberts and Marshalls to support the invasions of Makin and Tarawa in November 1943; battleships *Alabama* (left) and *Indiana* (in the distance) escort the light carrier U.S.S. *Monterey* (CVL-26) and other ships.

A campaign to save *Alabama* from the breakers' yard succeeded in raising the necessary funds, and the historic battleships was preserved as a museum ship in Mobile Bay, Alabama, in 1962. Today, *Alabama* is the main attraction of the Battleship Memorial Park. (U.S. Library of Congress)

Two years later, the vessel was towed to Mobile, Alabama, where it is now open as a museum ship, the main attraction of Battleship Memorial Park. The museum is also home to the World War II submarine U.S.S. *Drum*, as well as various aircraft such as a P-51 Mustang fighter and a B-52 bomber. During its career as a museum ship, *Alabama* has been used as a set for several Hollywood movies, including *Under Siege* (1992), in which it portrays the then-active battleship *Missouri*, and *U.S.S. Indianapolis: Men of Courage* (2016).

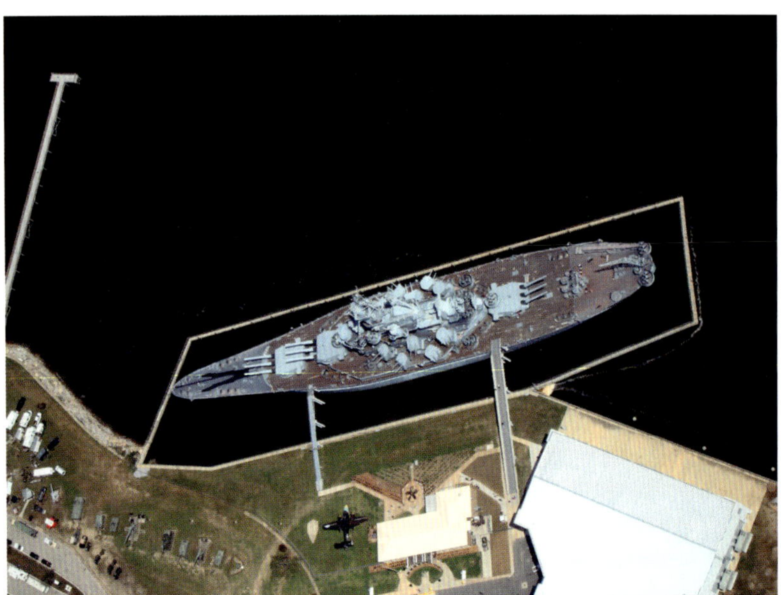

Aerial view of *Alabama* as a museum ship. The ship was damaged by Hurricane *Katrina* in September 2005, taking on water and a list to port, but was repaired. (Photo: Kevin King, CC-BY-2.0)

South Dakota-class General Characteristics (as built)

Class	*South Dakota*
Name	*South Dakota* (BB-57) *Indiana* (BB-58) *Massachusetts* (BB-59) *Alabama* (BB-60)
Shipyard	New York Shipbuilding Corporation, Camden (BB-57) Newport News Shipbuilding Company (BB-58) Fore River Shipyard, Quincy (BB-59) Norfolk Naval Shipyard, Virginia (BB-60)
Commissioning	March 20, 1942 (BB-57) April 30, 1942 (BB-58) May 12, 1942 (BB-59) August 16, 1942 (BB-60)
Displacement (normal) Displacement (full)	35,412 long tons (35,980 t) 44,519 long tons (45,233 t)
Length (overall)	680 ft (207 m)
Beam	108 ft 2 in (33 m)
Draft (max)	36 ft 2 in (11 m)
Propulsion	4 × steam turbines (130,000 shp / 97,000 kW)
Maximum speed	ca. 27.5 kn (50.9 km/h)
Range	15,000 nmi (28,000 km) at 15 knots
Complement	1,793–2,634
Armament	9 × 16-in (406 mm)/45 cal. Mark 6 16 or 20 × 5-in (127 mm)/38 cal. Various AA guns
Fate	Sold for scrap, 1962 (BB-57) Sold for scrap, 1963 (BB-58) Preserved as museum ship (BB-59 and BB-60)

Iowa-class

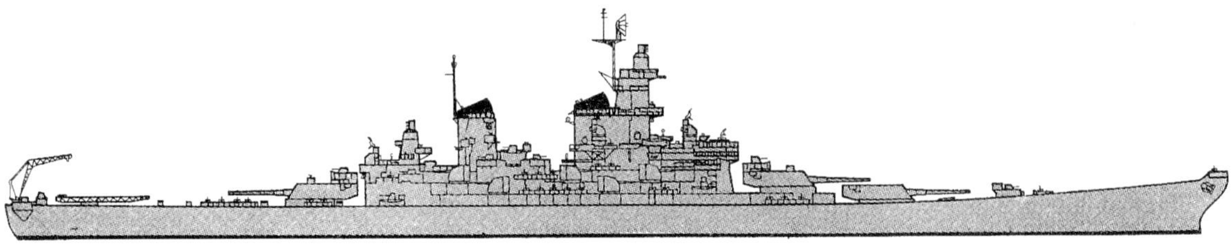

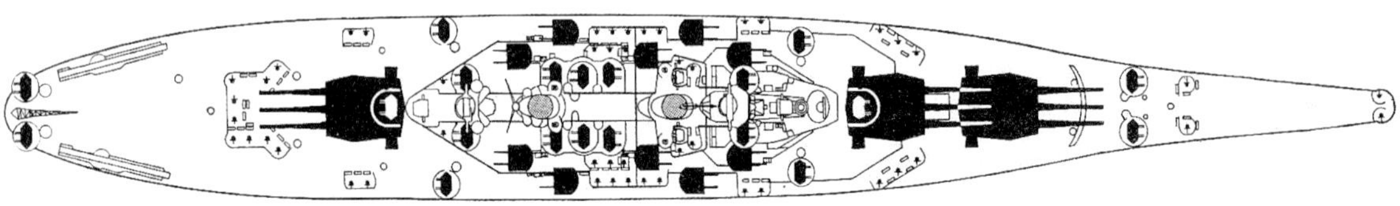

U.S.S. *Iowa* (BB-61) under construction at the New York Naval Shipyard, July 1942, looking forward from amidships.

Even during the development of the preceding *North Carolinas* and *South Dakotas*, battleship designs capable of speeds more than 30 knots (35 mph; 56 km/h) were considered to counter fast Japanese "big gun" ships. Simultaneously, the idea of a powerful strike force consisting of fast battleships operating with fast carriers and destroyers was taking shape. Although carriers were initially believed to be subordinate the battleships, this concept eventually became the Fast Carrier Task Force.

Another factor was the Second London Naval Treaty's "escalator clause," which allowed to raise the gun caliber limit from 14 inches (356 mm) to 16 inches (406 mm) after Japan had refused to sign the treaty. This meant that the Japanese did not accept the 14-inch gun caliber limit or the 5:5:3 ratio of warship tonnage limits for the United States Great Britain and Japan, respectively. This prompted the three western signatories (United States, Britain, and France) to invoke the escalator

Missouri's two forward 16-inch/50 caliber gun turrets are trained to the starboard during a gunnery exercise in the 1980s. This weapon is considered by experts to be one of the finest naval guns ever developed.

clause after April 1937. In addition, intelligence reports showed that the Japanese were building capital ships, violating naval treaties. This caused the three treaty powers to expand the escalator clause in June 1938 by also increasing the standard displacement limit of battleships from 35,000 long tons (35,560 t) to 45,000 long tons (45,720 t). Using the additional 10,000 long tons (10,160 t) over the two preceding *North Carolinas* and *South Dakotas*, various design studies included 27 knot (31 mph; 50 km/h) "slow" battleships with more powerful guns and improved protection as well as "fast" battleships capable of at least 33 knots (38 mph; 61 km/h). One of the slower designs was an expanded *South Dakota*-class armed with either 12 16-inch (406 mm)/45 caliber Mark 6 guns or nine 18-inch (457 mm)/48 guns and protected by additional armor. Eventually, priority was given to "fast" ship capable of defeating the Japanese 30-knot *Kongō*-class battlecruisers.

As a result, three improved designs, labeled "A," "B," and "C" were drawn up. All featured an increase in draft, considerable additions to the armor, and the substitution of 12 6-inch (152 mm) secondary guns.

"A" was the largest variant, with 59,060 long tons (60,010 t) standard displacement. It was the only one that retained the 12 16-inch guns in four three-gun turrets. To reach 32.5 knots (37.4 mph; 60.2 km/h), it required a power plant capable of 277,000 shp (207,000 kW).

"B" was the smallest ship, with 52,707 long tons (53,553 t) standard. Capable of the same top speed like variant "A," it only required 225,000 shp (168,000 kW), while carrying only nine 16-inch guns, in three three-gun turrets.

"C" was similar to "B" but it added 75,000 shp (56,000 kW), for a total of 300,000 shp (220,000 kW), to meet the initial demand for 35 knots. This caused additional weight, thus requiring a longer armor belt, resulting in a standard displacement of 55,771 long tons (56,666 t).

Further design developments convinced the General Board that a reasonably well-designed and balanced 33 knot "fast" battleship could be built within the terms of the "escalator clause." Due to a lack of communication during the design development, the Bureau of Ordnance believed the *Iowas* would carry the 16-inch/50 caliber Mark 2 guns, originally constructed for the canceled *Lexington*-class battlecruisers of the early 1920s. However, the Bureau of Construction and Repair believed that the ships would be armed with more compact (and lighter) 16-inch guns, thus designing the *Iowas* with barbettes that were too small to accommodate the 16-in/50 Mark

U.S.S. *New Jersey* (BB-62) ready for launching on December 7, 1942, the first anniversary of the attack on Pearl Harbor.

2 three-gun turrets that the Bureau of Ordnance had in mind. To solve this problem and to have a modern weapon at hand, the lightweight 16-in/50 Mark 7 was designed, which proved to be one of the finest naval guns ever built.

For half a century before the *Iowas* entered service, the U.S. Navy had always favored heavy armor and firepower at the expense of high speed. Even in designing the fast *North Carolinas*, it preferred the slower of two alternative versions. Still, the four *Iowas*, the largest battleships built by the United States, were little more than 33 knot variants of the 27 knot and 35,000 ton battleships that had preceded them. All in all, the *Iowas* offered no better protection than the *South Dakotas*, while the most important armament improvement was a more powerful 16-inch gun.

When entering service during the final years of the war, the *Iowas* were assigned to

Miss Margaret Truman christens U.S.S. *Missouri* (BB-63), during launching ceremonies at the New York Navy Yard, on January 29, 1944. Looking on are, from left: Rear Admiral Monroe R. Kelly, New York Navy Yard Commandant; Rear Admiral Sherman S. Kennedy, USN; and Senator Harry S. Truman of Missouri, Margaret's father.

operate in the Pacific. By this point, aircraft carriers had replaced battleships as the primary striking force. As a result, the *Iowas* and the other American fast battleships were relegated to the secondary role of carrier escorts and assigned to the fast carrier task forces to provide antiaircraft defense and perform shore bombardment.

U.S.S. *Iowa* (BB-61)

Commissioned in February 1943, *Iowa* (BB-61) conducted a shakedown cruise in Chesapeake Bay before sailing to Newfoundland. From here it was to engage the German battleship *Tirpitz*, *Bismarck*'s sister ship, in case it broke out into the Atlantic to attack Allied convoys, but this never happened. Transferred to the Pacific in 1944, *Iowa* made its combat debut in February when it participated in the campaign for the Marshall Islands. Later, the new battleship escorted carriers conducting air strikes in the Marianas campaign, followed by its participation in the battle of Leyte Gulf in October 1944, fighting off Japanese aircraft. In March 1945, *Iowa* supported the invasion of Okinawa and then bombarded various targets on the Japanese coastline with its powerful and accurate guns. On August 29, after Japan's surrender, *Iowa* entered Tokyo Bay and witnessed the surrender aboard *Missouri*.

U.S.S. *New Jersey* (BB-62)

Commissioned in May 1943, *New Jersey* (BB-62) transferred to the Pacific in advance of the planned assault on the Marshall Islands, where it screened American carriers from Japanese air attacks. During the battle of Leyte Gulf, the ship protected carriers with its massive antiaircraft armament, followed by shore bombardment missions on Iwo Jima and Okinawa. After protecting aircraft carriers during their attacks against the Japanese homeland toward the end of the war, *New Jersey* then participated in the repatriation of American troops (Operation *Magic Carpet*) in early 1946.

The new battleship *New Jersey* at anchor. At this time, it still had an open bridge in front of the massive conning tower.

U.S.S. *New Jersey*'s (BB-62) rounded bridge arrangement after reconstruction, October 1943.

New Jersey was refitted in 1945 with the now standard square-faced bridge, which was installed in its sister ships. The conning tower carries one large periscope (for the captain) and two smaller ones, with a Mark 27 radar abaft them. *New Jersey* has also been fitted with Mark 57 radar directors for its 40-mm guns.

Front view of *New Jersey*'s superstructure with the new square-faced bridge.

Rear of *New Jersey*'s superstructure. Note the 40-mm quadruple antiaircraft gun on top of No. 3 gun turret.

New Jersey and the French battleship *Richelieu* at anchor off New York, September 1943. After France's defeat, *Richelieu* was able to escape German capture and join the naval forces of Free France. The ship was repaired and modernized in the United States and then served with the British Fleet.

New Jersey in a stiff storm in the western Pacific, November 8, 1944. The carrier U.S.S. *Hancock* (CV-19) is in the background. The *Iowas* proved to be very seaworthy ships.

U.S.S. *Missouri* (BB-63) on its shakedown cruise in camouflage paint, August 1944. Note the parabolic antenna of the SK-2 air-search radar on top of the superstructure, which had a range of up to 86 nautical miles (161 km).

U.S.S. *Missouri* (BB-63)

Completed as the last of the four *Iowas* as the priority had shifted the construction of carriers, *Missouri* was commissioned in June 1944. After its transfer to the Pacific, it provided antiaircraft defense for carriers conducting strikes against Tokyo. After supporting the invasion of Iwo Jima and carrier-based air strikes against Tokyo and protecting the aircraft carriers around it (Task Group 58.4), it joined its sister ships *New Jersey* and *Wisconsin* for the shore bombardment of Okinawa in March 1945. After shelling the Japanese homeland and screening American carriers involved in combat operations, *Missouri* was chosen by American President Harry S. Truman to be the site of Japan's formal surrender in Tokyo Bay on September 2, 1945.

Missouri, nicknamed "*Mighty-Mo*," fires its two forward turrets consisting of six 16-inch guns, during gunnery practice. The projectiles are shown in flight at the upper right.

U.S.S. *Wisconsin* (BB-64) moored next to the hulk of U.S.S. *Oklahoma* in Pearl Harbor in November 1944. Note the anti-torpedo nets outboard of the ships and the great difference in lengths between *Wisconsin* and *Oklahoma*.

U.S.S. *Wisconsin* (BB-64)

Commissioned in April 1944, a few months before its sister ship *Missouri*, whose keel had been laid earlier, *Wisconsin* transferred to the Pacific to protect aircraft carriers involved in operations in the Philippines before being ordered to Iwo Jima in early 1945 to bombard the island in advance of the U.S. Marine invasion. The battleship then joined its sister ships *New Jersey* and *Missouri* for the shore bombardment of Okinawa in advance of the Allied amphibious assault in March 1945. In mid-1945 *Wisconsin* bombarded the Japanese homeland until the Japan's surrender in August.

U.S.S. *Illinois* (BB-65) and U.S.S. *Kentucky* (BB-66)

Although the hull numbers BB-65 and BB-66 were originally intended as the first and second ships of the subsequent *Montana*-class, the passage of the 1940 Two-Ocean Navy Act, which enlarged the American fleet

U.S.S. *Kentucky* (BB-66) being towed to the Boston Metals Company, Baltimore, Maryland, for scrapping, October 31, 1958. A few years earlier, its bow had been removed to repair the damaged bow of *Wisconsin*. Neither *Kentucky* nor *Illinois* (BB-65) was completed.

A battleship means firepower: *Iowa* firing a broadside with all its nine guns off the starboard side during a firepower demonstration, August 15, 1984.

by 70 percent, resulted in both hulls being reordered as *Iowa*-class ships to save time on construction. However, as the war ended before their completion, work was eventually stopped. Proposals to convert the hulls into aircraft carriers like the *Essex*-class were considered, but eventually abandoned. *Illinois* and *Kentucky* were broken up in the late 1950s.

Drawings of U.S.S. *Missouri* in its World War II configuration.

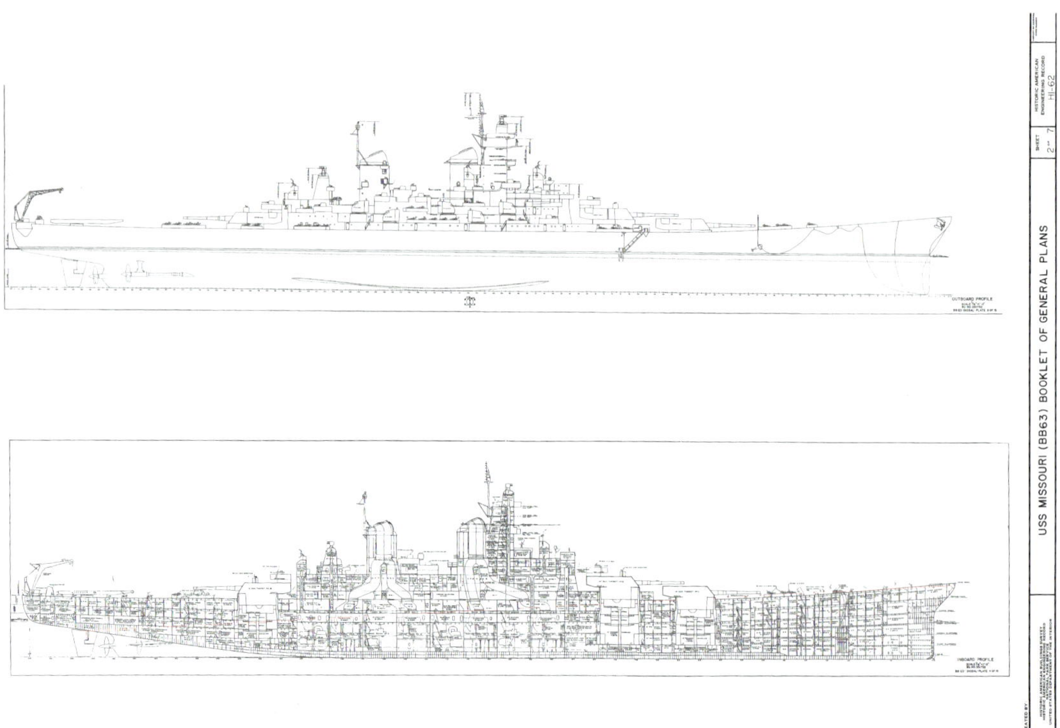

How Battleship Guns Work

The role of a battleship was to bring the largest and most powerful guns possible to sea. How did these complex weapons work? With the *Iowa*-class boasting some of the finest naval guns in history, it is worth having a closer look at them.

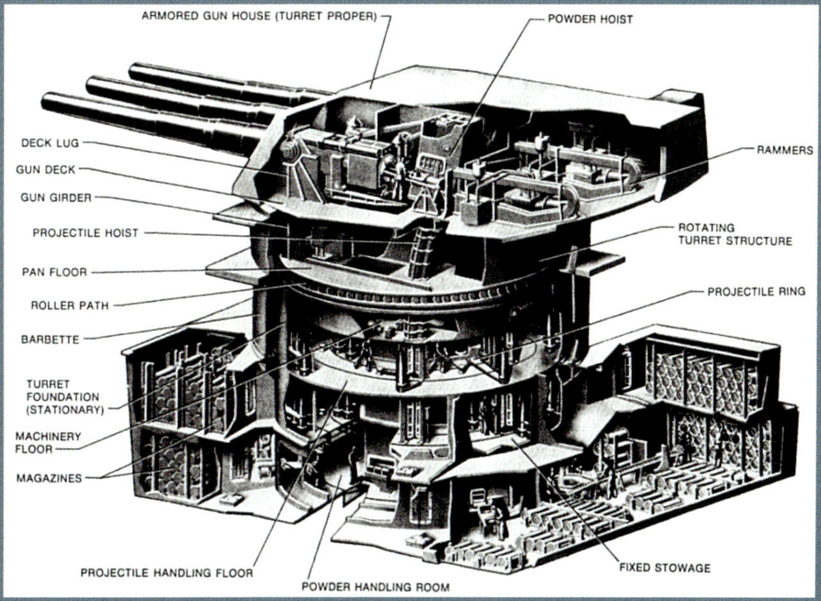

Cutaway of a 16-inch gun turret. (U.S. Navy)

Each ship of the *Iowa*-class carriers has nine breech-loading 16-inch (406 mm) naval guns. They are housed in three gun turrets—two forward and one aft. The guns are 66 feet (20.1 m) long and weigh 239,000 lb (108,409 kg) each. The number 16 indicates the projectile's diameter. For ship-to-ship engagements the *Iowa*-class fired 2,700 lb (1,225 kg) AP shells at a maximum speed of 2,690 feet (820 m) per second which could penetrate the other ship's armor plating and detonate with a short delay inside the hull. For shore bombardment the guns fired 1,900 lb (862 kg) HC explosive shells, which would detonate immediately upon impact.

At the maximum range of 40,500 yards (37 km) the projectile spent almost 90 seconds in flight. The maximum firing rate for each gun was 2 rounds per minute. When firing 2 broadsides per minute, the *Iowa*-class could put 36,000 lb (16,329 kg) of ordnance on a designated target every minute. This means that a second salvo could be fired while the first one was still in flight. In other words, 27 projectiles could hit the target within 90 seconds. Each of the 16-inch guns could rotate 300° and could fire independently. To minimize any rocking movement to the ship, the barrels recoiled 4 feet.

How does such a gun turret work and what does it take to hit a moving target that doesn't want to be hit?

Two gunner's mates attach lifting cables to a 16-inch projectile to move it below to the projectile flats for storage. The weight ranged from 1,900 lb (862 kg) to 2,700 lb (1,225 kg).

Powder bags arrive in the powder room aboard the U.S.S. *Iowa* (photographed in 1943) before being placed in the hoist (right) to be moved up to the 16-inch gun house.

You can only see a small portion of the whole 1,700-ton turret when standing on deck, so it is worthwhile having a closer look to understand why each turret required a crew of 77 to 110 men. On top there is the armored gun house, which has its thickest armor plating at the front. Its thickness measures 17 inches (430 mm) over an additional layer of 2.5 inches (64 mm) of STS. Below is the rotating structure that goes down four to five decks and rotates with the gun house. An armored circular cylinder known as the barbette surrounds this structure. It keeps the turrets in place, because they are not attached to the hull and would fall out if the ship were to capsize.

A 2,700 lb (1,225 kg) dummy projectile travels up a hoist from a handling room in one of the 16-inch gun turrets aboard *Iowa*, 1986.

Inside the gun there are the three gun slides, three powder trunks, sighting, elevating and training stations, a projectile hoist, and a cradle for each gun. The turret officer's booth contains the secondary rangefinder and fire-control equipment. Below the gun house or the gun deck, there are four more levels—the pan plate, where the power equipment for elevating the guns is located, the electric deck where the power equipment for training the guns can be found; the two decks below are the projectile handling platforms. There are stationary projectile storage areas that contain a ring for handling the projectiles.

The bottom deck contains the powder handling room, surrounded by the magazines. From here, the powder is moved to the powder hoists. Six powder bags weighing 110 lb (50 kg) each are necessary to fire one projectile. These

A ring on the projectile handling floor helps to move the enormously heavy 16-inch shell to its hoist to be raised up to the gun house.

After the gun captain has opened the gun breech, a 1,900 lb (862 kg) HC projectile is hoisted up to the spanning tray of the center 16-inch gun in the No. 2 turret aboard *Iowa*.

bags are taken from the magazine's scuttles and placed in the powder car, the doors are closed, and the car starts up through the hoist trunk to the gunroom. Simultaneously, a ring on the projectile handling floor helps move the enormously heavy 16-inch shell to its hoist to be raised up to the gun house. As soon as the projectile arrives at the top of the hoist, the 16-inch guns are brought into loading position. The gun captain opens the breech and the cradle and spanning tray are aligned with the gun. Once in position, a rammer moves the projectile into the gun. After retracting the rammer, the powder trunk door is opened, and three powder bags are rolled into the tray. Then the powder car moves down, and three more bags are rolled into the tray. Now all six bags can be rammed slowly into the gun. After

Six powder bags in total, weighing 110 lb (50 kg) each, are necessary to fire one 16-inch projectile.

After retracting the rammer and raising the cradle and the spanning tray, the gun captain closes the breech.

U.S.S. *New Jersey* firing a broadside in 1984.

retracting the rammer and raising the cradle and the spanning tray, the gun captain closes the breech and turns the "ready" switch to "ready." Then the gun automatically goes to firing position to be fired at any time.

Drawing of a 5-inch gun. Originally, the *Iowas* carried 20 5-inch (127 mm)/38 caliber Mark 12 guns in 10 gun turrets. During the 1980s modernization, four gun turrets were removed to make room for armored box launchers needed to fire Tomahawk missiles.

The 5-inch/38 caliber gun functioned as a dual-purpose gun, capable of firing at surface and air targets.

Fire Control

As a heavy bombardment weapon against surface and shore targets up to 40,500 yards (37 km) away, the 16-inch guns of the *Iowa*-class were valuable and accurate weapons. Even under ideal circumstances the crew could see only about 24,500 yards (22.5 km) from the deck of a battleship. But with two ships 35,000 yards (32 km) apart firing at each other it was possible to land a salvo of 16-inch projectiles accurately on the target. Although the fire could be directed from each gun turret individually, rangefinding was usually accomplished by remotely located directors operating through a central fire-control system. An early form of radar and optical rangefinders measured target motion and gave this information to the Mark 8 range-keeper computer deep down in the plotting room. Its technology dates to the 1920s and is fully analog. Like an old-fashioned

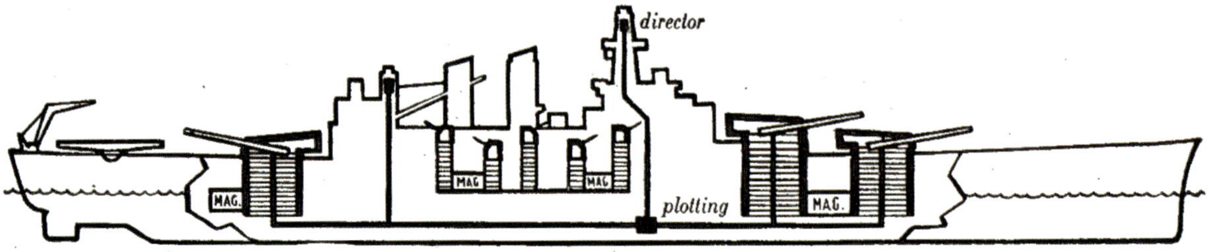

Diagram of the fire-control system aboard the *North Carolina*-, *South Dakota*-, and *Iowa*-classes.

One of the two main battery plotting rooms of the *Iowa*-class. Located below the waterline and inside the armor belt, it housed analog fire-control computers and switchboards, displays and communication devices.

The analog Mark 1 fire-control computer was a component of the Mark 37 gun fire-control system, which used tachymetric target motion prediction to compute a fire-control solution. It contained a target simulator, which was updated by further target tracking until it matched. The tachymetric system generated target position, speed, direction, and rate of target range change by computing these parameters directly from measured data.

Each plotting room had a Mark 41 stable vertical. This gimbaled gyroscope measured the ship's roll and pitch to generate level and cross-level corrections to the fire-control system's various elements. Mounted waist high on its side were the guns' firing keys: the left one was the salvo signal key, which sounded the salvo buzzer in each turret to warn the gun crews that the guns were about to fire. The center key was the automatic firing key. When this button was held closed, the Mark 41 could fire the guns automatically when the ship's deck was parallel to the horizontal plane. The right key was the hand-firing key that bypassed the Mark 41 and fired the guns directly.

View of *Wisconsin*'s forward 16-inch guns, taken in March 1952. Note the Mark 38 main battery director on top of the superstructure. A long-based stereoscopic rangefinder is enclosed in the armored extensions on both sides. A Mark 13 radar is mounted atop. When there was clear visibility, the Mark 48 was used for rangefinding, while the Mark 13 had a complete blind firing capability.

The SPS-49 air-search radar can provide contact bearing and range. It was installed during the 1980s modernization. The SPS-49 is used on numerous U.S. Navy ships and has a range of up to 256 nautical miles (474 km).

A crewmember monitors the SPS-49 radar screen aboard *Iowa*, 1984.

In addition to the rangefinders on the superstructures, the 16-inch (and 5-inch) gun turrets also had their own optical (stereoscopic) rangefinders. This one is *Iowa*'s No. 3 gun turret.

windup clock, all its calculations result from rotation switches, wheels, cams, and levers.

The data generated by the optical rangefinders and radars are processed in the plotting room and then used to direct the guns.

In addition to the battleship's course and speed, the target's course and speed, bearing and range, and additional information such as wind speed, air temperature, and magazine temperature were fed into the Mark 8. From these data, the computer calculated values for gun elevation and turret train orders and sent them to the turrets. With an astonishing accuracy of 20 feet (6 m) this amazing machine was so precise that it remained

The optical (stereoscopic) rangefinder inside *Iowa*'s No. 3 gun turret. This system served as a backup in case of failure of the main central fire-control system.

One of *Iowa*'s 40-mm antiaircraft quadruple gun mounts with its fire-control director is visible in the foreground.

the main computer for the massive 16-inch guns all the way through Operation *Desert Storm* (1991), when, augmented by modern radar, it precisely directed the fire on targets in Iraqi-occupied Kuwait.

Propulsion

The four ships of the *Iowa*-class are the fastest battleships ever launched, capable of a top speed of 33 knots

The *Iowas* were built with four screws: the outboard pair consisted of four-bladed propellers 18.25 feet (5.56 m) in diameter, while the inboard pair consisted of five-bladed propellers 17 feet (5.18 m) in diameter. The two inner shafts were housed in skegs to smooth the flow of water to the propellers and improve the stern's structural strength. Two semi-balanced rudders provided a tactical turning diameter of 814 yards (744 m) at 30 knots and 760 yards (695 m) at 20 knots.

U.S.S. *Iowa* under construction, looking aft, June 1941. The boilers and main engines are in place and the torpedo defense system is taking shape. The power plant consists of eight Babcock & Wilcox boilers and four turbine sets.

Control board in one of *New Jersey*'s engine rooms. The ship's speed is regulated by turning the wheels: the large black one for ahead, the small red one for astern.

No. 3 boiler room aboard *Iowa*, photographed in 1943. Each of the four boiler rooms housed two M-Type boilers operating at 600 psi (4,137 kPa; 42 kgf/cm^2) with a maximum superheater outlet temperature of 850°F (454°C) to generate steam for the turbines.

Close-up of *Iowa*'s main reduction gear, 1943. Each ship was built with four sets of double-reduction, cross-compound geared turbines, with each turbine set driving a single shaft.

Missouri's technicians service the boiler system during the 1980s.

Enginemen check fuel samples in an engineering space aboard *Missouri* during Exercise *RimPac '88*.

"Broadway" aboard *Iowa*. Located inside the armor citadel, this main fore and aft passageway on the third deck provides access to the machinery spaces and the 5-inch magazines. The removable overhead monorail allows the transport of 16-inch projectiles between gun turrets Nos. 2 and 3.

(38 mph; 61 km/h). Their engineering plant consists of four General Electric double-expansion steam turbine engines, each driving a single shaft that turns one screw. The steam produced by the eight Babcock & Wilcox boilers passes through the turbines, which turn at 2,000 rpm. Without refueling, the *Iowa*-class had a range of 15,000 nautical miles (27,780 km) at a cruising speed of 12 knots (22 km/h).

Armor Protection

As the four battleships of the *Iowa*-class represented one of the most modern designs completed during World War II, their protection scheme is worth studying.

The ship's hull includes an armored box, known as the citadel, ranging from forward of turret 1 to aft of turret 3. The top, sides, and ends of the citadel are heavily armored, protecting vital parts such as the powder

Diagram of the general armor distribution of the *North Carolina*-, *South Dakota*- and *Iowa*-classes.

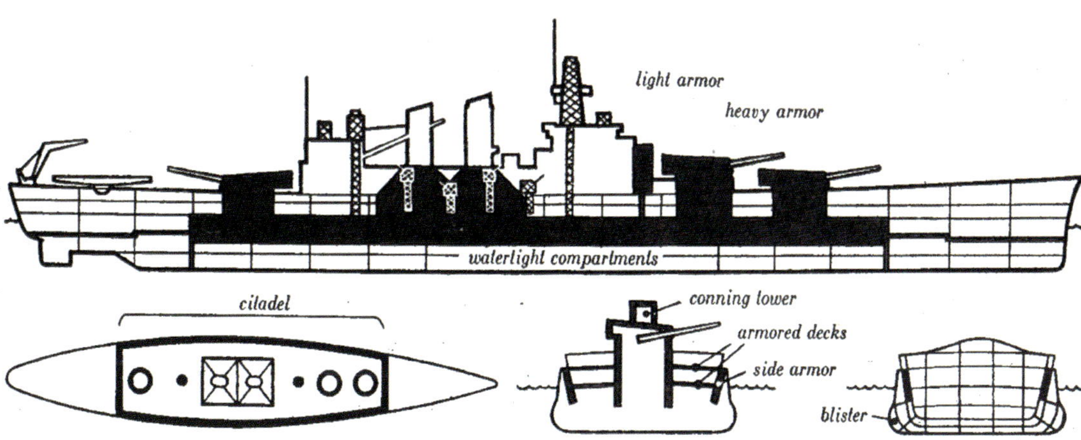

The heavily armored conning tower behind the bridge houses the helm and various observation and communication devices on two levels.

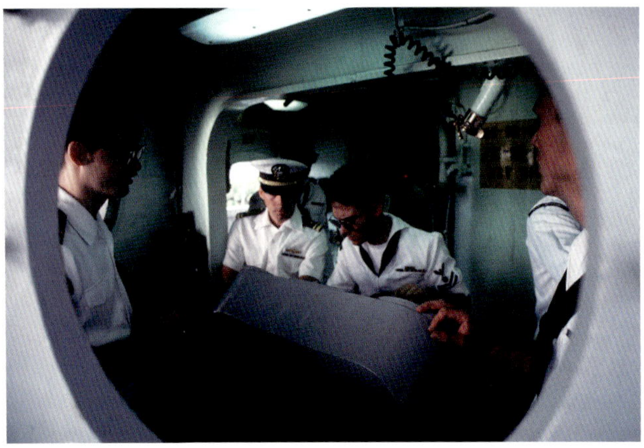

Missouri's helmsman mans the wheel while other crewmembers stand by during Exercise *RimPac '88*.

and magazines and the machinery. The vertical side armor consists of an upper and lower belt, inclined to an angle of 19°. The upper belt is Class A armor, 12.1 inches (307 mm) thick, while the lower belt is Class B armor, 12.1 inches thick at the top and tapered to 1.6 inches (41 mm) at the bottom.

The horizontal protection consists of three parts: first comes the main or bomb deck with a thickness of 1.5 inches (127 mm), designed to detonate general-purpose bombs on contact and arm armor-piercing bombs so they will explode between the bomb deck and the main armor deck below. Second is the armor deck, which has a thickness of 4.75 inches (121 mm) plus an additional layer of 1.25 inches. Its purpose is to defeat plunging shells, which may penetrate the bomb deck. Third comes the splinter deck, which is designed to contain any fragments and pieces of armor, which might be broken off from the main armor deck. All in all, this concept was far more resistant to aerial bombardment than World War I-era designs such as U.S.S. *Arizona* (BB-39).

Drawing from the lessons of World War I, the protection scheme of battleships designed during the interwar years incorporated a torpedo defense system. However, there were limits to the battleship's underwater protection scheme as well, as World War II saw the introduction of various new and punchy torpedo types. For instance, the torpedo defense system designed for the *South Dakota*- and *Iowa*-classes was to absorb the energy from an underwater explosion equivalent to 700 lb (317 kg) of TNT which was the U.S. Navy's estimation for the ability of Japanese torpedoes during the 1930s. The Japanese Navy, however, had secretly developed

Iowa under construction, looking forward, December 1940. Sections of the lower main armor belt and the traverse bulkheads are visible.

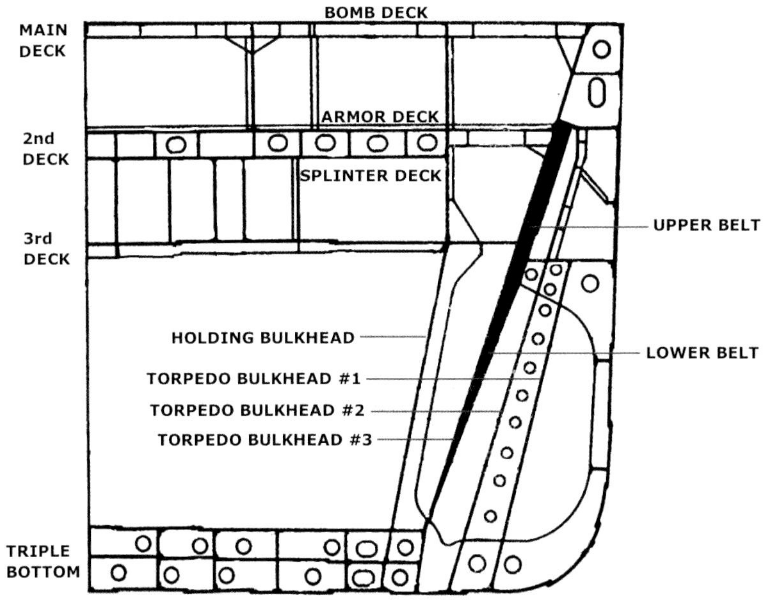

Illustration of the *Iowas'* protection system including the bomb decks, torpedo defense, and triple bottom.

the Type 93 torpedo carrying a charge equivalent to 891 lb (405 kg) of TNT.

The underwater protection of the *Iowas* consists of a torpedo defense system and triple bottom, which is designed to protect the ship from torpedoes, mines, and near-miss bombs equivalent to a 700 lb charge of TNT. The side protection system consists of two outboard tanks loaded with fuel oil or ballast water and two inboard tanks with a void space. The liquid layers are intended to deform and absorb the shock from the explosion and contain most of the shards from the damaged area. The innermost void is designed to contain potential leaks into the ship's interior. Torpedo bulkhead 3, also called the armor belt, between both tank sections is designed to stop any fragments that might have penetrated the second

Installation of *Kentucky*'s lower armor belt, July 1945. The pin brackets to attach the upper belt to the lower belt are visible. While the first four *Iowas* were completed with their upper and lower armored belts secured by key ways, *Illinois* and *Kentucky* were designed with a pin-securing arrangement.

The 19° slope of *Kentucky*'s armor belt.

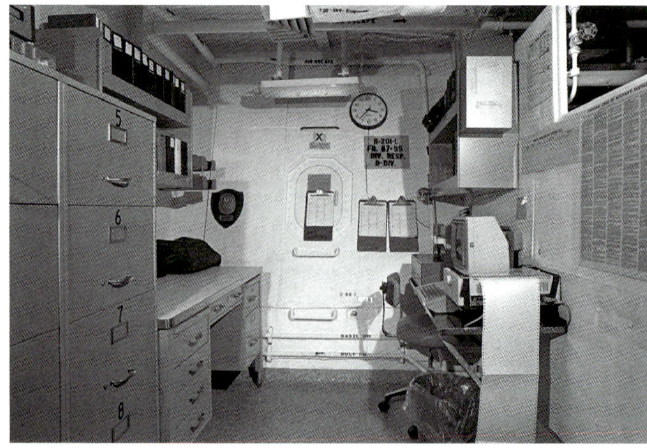

A dental office space aboard *Iowa*. The torpedo protection system is located behind the sloping ship's side.

Kentucky's stern, February 1946. The torpedo defense system is recognizable by the sloped and perforated struts on both sides.

torpedo bulkhead. Bulkheads 1 and 2 and the holding bulkhead each have a thickness of 0.625 inches (16 mm) of steel. The thickest is torpedo bulkhead number 3 measuring 12.1 inches (307 mm) and tapering down to one inch at the bottom with a 1.5-inch (38 mm) STS plate.

Aircraft

During World War II, *Iowa*-class was originally equipped with floatplanes. These aircraft were located on

An OS2N-1 Kingfisher floatplane is lowered onto its catapult cradle after a flight, during *Missouri*'s shakedown cruise, 1944.

A Sikorski HO3S-1 helicopter takes off from *New Jersey*, 1953.

A target drone about to take off from *Wisconsin*, 1945. Forty-six years later, reconnaissance drones were used in Operation *Desert Storm*.

A CH-53E Super Stallion lands on *Missouri*'s helicopter pad at the stern, 1986. Takeoffs and landings were controlled from the ship's helicopter control station on level 02 at the ship's fantail.

catapults at the ship's stern, whence they could be launched. Their duties usually included reconnaissance flights beyond the horizon and the observation and adjustment of the ship's gunfire. The plane had to land in the water next to the ship and was picked up by the stern crane. Because heavy seas could make recovery difficult and dangerous for the pilot, the ship would turn, thus forming a wide slick wake for landing. In the 1950s, a helicopter which was directly able to land on board, replaced the aircraft.

Iowa-class General Characteristics (as built)

Class	*Iowa*
Name	*Iowa* (BB-61) *New Jersey* (BB-62) *Missouri* (BB-63) *Wisconsin* (BB-64) *Illinois* (BB-65) *Kentucky* (BB-66)
Shipyard	New York Naval Shipyard (BB-61 and BB-63) Philadelphia Naval Shipyard (BB-62; BB-64; BB-65) Norfolk Naval Shipyard, Virginia (BB-66)
Commissioning	February 22, 1943 (BB-61) May 23, 1943 (BB-62) June 11, 1944 (BB-63) April 16, 1944 (BB-64) Canceled (BB-65 and BB-66)
Displacement (normal) Displacement (full)	48,110 long tons (48,880 t) 57,540 long tons (58,460 t)
Length (overall)	887 ft 3 in (270.43 m)
Beam	108 ft 2 in (32.97 m)
Draft (max)	ca. 37 ft 2 in (11.33 m)
Propulsion	4 × steam turbines (212,000 shp / 158,000 kW)
Maximum speed	33 kn (61.1 km/h)
Range	14,890 nmi (27,580 km) at 15 knots
Complement	ca. 2,700
Armament	9 × 16-in (406 mm)/50 cal. Mark 7 20 × 5-in (127 mm)/38 cal. Various AA guns
Fate	Preserved as museum ships (BB-61; BB-62; BB-63; BB-64) Sold for scrap, 1958/59 (BB-65 and BB-66)

Montana-class

In the interwar years, the U.S. Navy grew increasingly concerned with its strengthening rival in the Pacific, the Imperial Japanese Navy. The 1922 Washington Naval Treaty had accorded the United States and Great Britain superiority over Japan in terms of total tonnage. As the latter had already refused to abide by the terms of the 1936 Second London Naval Treaty, the other signatory nations, United States, Britain and France, loosened the restrictions on their own new capital ship designs.

The U.S. Navy now focused on two possible designs: a comparatively slow, heavily armed and armored vessel and a much faster, but lighter armed and armored type that was primarily capable of hunting down Japanese cruisers and countering the fast *Kongō*-class battleships. While the former was a 45,000-ton ship armed with 12 16-inch (406 mm) guns, and capable of 27 knots (31 mph; 50 km/h), the latter variant was as an improved *South Dakota* with a top speed of 33 knots (38 mph; 61 km/h)

An artist impression of the *Montana*-class, which was designed to carry four gun turrets boasting 12 16-inch guns.

Though the *Iowas* were built as a 33 knot design, the U.S. Navy's leadership considered this an exception to its normal doctrine, thus determining that the successor would be a 27 knot standard-type battleship. The primary consideration was the development of the super-heavy 2,700 lb (1,200 kg) AP shell. While standard design practice stated that American battleships should be immune to gunfire from their own calibers ("balanced armor"), the new shell had a significantly better penetrating power than older, lighter projectiles.

As none of the existing classes (*North Carolina, South Dakota, Iowa*) was resistant to the 2,700 lb shell, the General Board demanded better protection for the new *Montana*-class, asking the C&R for proposals conforming to the 45,000-ton limit, 12 16-inch guns, and a top speed of 27 knots.

C&R initially drew up a design named BB-65A based on *South Dakota*, but with a longer hull accommodating the fourth 16-inch main gun turret. This exceeded the displacement limit by about 435 long tons (442 t), while the ship was only protected against the older 2,250 lb (1,020 kg) AP projectile. The designers concluded that a sufficient protection scheme against the new 2700 lb shell would require more than 2,000 long tons (2,032 t). A second variant, BB-65B, featuring 12 new 6-inch (152 mm)/47 caliber secondary guns instead of the existing 20 5-inch (127 mm)/38 caliber guns increased the displacement even further. The subsequent designs, BB-65C and BB-65D, incorporated three quadruple main battery turrets instead of four triple turrets, resulting in about 1,600 long tons (1,626 t) of weight saving. Although these two proposals were only protected against the older 2,250 lb shell, they were below the displacement limit, thus prompting C&R to use the available weight to reinforce their armor by creating design BB-65E. This, however, increased the displacement to as much as 55,000 long tons (56,000 t).

While none of these four designs was considered acceptable, concerns also arose about the practical value of the quadruple turrets, which led to several (rather experimental) proposals incorporating 18-inch (457 mm) or 16-inch (406 mm) guns with mixed quadruple, triple, and double turrets for either 10 or 11 guns in total. The idea was to save weight while providing firepower greater than the *South Dakota*'s nine 16-inch guns. One design, BB-65J, even proposed a ship with 12 14-inch (356 mm) guns that would be well protected against the new 2,700 lb projectile.

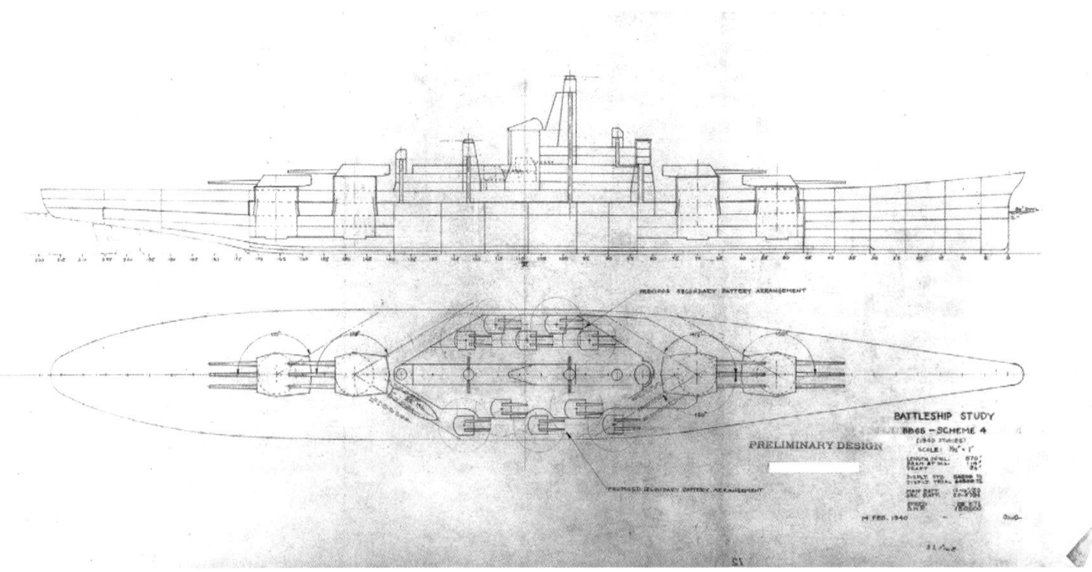

Drawing of one of the studies for the *Montana*-class.

The outbreak of World War II in Europe, the fall of France in June 1940, and Japan's expansionist actions in Asia increased the pressure to speed up construction of new American warships. To be prepared for a possible war with more than one enemy (Germany and Japan) both in the Atlantic and Pacific, the Two-Ocean Navy Act was passed on July 19, 1940. This was a federal law that enacted a 70 percent increase in fleet size. It included an increase of 385,000 long tons (391,000 t) for battleships alone, along with hundreds of thousands of tons for new aircraft carriers, cruisers, and destroyers.

In addition, the remaining limits imposed by the Washington and London Naval Treaties were now removed entirely. This was also done with regards of Japan's withdrawal from these agreements. The U.S. Navy therefore feared that the Japanese would soon build a class of super-battleships with a caliber of 16 inches or larger and a displacement of more than 60,000 tons. Indeed, this had already occurred with the keel-laying of the *Yamato*-class in 1937, which had nine 18.1-inch (460 mm) guns.

Model of the *Montana*-class (BB-67–BB-71), which was canceled during World War II. This model depicts the ship fitted with a heavy battery of antiaircraft guns, as would have been the case had the class been completed.

The new *Montana*-class would only be limited by logistical restrictions of existing naval infrastructure, most significantly available dry docks and the Panama Canal, then under American control. The Navy had been demanding a third, wider set of locks for the canal since 1938, which was eventually approved in 1940.

After requesting a new series of proposals in February 1940, the General Board selected one of the designs, labeled BB-65-5A, featuring 12 16-inch guns on a displacement of 57,500 long tons (58,400 t), and capable of 28 knots. This formed the basis for the additional refinements. As the last two *Iowa*-class battleships received the hull numbers BB-65 and BB-66, the final design series was named BB-67-1 to BB-67-4, which differed only slightly from each other.

In March 1941, BB-67-4 armed with 12 16-inch guns, displacing 60,500 long tons (61,500 t), and capable of about 27 knots eventually became the basis for the construction of the five planned *Montanas*. This design was immune to the new 2,700 lb AP shells when fired at ranges between 18,000 and 31,000 yards (16,460 and 28,350 m). The resistance to the older 16-inch AP shells extended to 16,500 and 34,500 yards (15,090 and 31,550 m).

Armament

The main armament featured 12 16-inch (406 mm)/50 caliber Mark 7 guns in four three-gun turrets. The guns fired two types of projectiles: a 2,700 lb (1,225 kg) AP shell and a 1,900 lb (862 kg) HC shell carrying a larger high-explosive bursting charge. The projectiles had muzzle velocities of 2,500 feet per second (760 m/s) and 2,690 feet per second (820 m/s) respectively.

Fired at the maximum elevation of 45°, the AP shells could reach targets up to 42,345 yards (38,720 m) away. The lighter HC shells had a range of 41,604 yards (38,043 m). At those distances, the projectiles' flight time was more than 80 seconds. At a realistic battle distance of 20,000 yards (18,290 m), the powerful AP shells could penetrate up to 20 inches (508 mm) of steel armor. The guns' rate of fire was about 2 shots per minute.

The secondary armament featured 20 5-inch (127 mm)/54 caliber Mark 16 dual-purpose guns (against aerial and surface targets) in 10 two-gun turrets. They fired a 70 lb (32 kg) shell at a muzzle velocity of 2,650 feet per second (810 m/s). The maximum range against surface targets was up to 25,909 yards (23,691 m), while the maximum ceiling against aerial targets was up to 51,600 ft (15,700 m). The rate of fire was up to 15 rounds per minute. The light antiaircraft (AA) armament was to consist of 30 40-mm Bofors guns in eight quadruple mounts and 20-mm Oerlikon guns mounted individually.

Protection

Designed with the "all or nothing" armor scheme, most of the armor was concentrated on the armored citadel containing the machinery spaces, tun turret barbettes, magazines, and command and control facilities. The armor belt was 16.1 inches (409 mm) thick and made of Class A face-hardened Krupp cemented armor mounted on 1 inch (25 mm) of STS. Inclined at 19°, the belt tapered to 10.2 inches (259 mm) below the waterline. To protect the ship's sides against potential underwater shell hits, a separate lower armor belt served as one of the torpedo bulkheads. It was up to 8.5 inches (216 mm) thick, inclined at 10°, and tapered to 1 inch at the triple bottom. The ends of the armored citadel would be closed by 18 inch (457 mm) thick bulkheads in the front and 15.25 inches (387 mm) in the aft.

The *Montana*'s deck armor was to be made of three layers: the first consisted of 0.75 inch (19 mm) STS laminated on 1.5 inch (38 mm) STS, thus totaling 2.25 inches (57 mm). The second and strongest deck was to be a 5.8 inch (147 mm) thick Class B armor laminated on 1.25 inch (32 mm) STS, totaling 7.05 inches (179 mm). The third deck was a 0.625 inch (16 mm) thick splinter deck (1 inch or 20-mm over the magazines). The ship's total horizontal armor thickness was to be 9.925 inches (252 mm) over the citadel and 10.3 inches (262 mm) over the magazines.

The main gun turrets were designed to be heavily protected, with turret faces made of 18 inches (457 mm) of Class B armor mounted on 4.5 inches (114 mm) of STS, totaling 22.5 inches (572 mm). The sides consisted of up to 10 inches (254 mm) of Class A, while the roofs had 9.15 inches (232 mm) of Class B. The massive barbettes were protected by up to 21.3 inches (541 mm) of Class A armor forward and 18 inches (457 mm) aft. The conning tower's Class A armor was up to 18 inches (457 mm) strong.

The torpedo and mine protection system incorporated lessons learned from the three preceding battleship classes. It featured four internal longitudinal torpedo bulkheads behind the outer hull plating, thus forming a multilayered bulge. The two outer compartments were liquid-filled, while the two inner ones were void with the lower Class B armor belt forming the holding bulkhead between them. As the protection system featured an external armor belt, the geometry of the multi-layered "bulge" rather resembled that of the *North Carolinas* than that of the *South Dakotas* and *Iowas*. The *Montana*'s greater beam allowed a higher system depth of up to 20.5 feet (6.25 m) compared to the *North Carolina*'s 18.5 feet (5.64 m).

Propulsion

The *Montanas* featured eight oil-fired Babcock & Wilcox two-drum boilers. Generating a steam pressure of 565 psi (3,900 kPa) and a temperature of 850°F (454°C), the boilers supplied their steam to four geared steam turbines. Driving one propeller each, the four turbines were rated at 43,000 shp (31,600 kW) each, totaling 172,000 hp (126,400 kW) to reach a top speed of 28 knots (32 mph; 52 km/h). The two inboard shafts were housed in skegs, which, while increasing hydrodynamic drag, strengthened the stern structure. The ships were designed to carry 7,500 long tons (7,620 t) of fuel oil, giving them a range of 15,000 nautical miles (17,300 mi; 27,800 km) at a cruising speed of 15 knots (17 mph; 28 km/h). While the standard displacement was 63,221 long tons (64,240 t), it would have reached 70,965 long tons (72,104 t) at full load.

Cancelation

After the authorization of five *Montanas* by the 1940 Two-Ocean Navy Act, all of them were canceled in July 1943 as production priorities had shifted decisively toward aircraft carriers, submarines, and destroyers.

Montana-class General Characteristics (as planned)

Class	*Montana*
Name	*Montana* (BB-67) *Ohio* (BB-68) *Maine* (BB-69) *New Hampshire* (BB-70) *Louisiana* (BB-71)
Shipyard	Philadelphia Naval Shipyard (BB-67 and BB-68) New York Naval Shipyard (BB-69 and BB-70) Norfolk Naval Shipyard, Virginia (BB-71)
Commissioning	Canceled
Displacement (normal) Displacement (full)	63,221 long tons (64,240 t) 70,965 long tons (72,104 t)
Length (overall)	921 ft 3 in (280.8 m)
Beam	121 ft 2 in (36.9 m)
Draft (max)	36 ft (11 m)
Propulsion	4 × steam turbines (172,000 shp / 126,506 kW)
Maximum speed	28 kn (52 km/h)
Range	15,000 nmi (27,800 km) at 15 knots
Complement	ca. 2,700
Armament	12 × 16 in (406 mm)/50 cal. Mark 7 20 × 5 in (127 mm)/54 cal. Various AA guns
Fate	Canceled

5

Battlecruisers and Large Cruisers

Founded in 1884, the Naval War College (NWC) is the "Home of Thought" at Naval Station Newport, Rhode Island. The institution educates and develops leaders, helps define the future U.S. Navy, its missions, and strengthens global maritime partnerships. As early as 1903, the NWC raised questions about the overall effectiveness of large, armored cruisers such as the then-new *Pennsylvania*- and *Tennessee*-classes.

As an alternative, its staff suggested a new cruiser type featuring a similar armament and armor like a battleship, proposing a vessel with four 12-inch (305 mm), 22 3-inch (76 mm) guns, four torpedo tubes and battleship-type protection.

In 1906, after preparing various studies over several years, the College strongly advocated the ships' construction for use in scouting and as fast wings in a fleet action, and for their resistance to 12-inch gunfire. However, the General Board and the Secretary of the Navy refused to adopt the proposed new armored cruiser (as an early variant of a battlecruiser). This occurred most likely because the U.S. Navy already had 10 new armored cruisers on hand. Nevertheless, the Naval War College continued to test its design against various foreign vessels, including the three British *Invincible*-class ships that entered service in 1908/9 as the world's first battlecruisers.

The British *Invincible*-class (here HMS *Inflexible*) boasted a significant increase in speed, displacement, and firepower compared to the most recent armored cruisers but had no more armor. (U.S. Library of Congress)

What is a Battlecruiser?

Battlecruisers resembled battleships in displacement, armament, and cost, but differed in form and balance of attributes. They typically had thinner armor and lighter main guns than contemporary battleships, installed on a longer hull with a more powerful power plant to attain greater speeds. The first battlecruisers were commissioned by the British Royal Navy, as a further development of the armored cruiser, at the same time as the dreadnought-type battleship succeeded pre-dreadnought designs shortly before World War I. They were designed to outrun warships with similar armament, and hunt down vessels with weaker weaponry. This meant that they were intended to hunt down slower armored cruisers and destroy them with superior fire while avoiding combat with the more powerful but slower battleships. The concept of the battlecruiser became obsolete with the introduction of battleships that could achieve the same speed while being more heavily armed and better protected.

Lexington-class

For years, the U.S. Navy did not focus on the construction of these ships as Japan, its potential main rival in the Pacific, continued to build armored cruisers. It did not react either when Germany and Britain built increasing numbers of battlecruisers prior to World War I. However, in early 1911, the navy changed its attitude when Japan laid down the first of four *Kongō*-class battlecruisers, thus demanding an American version of *Kongō* to counter it.

After approving six ships for the future *Lexington*-class, they were originally designed to mount a main armament of 10 14-inch (356 mm) guns and a secondary battery of up to 18 5-inch (127 mm) guns on a hull capable of 35 knots (40 mph; 65 km/h). Their construction was repeatedly postponed in favor of escort ships and submarines. This opened the opportunity for various redesigns, which had become apparent considering experience gained in the battle of Jutland in 1916, which was fought between British and German battleships and battlecruisers. This clash—where three British battlecruisers were sunk in part because of their weak armor protection—took place shortly after the original *Lexington* design was drawn up.

The construction of the Japanese *Kongō*-class battlecruisers eventually prompted the U.S. Navy to build similar ships, resulting in the *Lexington*-class.

An artist conception of the *Lexington*-class. This was the only battlecruiser class ever ordered by the U.S. Navy.

That the U.S. Navy had initially misinterpreted the essentials of the battle of Jutland was shown by its neglect of the *Lexington*'s protection. Instead, it increased the main armament to eight 16-inch (406 mm) guns and the secondary battery to up to 16 6-inch (152 mm) guns, while the top speed decreased to 33.25 knots (38.26 mph; 61.58 km/h).

Other factors for this modification were the discovery of British and Japanese plans for new battlecruisers armed with 15-inch (381 mm) and 16-inch guns, respectively. The combined requirements of enormous firepower, high speed, and sufficient protection provided considerable challenges to naval architects and the technology of the time. As the desired speed of 32 to 35 knots had been attained previously only in destroyers and smaller craft, a capital ship required a hull and a power plant of unprecedented size for a U.S. Navy vessel. As a result, careful planning was necessary to ensure the *Lexingtons* would have enough longitudinal strength to withstand bending forces underway and the added stresses on its structure during battle. In addition, it was a complex task to design a powerful propulsion system that was also compact enough to allow sufficient protection. None of the proposals made provision for aircraft. However, it was planned to add them later.

Armament

The initial *Lexington* design proposal featured a main armament consisting of 10 14-inch (356 mm) guns in four turrets (two triple superfiring over two double turrets). This gun was installed on the *Tennessee*- and *New Mexico*-class battleships. Later proposals called for eight 16-inch (406 mm) guns, which were also intended for the (eventually canceled) *South Dakota*-class battleships. A similar variant of this gun was used on the *Colorado*-class.

The initial secondary armament was to consist of 18 5-inch (127 mm)/51 caliber guns, which were mounted on every American battleship built prior to the 1922 Washington Naval Treaty (from the *Florida*- to the *Colorado*-class). This weaponry was upgraded to 14 6-inch (152 mm)/53 caliber guns, which were also intended as secondary armament on the *South Dakotas*. They fired a 105 lb (48 kg) shell at a muzzle velocity of 3,000 feet per second (914 m/s). Their rate of fire was up to 7 rounds per minute, while the range was up to 25,300 yards (23,100 m) at an elevation of 30°. The antiaircraft armament was to consist of several 3-inch (76 mm) Mark 11 guns, which were also used on other battleship classes such as the *Colorados*.

The torpedo armament featured up to eight 21-inch (533 mm) torpedoes. While four would be mounted inside the hull below the waterline, with two at either side of the bow, the other four would be installed above the waterline at the stern, with two at either side.

Protection

The armor belt tapered from to 7 to 5 inches (178–127 mm) in thickness from top to bottom. It was angled 11° outwards at the top, thus increasing the armor's relative thickness. On either end of the belt, a transverse bulkhead, 5 to 7 inches thick forward and 7 inches thick aft, connected both sides, thus forming an armored citadel for ship's vital parts. While the belt had a thickness like the pre-1914 armored cruisers, it was considerably thinner than that of contemporary battleships, thus providing no protection against gunfire from capital ships.

Made of two layers, the upper deck had a total thickness of 2.25 inches (57 mm). The deck over the machinery and magazines was also armored, with two layers of STS, totaling 2 inches (51 mm) in thickness. The turret faces were 11 inches (279 mm) thick, while their sides were 6 inches (152 mm), and the roof was 5 inches. The barbettes had a maximum of 9 inches (229 mm) of armor but were reduced in thickness in stages below decks to a minimum thickness of 5 inches. The conning tower armor was up to 12 inches (305 mm) thick. The torpedo defense system consisted of three to six medium steel protective bulkheads that ranged from 0.375 to 0.75 inches (10 to 19 mm) in thickness. The spaces between them could be left empty or used as fuel tanks to absorb a torpedo or mine detonation.

The incomplete hull of U.S.S. *Saratoga* (CV-3) at the New York Shipbuilding Corporation shipyard, Camden, New Jersey, March 8, 1922. Construction had been suspended, pending the ship's conversion to an aircraft carrier. Note barbette structures resting on blocks on its deck. (U.S. National Archives)

Propulsion

Turbo-electric propulsion was first used in the *New Mexico*-class battleships. Four General Electric turbogenerators powered each propeller shaft, with 16 water-tube boilers providing steam for the generators. The machinery was designed to produce a total of 180,000 shp (130,000 kW) for a top

This photo illustrates the genesis of the *Lexington*-class aircraft carrier. In the foreground is a model of the carrier design converted from the battlecruiser hull. (U.S. National Archives)

speed of 33.25 knots (38.26 mph; 61.58 km/h). However, after their completion as carriers, the ships reached about 202,000 shp (151,000 kW) and 34.5 knots (39.7 mph; 63.9 km/h) during sea trials in 1928.

Fate

In November 1921, one year after the *Lexington*'s construction had begun, the Washington Naval Conference was held. The goal was to limit the rapidly growing and expensive international naval construction programs. The Board noted that the expensive new battlecruisers, which some experts believed were already obsolete due to the introduction of fast battleships in foreign navies, would be attractive targets for cancelation. As a result, various studies investigated the possibilities of converting some of the *Lexingtons* to aircraft carriers, while another proposal contemplated a conversion to an Atlantic Ocean liner. Finally, the treaty allowed two of the six battlecruisers to be completed as aircraft carriers, while the remaining four were scrapped.

Commissioned in 1927, *Lexington* (CV-2) and *Saratoga* (CV-3) became the U.S. Navy's first operational fleet carriers. Both ships saw extensive action in World War II, with *Lexington* conducting several raids before being sunk during the battle of the Coral Sea in 1942. *Saratoga* served in multiple campaigns in the Pacific and the Indian Oceans. During the atomic bomb tests at Bikini Atoll in 1946, the carrier was severely damaged as a target ship and sank. To this day, the wreck is a popular destination for scuba divers.

The sister ships *Saratoga* (CV-3, front) and *Lexington* (CV-2, rear) off the coast of the Hawaiian island of Oahu during the 1930s. Diamond Head is visible in the background. This extinct volcano is the landmark of Hawaii.

Lexington-class General Characteristics (as planned)

Class	*Lexington*
Name	*Lexington* (*ex-Constitution*) (CC-1) *Constellation* (CC-2) *Saratoga* (CC-3) *Ranger* (*ex-Lexington*) (CC-4) *Constitution* (*ex-Ranger*) (CC-5) *United States* (CC-6)
Shipyard	Fore River Shipyard, Quincy (CC-1) Newport News Shipbuilding (CC-2 and CC-4) New York Shipbuilding Corporation, Camden (CC-3) Philadelphia Naval Shipyard (CC-5 and CC-6)
Commissioning	*Lexington* (CC-1): December 14, 1927 (aircraft carrier CV-2) *Saratoga* (CC-3): November 16, 1927 (aircraft carrier CV-3) Canceled: CC-2; CC-4; CC-5; CC-6
Displacement (normal) Displacement (full)	43,500 long tons (44,200 t) 44,638 long tons (45,354 t)
Length (overall)	874 ft (266.4 m)
Beam	105 ft 4 in (32.1 m)
Draft (max)	31 ft (9.4 m)
Propulsion	4 × steam turbines / turbo-electric (180,000 shp / 130,000 kW)
Maximum speed	33 kn (61 km/h)
Range	10,000 nmi (19,000 km) at 10 knots
Complement	ca. 1,297
Armament	8 × 16 in (406 mm) 14 × 6 in (152 mm) Various AA guns
Fate	*Lexington* (CV-2): sunk at battle of Coral Sea, May 8, 1942 *Saratoga* (CV-3): sunk as target (Operation *Crossroads*), July 25, 1946

Alaska-class

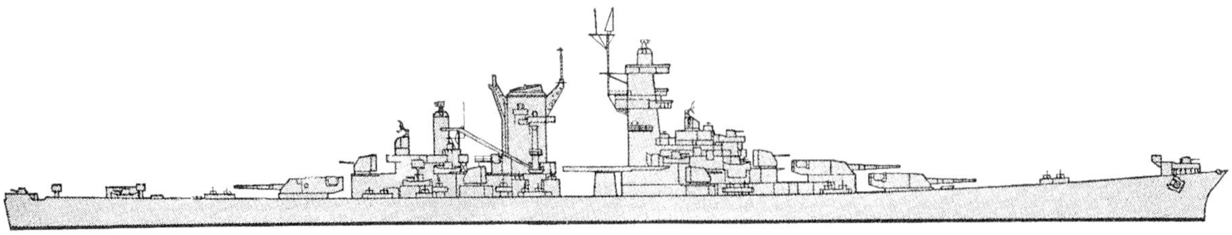

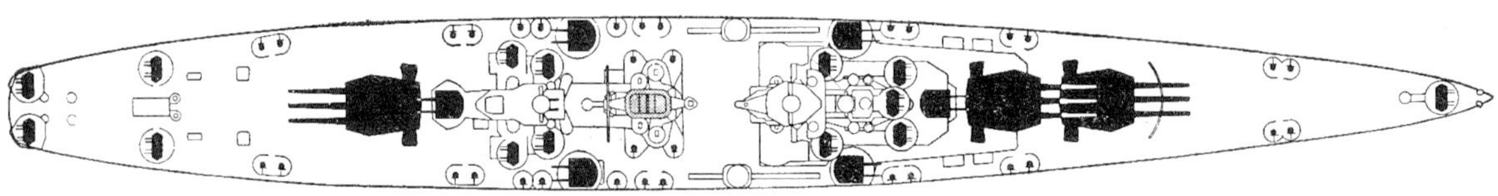

During the interwar years, heavy cruiser development was formalized due to the terms of the Washington Naval Treaty and subsequent treaties. The United States, Great Britain, Japan, France, and Italy agreed to limit heavy cruiser designs to a standard displacement of 10,000 long tons (10,160 t) and armament of 8-inch (203 mm) guns. Early proposals for a larger and more heavily armed cruiser design emerged in the early 1930s, when the U.S. Navy at one point contemplated designing a possible counterpart to the three German "pocket battleships" of the *Deutschland*-class, armed with six 11-inch (279 mm) guns. In the late 1930s, more design studies followed, after the two German *Scharnhorst*-class battleships, armed with nine 11-inch guns, were commissioned and American intelligence reports indicated that Japan was planning a large new cruiser (B-65) armed with nine 12.2-inch (310 mm) guns, which would outgun existing American cruisers. As a result, the U.S. Navy demanded a "cruiser-killer," capable of hunting and engaging these well-armed ships.

The designers drew up at least nine different layouts for the future *Alaska*-class. These ranged

The *Admiral Graf Spee*, one of Germany's three so-called "pocket battleships" (*Panzerschiffe*), built in the interwar period. Armed with six 11-inch guns in two turrets and capable of about 29 knots, these cruiser-like vessels could outrun all British battleships (except the three battlecruisers) and outgun all cruisers.

The German battleship *Gneisenau* of the *Scharnhorst*-class, launched in 1936, was armed with nine 11-inch guns in three turrets, which had a range of up to 44,760 yards (40,930 m) at 40° elevation. One of *Gneisenau*'s 11-inch turrets has survived as a coastal defense battery in Norway to this day.

from 6,000 long ton (6,096 t) antiaircraft cruisers to "oversized" heavy cruisers and even a 38,000 long ton (38,610 t) "miniature-battleship" armed with 12 12-inch (305 mm) and up to 16 5-inch (127 mm) guns. Nevertheless, to keep the displacement under 25,000 long tons (25,400 t), the General Board only allowed designs with a limited underwater protection. The final design was in many aspects an enlarged version of the *Baltimore*-class heavy cruisers, which had the same propulsion system as the fast *Essex*-class fleet aircraft carriers.

The *Alaska*-class featured a main armament of nine 12-inch guns, a protection system against 10-inch gunfire, and a top speed of 33 knots (38 mph; 61 km/h). The new ships were officially funded in September 1940 along with numerous other ships as a part of the Two-Ocean Navy Act that enlarged the fleet considerably.

By this time, their operational profile had changed slightly: in addition to their ship-to-ship engagement role, they were to protect fast carrier groups. With their bigger guns, greater size, and increased speed, they would be more valuable in this escort role than traditional heavy cruisers.

Moreover, the *Alaskas* would provide insurance against American intelligence reports that assumed that Japan was working on "super-cruisers" (B-65 design), which were considered more powerful than the American 8-inch-gun heavy cruisers. Moreover, the escort concept would also free up the few existing heavy cruisers for scouting operations, which was their original purpose.

U.S.S. *Alaska* (CB-1) in November 1944. Of the six ships ordered, only two were completed, which then entered service shortly toward the end of the war. The *Alaskas* were all named after territories or insular areas of the United States, signifying their intermediate status between larger battleships and smaller heavy and light cruisers.

A rare color photo of *Alaska* during its shakedown cruise in August 1944. Note the Measure 32 camouflage paint. The U.S. Navy designation for the ships of this class was "large cruiser" (CB).

Armament

The *Alaskas* featured nine 12-inch (305 mm)/50 caliber Mark 8 guns mounted in three triple turrets. The U.S. Navy's preceding 12-inch artillery was the Mark 7, which had been installed in the *Wyoming*-class battleships (1912). Designed in 1939, the Mark 8 was of significantly higher quality. The gun had a rate of fire of 2.4 to 3 rounds a minute. At an elevation of 45°, it could fire a 1,140 lb (520 kg) Mark 18 AP shell 38,573 yards (35,271 m). Boasting the heaviest main battery of any World War II cruiser design, the *Alaska*'s 12-inch guns were as capable as the old 14-inch (356 mm)/45 caliber gun used on American battleships built prior the 1922 Washington Naval Treaty.

The ships were built with 12 dual-purpose 5-inch (127 mm)/38 caliber guns against surface and aerial targets in six twin mounts. This weapon was originally intended for destroyers built in the 1930s, but it was installed on most American major warships, including the fast battleships, aircraft carriers, and cruisers. The ships were fitted with up to 56 40-mm Bofors guns and up to 34 20-mm Oerlikon antiaircraft guns.

Protection

The 9-inch (229-mm) thick armor belt extended from the front to the rear barbette. Inclined at 10°, it tapered to 5 inches (127 mm) towards the bottom. Together with 10.6 inch (269 mm) thick transverse bulkheads, the belt formed the armored citadel. The *Alaskas* had a total of three armored decks. The main (weather) deck had a thickness of 1.4 inches (36

Looking aft from *Hawaii*'s superstructure. The smokestack is in the foreground. While the main gun turrets have been installed, the foundations and platforms for the secondary armament, antiaircraft guns, and rangefinding equipment are empty.

mm), the armor (bomb) deck was up to 4 inches (102 mm) strong. The third deck was a splinter deck, which was 0.625 inches (15.9 mm) thick. The faces of the main guns had a thickness of 12.8 inches (330 mm), with up to 6-inch (152 mm) sides, 5.25 inch (133 mm) rear sides, and 5 inch (127 mm) roofs. The conning tower was armored with 10.6 inch (270 mm) sides and had a 5 inch (127 mm) thick roof.

Propulsion

The *Alaskas* were powered by four General Electric steam turbines, each driving a shaft and producing a total of 150,000 shp (110,325 kW), giving them a top speed of 33 knots (38 mph; 61 km/h). Steam was provided by eight Babcock & Wilcox water-tube boilers. The ships could carry up to 3,560 long tons (3,617 t) of fuel oil, giving them a range of up to 12,000 nautical miles (22,000 km) at a cruising speed of 15 knots (27 km/h).

Electronics

The fire control for the main guns consisted of two Mark 8 radars, which had a range of up to 45 nautical miles (83 km). The secondary armament was equipped with two Mark 12 fire-control radars with a range of up to 20 nautical miles (37 km). In addition, the *Alaskas* had a SG-1 surface-search radar with a range of 15 nautical miles (28 km) and an SK air-search radar (87 nmi; 161 km) installed. The ships carried up to four reconnaissance aircraft launched from catapults at the stern, allowing the ships to "see" beyond the horizon. In addition, the planes could observe the ship's own artillery fire more closely and correct its accuracy.

Alaska's starboard side. Note the floatplane catapult. Unlike the modern battleships of the *North Carolina*-, *South Dakota*-, and *Iowa*-classes, which carried their catapults at the stern, the *Alaska*'s two catapults were installed amidships and could be rotated outward for aircraft launching.

Conversion to Aircraft Carriers

In late 1941, shortly before and particularly after the Japanese attack on Pearl Harbor, the U.S. Navy realized the urgent need for more aircraft carriers to counter the Japanese carrier operations in the Pacific. As a result, numerous hulls of U.S. Navy ships under construction were considered for a potential conversion into carriers. This included the *Cleveland*-class light cruisers, the *Baltimore*-class heavy cruisers and the *Alaska*-class large cruisers. Finally, nine *Clevelands* under construction were rebuilt into the *Independence*-class light aircraft carriers.

Battleship *Missouri* (BB-63, top) and large cruiser *Alaska* (CB-1, bottom) at Norfolk Naval Base, Virginia, in 1944. Note the difference in size and proportion between the two ships.

A conversion of the *Alaskas* seemed to be logical as they shared several design similarities with the *Essex*-class aircraft carriers, including the same machinery. However, when compared to the *Essex*-class carriers, the operational range of the converted cruisers was about 8,000 nautical miles (14,800 km) shorter at a cruising speed of 15 knots (17 mph; 28 km/h). In addition, the *Alaskas'* conversion would have taken too long to meet the U.S. Navy's goal to have new carriers available quickly, which led to the cancelation of this plan in January 1942.

Only two of the planned six ships, *Alaska* (CB-1) and *Guam* (CB-2), were completed, while the third, *Hawaii* (CB-3), was suspended in 1947 when it was 84 percent complete. The keel-laying of the last three vessels, *Philippines* (CB-4), *Puerto Rico* (CB-5), and *Samoa* (CB-6), was delayed as all available materials and shipyards had been used for higher-priority ships, such as aircraft carriers, destroyers, and submarines. The U.S. Navy realized that these "cruiser-killers" no longer had an enemy to hunt: while American carriers and submarines had already destroyed the existing Japanese cruisers, the planned B-65 "super-cruisers"

U.S.S. *Hawaii* (CB-3), the third ship of the class, leaving the launching ways at the New York Shipbuilding Corporation, Camden, New Jersey, on November 3, 1945.

Hawaii in the final stage of construction, looking forward, January 1947. A few months later construction was suspended.

were never built. Thus, the last three *Alaskas* were considered expendable and canceled before construction began.

Operational History

Alaska and *Guam* saw action during the last year of the war, forming Cruiser Division 16. Like the *Iowas*, their accurate firepower was useful in shore bombardment, while their speed made them excellent fast carrier escorts. After *Alaska* had supported the landings on Okinawa in spring 1945, both ships, accompanied by four light cruisers and nine destroyers, sailed into the East China and Yellow Seas to conduct raids on Japanese shipping; they encountered only Chinese junks. In 1947, *Alaska* and *Guam* were decommissioned after only two and a half years of service and assigned to the Reserve Fleet.

Hawaii being towed away for scrapping on June 20, 1959.

In 1958, the U.S. Navy conducted studies to investigate the possible conversion of the *Alaskas* to guided-missile cruisers. One proposal involved the removal of all guns to install four different missile systems. As this was too costly, a second proposal suggested removing only the third turret in favor of missile systems. Since this plan was considered too expensive, it was also abandoned. Consequently, both ships were stricken from the naval register and sold for scrap in 1960. The still-incomplete *Hawaii* was also considered for conversion to a guided-missile cruiser, but when this idea did not materialize, it too was sold for scrap.

Alaska-class General Characteristics (as built)

Class	*Alaska*
Name	*Alaska* (CB-1) *Guam* (CB-2) *Hawaii* (CB-3) *Philippines* (CB-4) *Puerto Rico* (CB-5) *Samoa* (CB-6)
Shipyard	New York Shipbuilding Corporation, Camden (CB-1; CB-2; CB-3) Canceled: CB-4; CB-5; CB-6
Commissioning	June 17, 1944 (CB-1) September 17, 1944 (CB-2) Canceled: CB-3; CB-4; CB-5; CB-6
Displacement (normal) Displacement (full)	29,771 long tons (30,249 t) 34,253 long tons (34,803 t)
Length (overall)	808 ft 6 in (246.43 m)
Beam	91 ft 9.4 in (28.0 m)
Draft (max)	ca. 27 ft 1 in (8.26 m)
Propulsion	4 × steam turbines (150,000 shp / 110,000 kW)
Maximum speed	33 kn (61 km/h)
Range	12,000 nmi (22,000 km) at 15 knots
Complement	1,517–2,251
Armament	9 × 12 in (305 mm)/50 cal. Mark 8 12 × 5 in (127 mm)/38 cal. Various AA guns
Fate	Sold for scrap, 1959–1961 (CB-1; CB-2; CB-3) Canceled (CB-4; CB-5; CB-6)

"Large Cruisers" or "Battlecruisers"?

The *Alaskas*, along with the (never built) Japanese B-65 cruisers, were designed to counter the heavy cruisers of their naval rivals. Occasionally labeled as "super-cruisers" or "large cruisers" or even "battlecruisers," they were never officially classified as capital ships. Instead, the term "battlecruiser," abbreviated "CC," was reserved for the planned (but canceled) *Lexington*-class (1920). During the early development stages, the *Alaskas* carried the "CC" designation as well, but this was changed to "CB" to reflect their new status as "large cruisers." The U.S. Navy named each ship of the class after American territories (Alaska, Guam, Hawaii etc.), rather than American states (as was the tradition with battleships) or cities (for cruisers). This symbolized that the *Alaskas* were to play an intermediate role between heavy cruisers and battleships.

In overall terms, the *Alaska* design was a scaled-up variant of the *Baltimore*-class heavy cruisers, displacing twice as much, thus only 5,000 long tons less than 35,000 long ton battleships determined by the Washington Naval Treaty. The armor scheme was deemed to resist not only 8-inch (203 mm) heavy cruiser shells but even the larger 11-inch (279 mm) shells used by Germany's *Deutschland*-class "pocket battleships" and *Scharnhorst*-class battleships. However, the *Alaskas* did not have the effective underwater protection systems of larger battleships, making them as vulnerable to torpedoes as heavy cruisers. Despite their cruiser-like characteristics (including their speed), the *Alaskas* have occasionally been described as battlecruisers. The official navy magazine *All Hands* said, "The *Guam* and her sister ship *Alaska* are the first American battlecruisers ever to be completed as such."

The ships' percentage of armor tonnage (28.4 percent) was slightly less than that of the *Iowa*-class (32 percent). The *Lexington*-class battlecruisers incorporated a nearly identical armor percentage (28.5 percent). While the *Baltimores* were armed with nine 8-inch (203 mm) guns, the *Alaskas* carried nine 12-inch (305 mm) guns that were at least as effective as the old 14-inch (356 mm) guns used on pre-treaty battleships.

U.S.S. *Guam* (CB-2), the second ship of the class, during its shakedown cruise off Trinidad, in November 1944. Their top speed of 33 knots made the *Alaskas* excellent fast carrier escorts in the Pacific.

6

World War II—The Fighting Battleships

During the 1930s, all major naval powers designed and built modern battleships that incorporated the lessons learned from World War I and used new technologies such as radar. Although international agreements such as the naval treaties of Washington and London tried to avoid another naval arms race, no nation intended to end up without modern and capable ships in case of war.

However, battleship building of the 1930s did not reach the extent of the pre-World War I era, partly because of international treaties and the nascency of aircraft carriers diverting resources from the capital ship construction programs. By the eve of World War II, large fleets of battleships—with many inherited from the dreadnought era—remained as one of the decisive forces in naval thinking.

U.S.S. *Idaho* (foreground) and U.S.S. *Texas* steaming at the rear of the battle line, during battle fleet practice off the California coast, circa 1930. *Idaho*'s four triple 14-inch gun turrets are trained on the starboard beam.

The Japanese attack on Pearl Harbor was the culmination of a decade of deteriorating relations between Japan and the United States over the status of China and the security of Southeast Asia. Nationalistic and militaristic fervor in Imperial Japan and a strong belief in its destiny and divine right to rule all Southeast Asia brought Japan and the United States into increasing diplomatic confrontation throughout the 1930s. When Japan seized a major portion of Southeast Asia, the administration of President Franklin D. Roosevelt was moved to action. An American embargo cut off shipments of scrap steel, raw materials, oil, and high-octane gasoline, while freezing Japanese financial assets in the United States. The Japanese, having only a six-month supply of strategic fuel available for its armed forces, felt the only choice was to initiate the conquest of Southeast Asia, which meant an inevitable war with America, Great Britain, and the Netherlands. Moreover, Japan had viewed with great concern the United States expand its naval authority in the Pacific in the late 1930s.

Fearing that the U.S. Pacific Fleet would pose a formidable obstacle to their conquest of Southeast Asia, the Japanese visualized a bold attack on the Pacific Fleet while it lay at anchor at Pearl Harbor, Oahu, Hawaii.

The objective was to immobilize the Pacific Fleet so that the United States could not interfere with these invasion plans. The principal architect of the attack was Admiral Isoroku Yamamoto, Commander-in-Chief of the Japanese Combined Fleet. Though personally opposed to war with America, Yamamoto knew that Japan's only hope of success in such a war was to achieve a quick and decisive victory. In his opinion, America's superior economic and industrial potential would tip the scales in its favor during a prolonged conflict.

"In the first six to twelve months of a war with the United States and Great Britain I will run wild and win victory upon victory. But then, if the war continues after that, I have no expectation of success."

- Admiral Isoroku Yamamoto

Isoroku Yamamoto, Commander-in-Chief of the Combined Fleet of the Imperial Japanese Navy.

Meanwhile at Pearl Harbor, about 100 vessels of the U.S. Pacific Fleet lay calm and serene. Seven of the Fleet's nine battleships were tied up along "Battleship Row" on the southeast shore of Ford Island, while one, *Pennsylvania*, was in dry dock. Nobody anticipated that a Japanese task force of more than 30 ships, including six aircraft carriers, was on its way to Oahu. However, some of the primary targets, the three aircraft carriers *Saratoga*, *Lexington*, and *Enterprise* were not in port at that time. Early in the morning of December 7, 1941, the Japanese launched about 350 aircraft in two waves that shattered Hawaii's tranquility and the uneasy peace that existed between Japan and the United States.

While one group of planes concentrated on the ships in Pearl Harbor, the remaining planes attacked the individual airfields on Oahu. After achieving complete surprise in the skies over the island, all battleships in Pearl Harbor were bombarded and torpedoed. Although the Americans tried to fight back, their antiaircraft fire was no match for the formidably trained Japanese pilots. One after another, the mighty battleships—unable to use

Photograph taken from a Japanese plane during the torpedo attack on ships moored on both sides of Ford Island shortly after the beginning of the Pearl Harbor attack. View looks about east, with the supply depot, submarine base, and fuel tank farm in the right center distance. A torpedo has just hit U.S.S. *West Virginia* on the far side of Ford Island (center).

Pearl Harbor after the end of the attack with sunk and burning ships.

their powerful guns against aerial attacks—fell victim to a new and deadly weapon—the carrier-borne aircraft. In less than two hours the U.S. Pacific Fleet was in shambles: 21 ships of about 100 had been sunk or damaged. Of that number, eight battleships were casualties, five sunk, and three damaged. About 2,400 Americans were killed and over 1,100 wounded. The victory was bought for a low price: 29 Japanese planes were lost, 55 airmen killed. The surprise attack came as a shock to the American people and led directly to the United States' entry into World War II in both the Pacific and European theaters.

The attack left the Pacific Fleet in a state of chaos and impotence. Japan's goal had been achieved: the U.S. Navy was unable to oppose the Japanese invasion of Southwest Asia, the Philippines, and islands of the South Pacific. The main battle line of the fleet was out of action. Of growing concern was the location and intention of the Imperial Japanese Navy. The loss of its

U.S.S. *California* in dry dock after it was refloated. Most of the ships sunk and damaged during the attack were repaired and eventually returned to service. Some even witnessed the official Japanese surrender in Tokyo Bay in 1945.

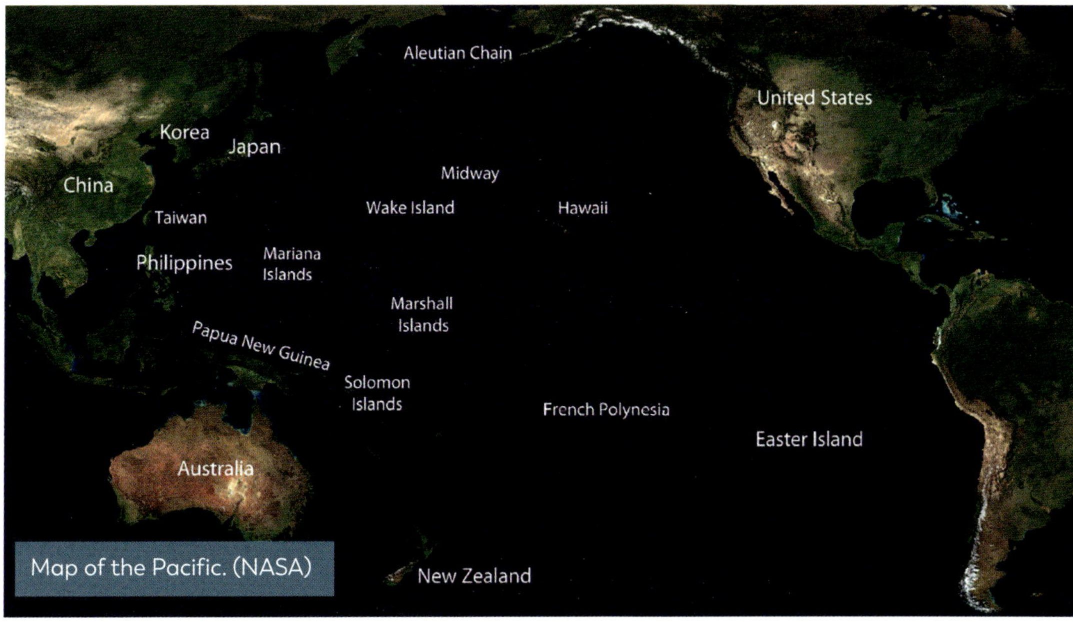

Map of the Pacific. (NASA)

battleships in the Pacific left the U.S. Navy with no choice but to rely on its submarines and aircraft carriers, both of which halted and eventually reversed the Japanese advance. The carriers distinguished themselves during the counterattacks against the Japanese during the Doolittle Raid (April 1942), the engagement of Japanese naval forces at the battle of the Coral Sea (May 1942), and the battle of Midway (June 1942). While six of the eight active battleships bombarded at Pearl Harbor were repaired and returned to service, their relatively low speed and high fuel consumption limited their deployment, thus mainly seeing them in shore bombardment roles until the end of the war. Although the Japanese had hoped to destroy them, they eventually would outlive the Japanese carriers which had launched the devastating attack against them.

Guadalcanal

In early 1942, after the attack on Pearl Harbor and the subsequent declaration of war on Japan, none of the nine U.S. Pacific Fleet battleships was available. While one, *Colorado*, was being overhauled at the West Coast, the remaining eight had fallen victim to the Japanese attack, with two, *Arizona* and *Oklahoma*, write-offs. Even if some of them had been available, they would have been unable to keep up with the fast fleet carriers due to their low top speed of 21 knots. At that time, the six new fast battleships of the *North Carolina*- and *South Dakota*-classes were still undergoing trials. Nevertheless, *North Carolina* and *South Dakota* became fully operational in mid-1942, thus providing crucial antiaircraft defense during the carrier battles of the Eastern Solomons and Santa Cruz Islands, both resulting in American victories.

The Guadalcanal campaign (1942–43) in the British Solomon Islands was the first major Allied offensive against Japan forces. While the battle of Midway had been a crushing defeat for the Japanese Navy, it did not stop Japanese offensives, which continued at sea and on land. After the Japanese had taken Guadalcanal, they were in the position to attack Australia's supply lines and New Guinea. However, the Allied victories at Guadalcanal and its recapture marked the Allied transition from defensive operations to the strategic initiative in the Pacific, leading to offensive campaigns in the Solomon Islands, New Guinea, and the Central Pacific, thus forcing the Japanese into retreat.

At the same time, in early 1942, the Imperial Japanese Navy enjoyed the advantage of a dozen operational battleships but decided not to use them offensively in any significant battles. While the two *Fusō*- and two *Ise*-class battleships, although extensively modernized and capable of 25 knots, were relegated to home defense and training duties, the two more powerful *Nagato*- and two *Yamato*-class battleships were being saved due to fuel

South Dakota firing its antiaircraft guns at Japanese planes during the battle of Santa Cruz (Solomon Sea), October 26, 1942. A Japanese Type 97 Nakajima B5N2 torpedo plane ("Kate") is visible at right, apparently leaving the area after having dropped its torpedo. The smoke around the battleship is from the ship's antiaircraft guns.

shortages for a "decisive battle" following Alfred Thayer Mahan's doctrine—written more than half a century earlier—of a battle that never came. The only Japanese capital ships seeing significant action except the carriers in the early stages of the Pacific War were the four fast battleships (converted from battlecruisers) of the *Kongō*-class serving mostly as carrier escorts thanks to their top speed of 29 knots and powerful antiaircraft armament.

In November 1942, when the Japanese made a last attempt to recapture Guadalcanal, the American and Japanese navies had to deploy their battleships to surface combat, mostly due to the exhaustion of their carrier forces. While the Japanese had their landing ships protected by the battleships *Hiei* and *Kirishima*, both were attacked by American cruisers and destroyers. During the action, several American ships were sunk or disabled, but they managed to cause critical damage to *Hiei*. After suffering additional bomb and torpedo hits by aerial attacks, it had to be abandoned; its escorting destroyers scuttled it with torpedoes. *Hiei* sank in the evening on November 14 with the loss of about 190 of its crew. On the following evening, the American battleships U.S.S. *South Dakota* and *Washington*, both armed with nine 16-inch guns

The battleship *South Dakota* and two destroyers alongside the repair ship U.S.S. *Prometheus* (AR-3) for repairs, probably at Noumea, New Caledonia, in November 1942.

each and equipped with the latest radar, sank *Hiei*'s sister ship, *Kirishima*, armed with eight 14-inch guns and fitted with inferior radar, with the loss of more than 200 men. However, before *Kirishima* sank, it was able to inflict heavy damage on *South Dakota*. Moreover, *North Carolina* was temporarily disabled by the Japanese submarine *I-19*.

Battle of the Philippine Sea

After the victorious battles of Midway and Guadalcanal the American military developed a strategy of "island hopping." The idea was to bypass heavily fortified Japanese positions and instead invade strategically important islands that were not well defended but capable of supporting the Allied drive to the main islands of Japan. After successfully applying this strategy during the capture of the Gilbert and Marshall Islands, the United States planned to invade the Mariana Islands as an important step for the recapture of the Philippines which had been invaded and occupied by the Japanese in 1942.

Admiral Isoroku Yamamoto was killed in April 1943, when his plane was shot down by American aircraft. His successor, Admiral Mineichi Koga, wanted the Imperial Japanese Navy to engage the American fleet in a single decisive battle in early 1944. However, in March 1944, he was killed when his plane crashed in a typhoon. The new Commander-in-Chief of the Combined Fleet, Admiral Soemu Toyoda, continued the current work, finalizing the Japanese plans known as Operation *A-Go*. The plan was adopted in early June 1944 and had to be put into place quickly to engage the American fleet which had been detected heading for the island of Saipan in the Marianas. The subsequent battle of the Philippine Sea (June 19–20, 1944) would become the largest carrier-to-carrier battle in history. The American force, the Fifth Fleet, commanded by Admiral Raymond Spruance and Vice Admiral Marc Mitscher, boasted seven fleet carriers, eight light carriers, seven new battleships, eight heavy cruisers, 13 light cruisers, 68 destroyers, and 28 submarines. The battleships were the *North Carolina* and *Washington* (both *North Carolina*-class), *South Dakota*, *Indiana*, and *Alabama* (all *South Dakota*-class), as well as the U.S. Navy's newest and largest battleships, *Iowa* and *New Jersey* (both *Iowa*-class). The Japanese fleet, commanded by Vice-Admiral Jisaburō Ozawa, consisted of three large fast fleet carriers, two slower second-rate fleet carriers, four light carriers, five battleships, 11 heavy cruisers, two light cruisers, 31 destroyers, and 24 submarines. The battleships were *Yamato* and *Musashi*—the world's largest and most powerful battleships—as well as *Kongō* and *Haruna* (both *Kongō*-class), and *Nagato*. During this epic battle, the Japanese fleet

Japanese 3rd Carrier Division under attack by Task Force 38 planes during the battle of the Philippine Sea, June 20, 1944. The battleship in the lower center is either *Haruna* or *Kongō*. The carrier *Chiyoda* is at right.

> The battle of Leyte Gulf is generally considered to have been the largest naval engagement of World War II and, by some criteria, possibly history's largest naval battle. It consisted of several separate engagements between opposing forces at the battle of the Sibuyan Sea, the battle of Surigao Strait, the battle of Cape Engaño, and the battle off Samar.

lost three carriers, several hundred aircraft, and almost 3,000 men, and therefore the bulk of their carrier air strength; they would never recover.

Battle of Leyte Gulf

With the elimination of the Japanese Navy's ability to conduct large-scale carrier actions, it was finally forced to commit its battleships, both new and old, to the upcoming Leyte campaign. The Japanese objective in this "decisive battle" was the last Japanese attempt to prevent the Allies from capturing the Philippines and therefore coming dangerously close to the Japanese homeland. When the battle of Leyte Gulf (October 23–26, 1944) began, the American fleet comprised about 300 ships, including eight fleet carriers, eight light carriers, 18 escort carriers, 12 battleships, 24 destroyers, more than 160 destroyers and destroyer escorts, and about 1,500 aircraft. The Japanese fleet was significantly smaller, consisting of 76 ships, including just one fleet carrier, three light carriers, nine battleships, 20 cruisers, about 35 destroyers and more than 300 aircraft, many of which were land-based. With just a small number of aircraft carriers available, Japan's battleships had to play a more offensive role than in the past.

Two Japanese battleship forces were to converge on the American invasion forces at Leyte Gulf. While one task force, called the Center Force, including the five fast battleships *Yamato*, *Musashi*, *Nagato*, *Kongō*, and *Haruna*, and about 12 cruisers, and 13 destroyers, attacked from the north, the second force, including the two slower old battleships *Fusō* and *Yamashiro*, attacked from the south, thus serving as a decoy so that the Center Force could freely destroy General Douglas MacArthur's invasion forces on the Leyte beaches.

In the battle of the Sibuyan Sea on October 24, 1944, however, the Center Force, commanded by Vice-Admiral Takeo Kurita and operating without air cover, was attacked by American aircraft launched from the

The Japanese *Nagato* firing at attacking planes, during the battle of Sibuyan Sea on October 24, 1944. It was the only Japanese battleship that survived World War II relatively intact.

Explosion aboard the escort carrier U.S.S. *St. Lo* (CVE-63) after it was hit by a Japanese *kamikaze* off Samar on October 25, 1944. The ship sank a little later.

Japanese binoculars captured at the battle of Leyte.

Naval ensign flown from U.S.S. *LCI(L)-711* during the American invasion of Leyte in the fall of 1944.

carriers *Intrepid* and *Cabot*, damaging *Yamato*, *Musashi*, and *Nagato*. The second attack from the carriers *Intrepid*, *Essex*, and *Lexington*, concentrated on *Musashi*, damaging it further. Finally, already listing to port, it was hit by a third wave launched from *Enterprise* and *Franklin*. Although its crew, under the command of Captain Toshihira Inoguchi, tried to run it aground, it eventually capsized and sank that evening before reaching shallow waters.

A day after *Musashi*'s loss, during the battle of Surigao Strait on October 25, 1944, the Japanese Southern Force, including the battleships *Fusō* and *Yamashiro* under the command of Vice-Admiral Jisaburō Ozawa, encountered an American task force including the six modernized World War I-era battleships *West Virginia*, *Maryland*, *Mississippi*, *Tennessee*, *California*, and *Pennsylvania* commanded by Admiral Jesse Oldendorf of the

Japanese battleship *Musashi* under heavy attack during the battle of the Sibuyan Sea on October 24, 1944.

U.S.S. *Idaho* fires its 14-inch guns of turret No. 3 at nearly point-blank range, during the bombardment of Okinawa in support of the Allied invasion in April 1945.

U.S. Seventh Fleet. All of them, except *Mississippi*, had been sunk or damaged in the attack on Pearl Harbor and repaired. During the engagement, *Fusō* was sunk by torpedoes fired by American destroyers, while its sister ship *Yamashiro* suffered shell damage from the American battleships but was eventually also sunk by a torpedo fired by an American destroyer. In total, more than 3,200 Japanese sailors lost their lives. This engagement marked the last time in history when battleships engaged each other.

U.S.S. *Tennessee* shelling Okinawa with its 14-inch guns, as LVTs (Amphibious Vehicle, Tracked) in the foreground carry troops to the invasion beaches.

Nearing the End

By the end of the war, battleship construction was all but halted, due to the shift to aircraft carriers or the sheer lack of resources, and almost every remaining battleship was retired or scrapped within a few years. Although battleships did not play a decisive role in ship-to-ship engagements in World War II, their enormous firepower enabled them to conduct fire support operations (shore bombardment), during the Allied landings in Italy, French North Africa, Normandy, Iwo Jima, and Okinawa. The battleships' accurate shellfire destroyed enemy gun emplacements, bunkers, railroads, and killed troops, thus enabling Allied landing forces to go ashore without having to face the full defensive capacities of the enemy. Although aircraft could also be used for the support of amphibious operations, they could be more easily destroyed than a battleship off the coast. During July and August 1945 several U.S. Navy battleships conducted naval bombardments of several Japanese coastal cities, targeting harbors, major factories, and rail infrastructure. Japan had no means to defend its coasts anymore, as its navy and air force had practically ceased to exist as effective fighting forces.

During World War II American battleships were equipped with large antiaircraft (AA) batteries, using primarily 5-inch (127 mm), 40-mm, and 20-mm guns. The development of proximity fuzes and radar significantly increased their effectiveness.

While one or two battleships operating alone proved vulnerable, as the sinking of the British battleship HMS *Prince of Wales* and the battlecruiser HMS *Repulse* by Japanese bombers had shown, the U.S. Navy arrayed its forces in complex defense formations. The first line of protection was a carrier-based radar-vectored combat air patrol (CAP), and any attackers who managed to get through would face antiaircraft fire from a line of screening battleships and cruisers looking like a fire-spitting floating fortress when opening fire against attacking aircraft. This system of aerial defense inflicted such a heavy toll on the Japanese aircraft during the battle of the Philippine Sea (1944) that they failed to sink or disable their main targets, the American carriers. Although the U.S. Navy lost a few aircraft carriers due to their higher vulnerability, it did not lose any of its battleships by aerial attacks in open seas during the war. Powerful antiaircraft batteries proved a crucial defense against Japanese kamikaze aircraft in the final two years of the conflict.

With the relentless American advance towards the Japanese home islands in 1944, Japan decided to launch suicide air attacks—the so-called kamikaze ("divine wind")—against Allied ships, in particular aircraft carriers. While these attacks also struck several U.S. battleships, none was seriously damaged due to their thick armor. Moreover, Japan's kamikaze operations could not stop the American advance. One of the ships attacked was the U.S.S. *Missouri.* On April 11, 1945, during the heat of the battle for Okinawa, a low-flying Japanese Mitsubishi A6M Zero fighter penetrated its antiaircraft fire and crashed into the ship's starboard side. The aviation fuel in the wing caused a fire and one of the Zero's machine guns was impaled in the barrel of a 40-mm gun on *Missouri*'s quarterdeck. Fortunately, the ship did not suffer any casualties and the fire was extinguished quickly. But the dent caused by the aircraft's impact remains to this day. The only casualty was the Japanese pilot, whose remains were found in the debris. He was one of nearly 4,000 kamikaze pilots who sacrificed their lives for Japan.

U.S.S. *Missouri* conducting air defense drills. Note the 40-mm quad mount atop No. 2 turret and the deck-mounted single 20-mm mounts. An air defense officer and lookout in the foreground view the results.

Japanese Mitsubishi A6M Zero about to strike the side of U.S.S. *Missouri* on April 11, 1945. The pilot who was killed received a burial at sea with military honors.

Japanese Foreign Minister Mamoru Shigemitsu (wearing top hat) boards U.S.S. *Missouri* for the surrender ceremonies, in Tokyo Bay on September 2, 1945. (U.S. Army Signal Corps)

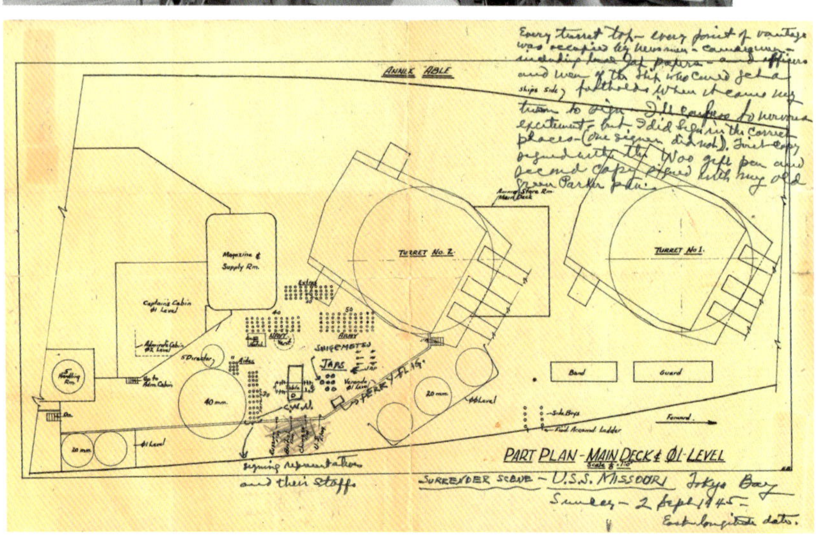

Deck plan for the Japanese surrender procedure aboard *Missouri*. Harry S. Truman, whose daughter Margaret had christened the ship, became president after the death of Franklin Roosevelt in April 1945. Because of his close association with the *Missouri*, he chose it as the site for Japan's surrender.

Japanese representatives on board during the surrender ceremonies. Standing in front are: Foreign Minister Mamoru Shigemitsu (wearing top hat) and General Yoshijiro Umezu, chief of the army general staff. Behind them are representatives of the foreign ministry, the army, and the navy.

One Final Duty

After two atomic bombs had destroyed Hiroshima and Nagasaki, Japan finally agreed to the Allied terms of unconditional surrender. In late August 1945, the new battleship U.S.S. *Missouri*, along with more than 200 other American and Allied warships, sailed into Tokyo Bay. Harry S. Truman, who had attended *Missouri*'s launch a year earlier as a senator, was now President of the United States following Roosevelt's death in April. Due to his personal ties to the ship, the "*Mighty Mo*" became his choice as the site of the formal Japanese surrender on September 2, 1945. On that historic day, *Missouri* was crammed with people who wanted to get a look at the Japanese delegation and the surrender ceremony. High-ranking military officials from all the Allied Powers were present, including representatives from the United States, Great Britain, the Soviet Union, Canada, France, the Netherlands, Australia, New Zealand, and China. U.S. Fleet Admiral Chester Nimitz boarded *Missouri* shortly after 8:00 a.m., followed by General Douglas MacArthur, Supreme Commander of the Allied Powers at 8:43 a.m. The Japanese representatives, headed by Foreign Minister Mamoru Shigemitsu, arrived a few minutes before 9:00 a.m. The Japanese felt that millions of eyes were bearing down on them, many filled with hatred. At 9:02 a.m., two minutes later than originally scheduled, MacArthur made a grand entrance down the ladder and stepped to the microphone:

> We are gathered here … It is my earnest hope and indeed the hope of all mankind that from this solemn occasion a better world shall emerge out of the blood and carnage of the past—a world founded upon faith and understanding—a world dedicated to the dignity of man and the fulfillment of his most cherished wish—for freedom, tolerance and justice.

MacArthur speaking during the surrender ceremony. The framed flag in upper left is that flown by Commodore Matthew Perry's flagship when it entered Tokyo Bay in 1853, forcing Japan to open itself to foreign trade. Borrowed from the U.S. Naval Academy Museum, it was displayed at the request of MacArthur, who was a blood relative of Perry.

Japanese Foreign Minister Mamoru Shigemitsu signs the Instrument of Surrender on behalf of the Japanese Government. Lieutenant General Richard K. Sutherland, U.S. Army, watches from the opposite side of the table. Foreign Ministry representative Toshikazu Kase is assisting Foreign Minister Shigemitsu. (U.S. Army Signal Corps)

Toshikazu Kase, one of the Japanese delegates, spoke fluent English and as he listened to the speech, he felt a deep gratitude for MacArthur's call for justice, tolerance, and rebuilding. Kase later wrote: "After all, we were not beaten on the battlefields by dint of superior arms. We were defeated by a nobler ideal. The real issue was moral—beyond all the powers of algebra to compute…"

The first person to sign that morning was Japan's Foreign Minister Shigemitsu. History was satisfied when he set his name and the exact time on the assigned line on the American copy of the surrender document: 9:04 a.m. on September 2, 1945, the day when peace was restored to the world. After signing the Japanese copy as well, General Yoshijiro Umezu, Chief of the Imperial General Staff, came forward, refused to sit down, and signed on behalf of the Japanese military.

Japanese Foreign Ministry representatives Katsuo Okazaki and Toshikazu Kase, and Lieutenant General Richard K. Sutherland, U.S. Army, correcting an error on the Japanese copy of the Instrument of Surrender, at the conclusion of the surrender ceremonies. At this historic moment, the ship was crowded with people who all wanted to catch a glimpse of the event.

Next, General MacArthur sat down and signed at 9:08 a.m. representing the victorious Allied powers. Finally, he concluded the ceremony with the following words: "Let us pray to peace, that peace be now restored to the world and that God will preserve it always. These proceedings are closed."

After the 23-minute ceremony the sun suddenly came out and hundreds of carrier planes and bombers flew over the anchored fleet just as the Japanese delegation was departing *Missouri*. Later, a plaque was placed in the deck where the surrender had taken place. It reads (on the opposite page):

Douglas MacArthur, General of the Army and Supreme Allied Commander, signs the Instrument of Surrender, thus officially accepting Japan's surrender. Behind him are Lieutenant General Jonathan M. Wainwright, U.S. Army, and Lieutenant General Sir Arthur E. Percival, British Army, both of whom had just been released from Japanese prison camps. Both had been captured at the fall of Singapore in February 1942.

OVER THIS SPOT ON 2 SEPTEMBER 1945 THE INSTRUMENT OF FORMAL SURRENDER OF JAPAN TO THE ALLIED POWERS WAS SIGNED THUS BRINGING TO A CLOSE THE SECOND WORLD WAR—THE SHIP AT THAT TIME WAS AT ANCHOR IN TOKYO BAY

Historical marker on *Missouri*'s deck, noting the location where the instrument of Japan's surrender was signed. The plate was selected by Captain Stuart S. Murray, and installed at the Norfolk Naval Shipyard, Virginia.

U.S. Navy carrier aircraft flying in formation over the American and British ships in Tokyo Bay at the conclusion of the surrender ceremony. U.S.S. *Missouri* is at left. The message of this impressive air show to the Japanese was clear.

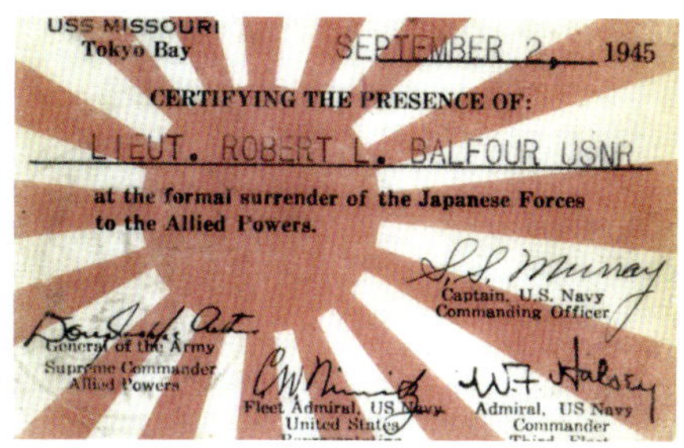

Wallet card souvenir of the surrender, produced by U.S.S. *Missouri*'s print shop. One was issued to each man who was on board the ship when Japan's surrender was formalized on its decks. The cards contain the facsimile signatures of Captain Stuart S. Murray, *Missouri*'s commanding officer, General of the Army Douglas MacArthur, Fleet Admiral Chester W. Nimitz, and Admiral William F. Halsey.

Fleet Admiral Chester W. Nimitz with the Instrument of Surrender of the Japanese Empire, which he also signed as a representative of the United States.

7

Battleships in the Cold War

During World War II, aircraft carriers had replaced battleships as the most powerful surface warships. Six years of war on various oceans had demonstrated that battleship-to-battleship engagements like the battle of Surigao Strait (1944) were just exceptions and not the rule. However, when battleships were conceived, there were no submarines, aircraft, or aircraft carriers posing a threat to them.

With the growing role of aircraft engagement ranges becoming wider and the introduction of missiles, large-caliber naval guns of battleships with a maximum range of about 46,000 yards (42 km) became less relevant. Battleship armor, for decades essential for the vessel's survival in battle, became insignificant in the face of a nuclear attack, as tactical missiles with a range of 110,000 yards (100 km) or more could be launched from cruisers, destroyers, and submarines. One of the first (experimental) floating platforms for missile launches was a battleship—the American World War I-era dreadnought U.S.S. *Mississippi*.

By the end of the 1950s, destroyers, which had been of no noteworthy opposition to battleships in previous decades, were now capable of launching powerful missiles and of eliminating battleships from outside the range of the ship's heavy guns.

A battleship in the missile age: U.S.S. *Mississippi* (reclassified as EAG-128), converted to a test platform, fires a SAM-7 Terrier test missile, circa 1954.

The Nuclear Age

"Now I am become Death, the destroyer of worlds."

—Julius Robert Oppenheimer, the "father" of the atomic bomb, quoting from the *Bhagavad Gita*, a central scripture of Hinduism

Julius Robert Oppenheimer, director of the *Manhattan Project* that led to the development of the atomic bomb.

Trinity was the first atomic detonation, conducted by the U.S. Army in a New Mexico desert on July 16, 1945. This test had heralded the atomic age.

After the dropping of two atomic bombs on Japan in August 1945 had ended World War II, the American military was eager to test this new devastating weapon on warships. Interestingly, there were parallels between these new tests and Billy Mitchell's aerial bombing tests on the ex-German dreadnought *Ostfriesland*—while the U.S. Army Air Forces (the predecessor of the Air Force) wanted to prove that any fleet could be destroyed by aircraft dropping atomic bombs, the Navy wanted to determine, if warships could withstand an atomic attack. Named Operation *Crossroads*, the tests were to be conducted at Bikini Atoll, Marshall Islands, in the Pacific in mid-1946 by Joint Army/Navy Task Force I, headed by Vice Admiral William H. P. Blandy, who was later quoted:

> The bomb will not start a chain-reaction in the water converting it all to gas and letting all the ships on all the oceans drop down to the bottom. It will not blow out the bottom of the sea and let all the water run down the hole. It will not destroy gravity. I am not an atomic playboy, as one of my critics labeled me, exploding these bombs to satisfy my personal whim.

The American entertainer Bob Hope commented on the decision to use Bikini for the atomic tests: "As soon as the war ended, we located the one spot on earth that hadn't been touched by the war and blew it to hell."

Operation *Crossroads* comprised a fleet of about 100 warships anchored in Bikini Lagoon, including

The target fleet included several famous Allied and Axis vessels such as the aircraft carrier *Saratoga*, the battleships *Arkansas*, *New York*, *Nevada* and *Pennsylvania*, as well as two war prizes—the German cruiser *Prinz Eugen* and the Japanese battleship *Nagato*.

World War I-era battleships, aircraft carriers, cruisers, destroyers, submarines, and other types of vessels. A support fleet of more than 150 ships provided quarters, experimental stations, and workshops for the 42,000 men participating in the tests. To get as much empirical data as possible, numerous cameras and various measurement devices were positioned on different islands and on board the target ships. To simulate the effects of a nuclear blast and radiation on human beings, the ships were "crewed" with about 5,600 living animals such as pigs, sheep, rats, and mice. The first test was named *Able*.

Sailors aboard an aircraft carrier cover their eyes during the Operation *Crossroads* atomic tests. At that time, people were not aware of the danger of radioactivity as they are today.

Aerial view of the *Baker* explosion. The condensation cloud covers large portions of the water column and some of the target ships. (U.S. Army Signal Corps)

The most impressive photograph of *Baker*: The condensation cloud has partially dissolved, so that the water column, explosion mushroom cloud, and target ships are clearly visible. The palm trees in the foreground have markers to estimate the height of the expected tidal wave. Slightly to the left of the water column is the cruiser U.S.S. *Pensacola* (CA-24). The dark spot probably marks the sinking point of the battleship U.S.S. *Arkansas* (BB-33). *Eugen* is on the far right.

The ex-Japanese *Nagato* survived both tests but suffered severe damage and leakage, eventually sinking after several days.

On July 1, 1946, a B-29 Superfortress dropped a bomb with a yield of 23 kilotons of TNT, which detonated 520 feet (158 m) above the target fleet and caused less than the expected amount of ship damage because it missed its aim point by 2,130 feet (649 m).

To reduce contamination aboard *Prinz Eugen* and the other ships, the decks and superstructures were sprayed with—partially contaminated—seawater.

Test *Baker* caused eight ships to sink or capsize, and eight more were severely damaged. Sunk vessels were the *Saratoga*, *Arkansas*, *Nagato*, the submarines *Apogon* and *Pilotfish*, and several smaller vessels.

On July 25, 1946, the second bomb named *Baker* (with a yield of 23 kilotons of TNT) was detonated 90 feet (27 m) underwater. *Baker*'s blast generated an underwater fireball taking the form of a rapidly expanding hot gas bubble, reaching the sea floor and the sea surface simultaneously, thus creating a shallow crater on the seafloor 30 feet (9 m) deep and 2,000 feet (600 m) wide. At the top, water burst through the surface like a giant geyser, creating a massive "spray dome" containing 2 million tons of water. The expanding dome stretched into a hollow chimney of spray called the "column" at 6,000 feet (1,800 m) tall and 2,000 (600 m) feet wide with "water walls" 300 feet (90 m) thick. The space vacated by the rising gas bubble caused a tsunami generating a wave 94 feet (29 m) high. By the time the wave reached the beach of Bikini Island 3.5 miles (5.6 km) away, 15 foot (24 m) waves tossed landing craft onto the beach. Ten seconds after the detonation, falling water from the column created a 900 foot (275 m) "base surge" rolling over many of the target ships, covering them with extensive radioactivity.

The battleship *Arkansas* was the closest ship to the *Baker* blast (170 yards from ground zero) and was lifted upwards by the rising water column. At 562 feet (171 m) long, and therefore more than three times as long as the water was deep at its position, the 27,000-long-ton *Arkansas* was (according to most observers) bow-pinned to the seafloor and toppled backward into the water curtain of the spray column. *Arkansas*'s crushed wreck came to rest in an inverted position in about 180 feet of water at the bottom of Bikini Lagoon.

Rear Admiral Robert Conard, who served as a young radiation protection officer, later remarked in an interview with the U.S. Naval Historical Center:

> We had goggles on. It was a very awe-inspiring experience, particularly the *Baker* shot, the underwater shot, where this big dome of water rose out of the lagoon. One ship [U.S.S. *Arkansas*] was just pushed upright into this dome of water, and then it went right down and sank. So that was very impressive, and, as I said, we learned a lot from the Bikini experience. We learned about how little we knew, too. But the experiences we had certainly served us well in subsequent tests.

A third deep-water test named *Charlie* was planned for 1947 but was canceled. The official reason was that the program staff felt it was unnecessary due to the success of the *Able* and *Baker* tests. Prior to the tests,

The damaged and contaminated battleship *Nevada*.

Destroyed vehicles on *Nevada*'s deck. Military members examine the effects of the test. Although *Nevada* was the primary target for the first test, *Able*, the bomb missed it, saving it from destruction. The battleship would survive the second test as well.

Bikini's native residents agreed to leave the island, and were evacuated to other atolls. In the 1950s, a series of large thermonuclear tests rendered Bikini unfit for subsistence farming and fishing due to radioactive contamination. The subsequent debate of reimbursing the Bikinians for the loss of their home islands continues to this day.

Operation *Crossroads* demonstrated that warships, even robust battleships, could be destroyed by the enormous blast of atomic explosions, and even if a ship survived the blast, its crew would be exposed to a deadly dose of radiation. After the tests, about 20 surviving target ships were brought back to the United States and Hawaii for radiological inspection. While some could be scrapped, the remaining target ships had to be scuttled near the Hawaiian Islands or the California coast. However, after *Arkansas* had sunk due to its proximity to *Baker*'s detonation, the remaining battleships were still afloat. *Nagato*, positioned 950 yards from ground zero and dangerously radioactive, eventually sank a few days later during the night due to flooding. *Pennsylvania* was towed to the Kwajalein Lagoon, Marshall Islands, where it remained for radiological and structural studies until February 1948, when it was sunk stern first off Kwajalein. *New York* and *Nevada* were towed to Pearl Harbor for further studies and eventually sunk in 1948 during target practice. Robert Conard witnessed *Nevada*'s sinking:

> There were some experts in the different types of Navy bombs there. The *Nevada* was towed out south of Honolulu about thirty or forty miles or so, and our destroyer then went up to the *Nevada*. The men were setting tremendous bombs on the deck of the ship. They were 500-pound bombs. They were being set all around the deck of the *Nevada*. As I remember, there were three experts to prime the bombs and get them ready for detonation. Eventually the bombs were set off by what I think were radio signals. … There were tremendous explosions all over the *Nevada*, which must have made holes way down into the bowels of the ship. But you know, she didn't go down. She was still floated. Pretty soon the Navy sent in torpedo planes from Honolulu and, after a long siege, the ship finally sank. But that ship didn't want to give up easily.

Nevada being sunk in ordnance tests off Pearl Harbor on July 31, 1948. In 2020, its wreck resting upside down, was discovered in a depth of 15,400 feet (4,700 m). Nearby is a debris field with the gun turrets, which fell off the ship when it capsized.

U.S.S. *Missouri* firing a 16-inch salvo from its No. 2 turret during the bombardment of Chongjin, North Korea, to cut enemy communications, October 1950.

The Korean War

During the 1950s, amid the demise of the battleships, there was one armed conflict involving battleship action. Korea, which had been liberated from Japanese rule at the end of World War II, was facing a civil war, when the pro-western South was invaded by the communistic North in June 1950. The United Nations, with the United States as the principal force, came to the aid of South Korea. China came to the aid of North Korea, while the Soviet Union also gave some assistance to the North.

Wisconsin in a floating dry dock at Guam in the Pacific in 1952. The use of such docks allowed the repair of large warships even in regions without developed ports.

Although caught off guard when the invasion struck, American President Harry S. Truman quickly ordered American forces stationed in Japan into South Korea. As part of the naval mobilization, *Missouri*, then the only American battleship in active service, was called up from the Atlantic Fleet and dispatched to support UN forces commanded by General Douglas MacArthur on the Korean peninsula. After arriving in Korean waters in September 1950, its feared 16-inch guns opened fire on Samchok in support of the amphibious landings of U.S. Marine and Army divisions at Inchon, the port area of Seoul.

During the war, the other three *Iowas* were reactivated to follow their sister ship into combat. They bombarded coastal targets and patrolled along the Korean coast to support troops ashore. When Red Chinese troops entered the conflict on the side of the North Koreans and launched a full-scale assault against advancing UN troops, the latter were forced to retreat. After the battle lines had been stabilized near the 38th parallel, the Korean War ended

Battleship Division 2 steaming in formation, June 7, 1954, off the Virginia Capes (Chesapeake Bay). This was the only occasion that all four *Iowas* were photographed together. The ship closest to the camera is *Iowa*. The others are (from near to far): *Wisconsin*, *Missouri*, and *New Jersey*.

with the signing of a truce on July 27, 1953, thus splitting Korea into two separate countries. After fighting their second war, all four ships of the *Iowa*-class were decommissioned between 1955 and 1958 to join the mothballed fleet. However, the Korean War was not their last call to action.

Postwar Modification Proposals

In 1954, the Ship Characteristics Board (SCB), responsible for coordinating the creation and improvement of ship characteristics and capabilities, suggested that the decommissioned *North Carolinas* and *South Dakotas* would be excellent additions to carrier task forces. For this purpose, the ships had to be capable of 31 knots (36 mph; 57 km/h).

For a *North Carolina* to obtain this speed, its power output of 121,000 shp had to be increased to 240,000 shp, making the installation of an extremely large power plant necessary, one which would not fit into the hull—even if the third turret was removed. If the external belt armor and other parts were removed to lighten the ships from 45,000 longs tons (45,720 t) (full load) to around 38,400 long tons (39,000 t), 186,000 shp (139,000 kW) would still be required. However, the hull form aft would also have to be significantly modified to accommodate larger propellers.

To give the four *South Dakotas* the required 31 knot speed for operations with fleet carriers, SCB's designers proposed to remove the after turret, modify the hull, and use the weight and space gained to install either a set of improved steam turbines or a set of gas turbines. Either system would have to produce at least 256,000 shp to achieve the 31 knots. However, the high estimated costs, finally put an end to the conversion plans.

Early design proposals for helicopter carriers also included a conversion plan for the *North Carolinas.* However, it was found that a purpose-built helicopter carrier would be more economical, so the plans were canceled.

The *Iowas* were the only battleships with the speed required for postwar operations with fast aircraft carriers. There were several conversion proposals that included plans to equip them with nuclear missiles or add aircraft capability. There was also a study to rebuild *Illinois* and *Kentucky*, both still incomplete, as aircraft

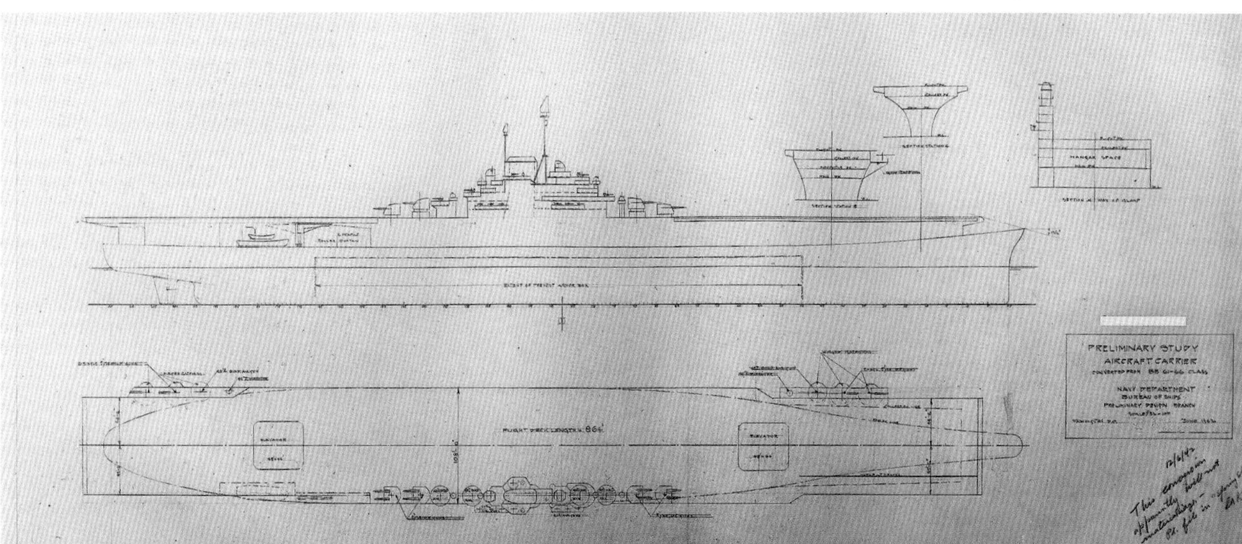

Plan for an *Iowa*-class conversion to aircraft carriers. This proposal dates from World War II but was reconsidered in the postwar period in a modified form as a hybrid of battleship and carrier.

carriers. However, while the former was scrapped, the latter was briefly considered to be completed as a guided missile battleship (BBG) by removing the aft turret like the conversion performed on *Mississippi*. As this never materialized, *Kentucky* was scrapped as well.

During the 1950s, a similar BBG conversion plan was proposed for *Iowa*, *New Jersey*, *Missouri*, and *Wisconsin*. This suggested the replacement of some of or all the 16- and 5-inch guns with various missile systems (Talos, Tartar, ASROC, Regulus II), turning the *Iowas* into capable missile platforms that were more resilient, yet more expensive than contemporary guided missile cruisers or destroyers. Although various conversion proposals were made into the 1970s, none materialized, primarily because of the high cost.

Eventually, the U.S. Navy decided to scrap all old battleships (except *Texas*), some of the newer ones (*Washington*, *South Dakota*, and *Indiana*), and its *Alaska*-class battlecruisers. With all other naval powers also scrapping their battleships in the 1950s and early 1960s, the United States ended up being the last nation with battleships—at least in its mothballed fleet.

Vietnam to *Desert Storm*

After the outbreak of the Vietnam War (1955–75), the United States and other nations supported the pro-western South, while the Soviet Union and other communist allies aided the communist North. As in the Korean War, the U.S. Navy decided to use battleships for shore bombardment missions. With all battleships mothballed since the late 1950s, U.S.S. *New Jersey* was called back from its retirement in 1968, because it was in better condition than its sisters, due to its overhaul prior to its decommissioning in 1957: "*Big J*" underwent a period of modernization during which its obsolete 20-mm and 40-mm antiaircraft guns were removed and received improved electronic warfare and radar systems.

After being recommissioned in April 1968, *New Jersey* set the battleship world speed record by achieving a top speed of 35.2 knots (40.5 mph; 62.5 km/h), maintaining it for six hours.

New Jersey bombarding enemy targets near Tuy Hòa, on South Vietnam's central coast, in March 1969. At that time, she was the only active battleship in the world, as her sister ships remained in the Reserve Fleet and all foreign battleships had either been scrapped or were about to be scrapped.

Nearly three decades in the Reserve Fleet have left their toll on *Wisconsin*. When this photo was taken in 1980, it was inconceivable that 11 years later these 16-inch guns would play their part in liberating Kuwait from Saddam Hussein's occupation.

In 1969 *New Jersey* supported American troops fighting on land by shelling various targets including, bunkers, gun emplacement, troop movements, and supply lines, firing about 5,600 rounds of 16-inch shells and 14,800 rounds of 5-inch projectiles—seven times more rounds against shore targets than it had fired in World War II. On December 17, 1969, *New Jersey* was decommissioned for the second time, entering the inactive fleet again. When its colors were hauled down, *New Jersey*'s commanding officer, Captain Robert C. Peniston, gave his last order: "Rest well, yet sleep lightly; and hear the call, if again sounded, to provide fire power for freedom." *New Jersey* and its sisters would hear the call…

During the early 1980s, long after the last battleship in any navy had been retired, President Reagan's administration proposed to build a 600-ship fleet as a counter to the powerful Soviet Navy. At that time, the Soviet Navy was in the process of commissioning the nuclear-powered *Kirov*-class of guided missile cruisers displacing 24,000 tons and armed with numerous missile systems, giving these ships an enormous long-range firepower. The *Kirov*-class was the largest type of surface warship—other than aircraft carriers or amphibious assault vessels—completed since World War II. Due to their size and general appearance, these ships were often referred to as battlecruisers in the west. Therefore, as part of Reagan's 600-ship navy policy and to act as a counter to the *Kirov*-class, the U.S. Navy decided to reactivate the four *Iowa*-class battleships and modernize them for service in the 1980s. Their unique firepower, high speed, and unsurpassed survivability made them feasible for naval fire-support missions in so-called "high-threat" areas where they could support amphibious landings and reduce the risk of using manned aircraft.

Iowa (right) and *Wisconsin* in mothball storage at the Philadelphia Naval Shipyard, Pennsylvania, in February 1982, shortly before they were slated to return to active service. Visible on the left is the aircraft carrier *Shangri-La* (CVS-38). *New Jersey* and *Missouri* spent their period of inactivity at Puget Sound Naval Shipyard, Washington.

The four nuclear-powered, guided-missile battlecruisers of the *Kirov*-class entered service in the 1980s as part of the increasingly powerful Soviet fleet. Their main armament consists of anti-ship, anti-submarine, and surface-to-air missile weapon systems.

Beginning with *New Jersey* in 1981, which was in the best condition due to its 1968 reactivation, all four ships underwent extensive modernization and were recommissioned until 1988. The old warriors were upgraded with modern radar and computer-guided Tomahawk and Harpoon missile launchers, thus extending the firepower of the historic 16-inch guns and making the battleships a formidable and versatile strike platform conforming to the modern fleet.

While the *Iowa*-class was modernized, former crewmembers who served aboard in the 1950s, trained the young 18- and 19-year-old crewmembers on how to operate the steam turbines and naval guns designed in the late 1930s.

Iowa's superstructure and bridge with its massive conning tower during modernization at Ingalls Shipbuilding Corporation, Pascagoula, Mississippi, September 1983.

Starboard bow view of *Missouri* in dry dock during its modernization at Long Beach Naval Shipyard, February 1985.

A famous battleship gets its name back—with brush and paint.

Iowa left the Reserve Fleet to be modernized for its role in the Cold War, September 1982. The reactivation of the four *Iowas*, upgraded with various missiles in addition to their existing 16-inch battery, would be America's answer to the *Kirovs*.

Missiles

During the *Iowas*' modernization, only the 16-inch guns and 12 of its original 5-inch guns were retained. The ships received two cruise missile systems providing a long-range capability against both surface and land targets. One was the BGM-109 Tomahawk, which could reach a speed of 550 mph (885 km/h) and had a weight of 3,200 lb (1,450 kg). Each ship carried eight Mark 143 armored box launchers containing four Tomahawk missiles each. These missiles extended the ships' 23-mile gun-range up to 1,500 nautical miles (2,780 km).

A view of two Mark 143 armored box launchers (ABLs), one in the raised position, aboard *Missouri*. Each ship of the *Iowa*-class was fitted with eight ABLs to launch BGM-109 Tomahawk anti-ship missiles (TASMs) and Tomahawk land attack missiles (TLAMs).

The *Iowa*-class also carried a total number of 16 Boeing RGM-84 Harpoon missile launchers in four quad-cell Mark 141 canister launchers. The Harpoon Weapons System is an anti-ship missile

Launch of a Tomahawk from *Missouri* in 1988.

One of *Iowa*'s 16 Harpoon anti-ship missile launchers, with two Tomahawk ABLs in the background.

system giving the battleships an over-the-horizon strike capability against surface targets. With a weight of 1,385 lb (628 kg), the Harpoon could reach a cruising speed of 537 miles per hour (860 km/h) and had a range of up to 85 nautical miles (157 km). Due to the lack of surface targets the Harpoon was not used during Operation *Desert Storm* in 1991.

Close-in Weapons System

During the modernization, all the original World War II 40-mm and 20-mm antiaircraft guns, now useless against modern jet aircraft or missiles, were removed and replaced with four Mark 16 Phalanx CIWS (close-in) weapon system mounts. This CIWS is a 20-mm Gatling gun, developed to engage enemy aircraft and incoming missiles. It can be operated in either automatic or manual mode. When in automatic, the system will search, track, fire, and destroy a potential target. In manual, an operator must push a button to begin the operation. The system has no IFF (Identification Friend or Foe) and any incoming high-speed object will be attacked. Firing out of six individual barrels simultaneously, the Phalanx can fire 50 rounds per second or 3,000 rounds per minute.

One of *Missouri*'s four Phalanx close-in weapon systems (CIWS) firing its 20-mm projectiles during gunnery practice. The effective firing range was 1,625 yards, while the maximum range was up to 6,000 yards.

Captain Albert L. Kaiss became the commanding officer of the *Missouri*, while Margaret Truman Daniels, who had christened the ship back in 1944, also became the sponsor for the recommissioning.

Tugs spray water into the air around *Missouri* as it arrives in San Francisco for recommissioning, which took place on May 10, 1986. Margaret Truman gave a short speech especially aimed at the ship's crew, which ended with, "Now take care of my baby." Her remarks were met with rounds of applause from the crew.

An elevated starboard bow view of *Missouri* during the 1986 around-the-world shakedown cruise. Despite its modernization, the battleship retained its elegant lines.

A sailor poses in one of *Missouri*'s 16-inch guns.

Visible on the left, a view of *Iowa*'s modernized aft Mark 37 fire-control system with its Mark 25 radar dish mounted on top, 1983. In the center, the Mark 38 fire director with the Mark 13 radar antenna mounted atop. The long-based Mark 48 stereoscopic rangefinder is enclosed in the armored extensions.

A radar technician operating a SPS-67 surface-search radar aboard *Missouri* during Exercise *RimPac '88.*

A port side view of the modernized *Iowa* at sunset, moored off Puerto Caldera, Costa Rica, 1986.

Iowa's two forward 16-inch gun turrets are trained to starboard during gunnery exercises, ready to fire.

A round is fired from *Iowa*'s 16-inch gun turret with a projectile visible at the edge of the burst.

One of the most iconic photographs of the *Iowa*-class: U.S.S. *Iowa* firing a full broadside of its nine 16-inch main and six 5-inch secondary guns during a target exercise off Puerto Rico, July 1, 1984. Note the concussion effects on the water surface, and the 16-inch gun barrels in varying degrees of recoil. The arrangement of the eight box-like Tomahawk launchers and the tube-like Harpoon launchers in the center of the ship is clearly visible.

Heavy smoke pours from *Iowa*'s turret No. 2 during or shortly after an internal explosion, which occurred on April 19, 1989 during gunnery exercises off Puerto Rico, killing 47 men. An independent investigation concluded that the gun's powder bags had likely been rammed farther into the gun breech and at a higher speed than designed ("overram"), resulting in the powder igniting while loading was still in progress. The U.S. Navy, however, concluded that the explosion's cause could not be determined.

New Jersey leading the American battle line off the coast of Yokosuka, Japan, followed by *Missouri* and the nuclear-powered guided missile cruiser *Log Beach* (CGN-9) with vessels following, 1982. *New Jersey* was modernized first as it was in the best condition of all *Iowas* due to its previous iteration during the Vietnam War in the 1960s.

New Jersey firing its nine 16-inch guns to both sides simultaneously. The *Iowas* are probably the best-photographed battleships in history, contributing to their timeless fame.

Rings of fire erupt from one of the 5-inch twin-gun mounts of *New Jersey* during practice firing off the coast of Beirut, Lebanon, 1983.

Waves break over *Missouri*'s bow in rough seas. Note the large discone antenna for the Navy Tactical Data System, installed during the 1980s.

Missouri transiting the Gatun Locks in the Panama Canal on the final leg of its 1986 around-the-world shakedown cruise. The beam of the *Iowas* (and preceding American capital ships) was determined by the width of the locks. Therefore, the 108 feet, 2 inch (33 m) wide ships just fit through the locks, while the subsequent *Montanas* would have been 13 feet too wide.

A show of force: Battle Group Echo in formation, 1987. Steaming ahead is *Missouri*, followed by the carrier *Ranger* (CV-61) and the guided-missile cruiser *Long Beach* (CGN-9). The escorting ships on both sides are guided-missile destroyers, frigates, and supply vessels.

In 1983, *New Jersey* participated in American operations during the Lebanese Civil War. With its sister ships entering service over the subsequent years, the *Iowa*-class participated in various fleet exercises and Operation *Earnest Will* from 1987 to 1988; the class helped protect Kuwaiti-owned oil tankers from Iranian attacks during the Iran–Iraq War. On August 2, 1990, Iraqi troops invaded and occupied their smaller neighbor Kuwait. U.S. President George H. W. Bush gave Saddam Hussein a deadline to withdraw all Iraqi forces by January 15, 1991. Should he refuse to do so, American General Norman Schwarzkopf would lead a multinational coalition force to liberate Kuwait. At that time, only two battleships, *Missouri* and *Wisconsin*, were still available for combat. Due to the approaching end of the Cold War, the other two, *Iowa* and *New Jersey*, had already entered their deactivation process. As in their previous wars, the battleships would provide fire support with their 16-inch artillery, knocking out targets along the coast of Kuwait. They were now even capable of hitting targets inside Iraq, because their Tomahawk missiles had a range of more than 1,000 miles compared to the 23-mile range of their historic guns. The deadline expired and Saddam Hussein's forces remained in Kuwait, so the crews of both battleships were ordered to battle stations.

Wisconsin was the last of the *Iowas* to be recommissioned, in October 1988. Along with *Missouri*, it would fight another war, in 1991.

Wisconsin firing its 16-inch guns to port during a firepower demonstration in the Gulf of Mexico, August 1988. A projectile fired from turret No. 1 can be seen in flight.

In 1989, the historic battleship became the stage for Cher's music video titled "If I Could Turn Back Time." The song became the unofficial ship's anthem during *Missouri*'s service and Operation *Desert Storm*.

While this was the third war for the battle-hardened battleships, it was certainly the first for most of its young crewmembers. The old warriors entered the modern age of warfare, when they launched their first Tomahawk missiles against targets in Iraq.

On February 3, 1991, for the first time since the Korean War 38 years earlier, *Missouri*'s powerful 16-inch guns opened fire on hostile targets and bombarded Iraqi military installations around Kuwait City and Khafji. Some crewmembers cheered when they heard the guns firing. *Wisconsin* relieved *Missouri* on February 6, then answered its first combat call for fire support since March 1952 when also opening fire with its main battery. Remarkably, the battleships' original World War II plotting computers, now integrated into a modern radar-guiding system, were still able to direct fire with pinpoint accuracy. Coastal surveillance was provided by *Pioneer* unmanned aerial vehicles (drones) launched from the decks, which also helped locate targets and direct the guns. *Missouri* also located and detonated floating Iraqi mines that posed a serious threat to naval operations. Compared to all other naval ships afloat, the battleships were much more

In August of 1990, Iraq's dictator Saddam Hussein ordered his troops to invade neighboring Kuwait. (Iraqi News Agency)

Return to combat: *Missouri* launches a Tomahawk land-attack missile (TLAM) toward an Iraqi target at the start of Operation *Desert Storm*, in January 1991.

Missouri fires its 16-inch guns as night shelling of Iraqi targets takes place along the northern Kuwaiti coast during Operation *Desert Storm.*

capable of surviving a mine strike due to its robust construction.

On February 24, 1991, General Schwarzkopf ordered the ground offensive to launch, from Saudi Arabia. *Wisconsin* and *Missouri* fired their guns into occupied Kuwait territory, Faylaka Island, to make the enemy think there would be an amphibious landing. The ground attack, which came from the opposite direction, ultimately resulted in Iraq's defeat. It was on this morning that Iraqi forces fired a Silkworm anti-ship-missile at the *Missouri*. Fortunately, the Silkworm was intercepted and destroyed by a missile launched from the British destroyer HMS *Gloucester*. The success of the ground attack required no further battleship support—it was time for *Wisconsin* and *Missouri* to return home.

Farewell—The End of an Era

It was clear that the two battleships would soon follow their sister ships into retirement. Without an enemy, they had become too costly to operate. While *Wisconsin* was decommissioned for the third and final time on September 30, 1991, *Missouri* was assigned one last honorary mission: on December 7, 1991, the "*Mighty Mo*" attended the 50th anniversary of the attack on Pearl Harbor paying tribute to the sunken battleship

A Pioneer is caught in a recovery net after returning from its mission. In one instance, a drone launched from *Wisconsin* was assessing the result of naval fire support near Kuwait's Faylaka Island. Iraqi soldiers stationed there surrendered to the loitering drone, hoping it wouldn't bring with it a flaming death from above that had befallen so many Iraqi troops in Kuwait. This was the first-ever surrender of humans to an UAV.

Launch of a Pioneer I UAV. It carried a stabilized TV camera and a laser designator for fire support with over-the-horizon targeting and reconnaissance capabilities.

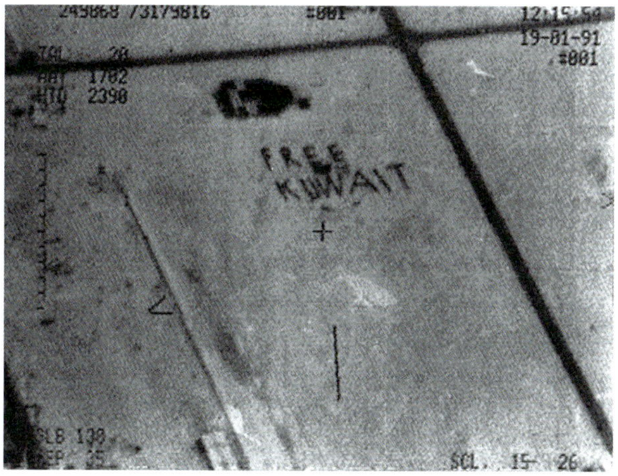

A Pioneer UAV videotaping a Kuwaiti call for help.

Arizona and all the lives lost on December 7, 1941. Just a few months later, March 31, 1992 marked the end of the battleship era—the most elegant warships to ever sail the seas.

On that day, *Missouri* was decommissioned for the third and final time. Its last commanding officer, Captain Albert L. Kaiss, wrote in the ship's final Plan of the Day:

> Our final day has arrived. Today the final chapter in battleship *Missouri*'s history will be written. It's often said that the crew makes the command. There is no truer statement—for it's the crew of this great ship that made this a great command. You are a special breed of sailors and Marines and I am proud to have served with each and every one of you. To you who have made the painful journey of

On February 24, 1991, an Iraqi HY-2 Silkworm missile was fired at *Missouri*; it was intercepted by a Sea Dart missile launched from the British destroyer HMS *Gloucester* and crashed into the sea, roughly 700 yards in front of *Missouri*. Shortly afterwards, the battleship's UAV located the missile launchers and neutralized them with its 16-inch guns. (Oil painting by John Charles Roach/U.S. Naval History and Heritage Command/92-007-U)

The setting sun silhouettes the *Missouri*.

The end of the battleship era: a crewmember lowers the colors on *Missouri* for the last time at its decommissioning ceremony, March 31, 1992.

putting this great lady to sleep, I thank you. For you have had the toughest job. To put away a ship that has become as much a part of you as you are to her is a sad ending to a great tour. But take solace in this—you have lived up to the history of the ship and those who sailed her before us. We took her to war, performed magnificently and added another chapter in her history, standing side by side our forerunners in true naval tradition. God bless you all.

People gather on the beach to see *Missouri* enter the channel into Pearl Harbor, Hawaii, on June 22, 1998.

Tugs move *Missouri* to its berth at Ford Island, Pearl Harbor. This berth is roughly where the battleships *Maryland* and *Oklahoma* were moored on December 7, 1941. The 184-foot-long U.S.S. *Arizona* Memorial in the foreground spans the mid-portion of the sunken *Arizona*.

8

U.S.S. *Missouri*—A Guided Tour

Of the numerous battleships and battlecruisers of the U.S. Navy, only eight have survived to this day as floating museums. One is U.S.S. *Missouri* (BB-63) of the *Iowa*-class. It fought in World War II, became the site of the Japanese surrender, served during the Korean War and was finally deployed during Operation *Desert Storm*, the liberation of Kuwait in 1991.

Today, you can visit *Missouri* in Pearl Harbor and immerse yourself in the history and technology of capital ships. The historic ship is representative of the other seven preserved battleships, U.S.S. *Texas*, U.S.S. *North Carolina*, U.S.S. *Massachusetts*, U.S.S. *Alabama*, U.S.S. *Iowa*, U.S.S. *New Jersey*, and U.S.S. *Wisconsin*, all of which are also open to the public. Let's go aboard the "*Mighty Mo*" and explore this famous ship.

Except for aircraft carriers, battleships were and still would be the largest ships in the fleet. Manned by a crew of up to 3,000, a battleship was like a city gone to sea. It provided several galleys, a bakery, and mess decks where the crew ate. It had laundry facilities, a barbershop, a post office, a library, stores, a chapel, a pharmacy and a prison (the "brig"). There was even a hospital ("sickbay"), which included dental officers—helpful since the crew's meals included treats like ice cream.

People visiting museum battleships often wonder why the deck under their feet is teak wood. In all, tens

U.S.S. *Missouri* moored as a museum ship in Pearl Harbor.

Main deck with 16-inch gun turrets.

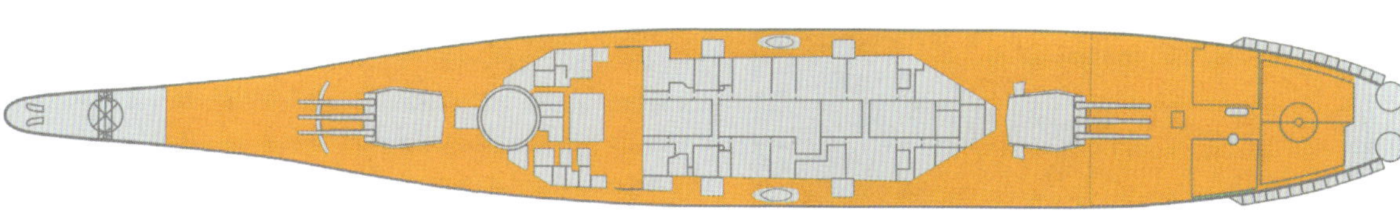

The massive forward 16-inch guns, here on the *Iowa*, are surrounded by teak on the steel deck.

of thousands of square feet are attached to the steel decks below. Teak is very hard and resistant to rot, even with constant exposure to seawater. Since it is not slippery when wet, it makes the deck safer for the crew. It also provided some insulation for the decks below in the days before air-conditioning.

Kamikaze Deck

On April 11, 1945, at 2:43 p.m., a Japanese kamikaze struck the ship during the battle for Okinawa. While fire erupted briefly, no crewmember was seriously wounded. The deceased pilot, believed to be Petty Officer 2nd Class Setsuo Ishino, was given a military burial at sea the following day.

Fantail

Originally, the fantail had two catapults used to launch floatplanes serving primarily as spotters to confirm target positions and gunfire accuracy. By 1949, the catapults were removed and replaced by a helicopter landing pad, which was later modernized when the ship was reactivated in 1986. UAVs were launched from the fantail during Operation *Desert Storm* in 1991.

Wardroom and Officer's Country

This area was reserved for the ship's officers and was where they gathered for meals. The mural was originally painted by crewmembers in 1945 while they were on their way home following the end of World War II. The mural was modified during each subsequent cruise including Operation *Desert Storm*.

Level 1

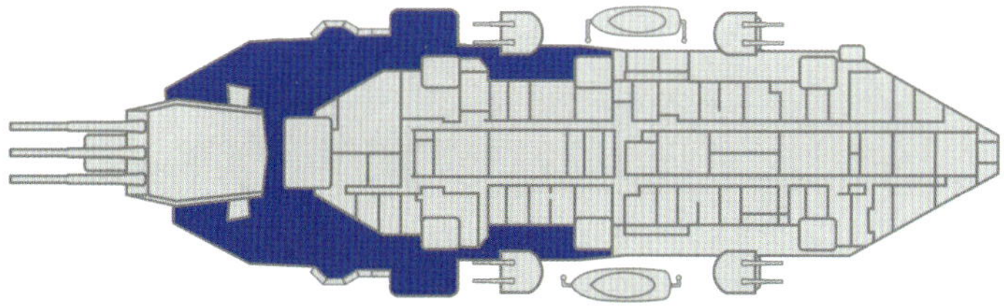

Surrender Deck

The surrender plaque, installed in October 1945, marks the spot where the surrender table was located and indicates the ship's coordinates in Tokyo Bay during the ceremony on September 2, 1945. The captain's in-port cabin is located behind the surrender deck, which was used to host formal dinners and for operational meetings.

5-inch Armament

The *Iowas* were originally commissioned with 10 5-inch mounts to engage surface and aircraft targets. During the 1980s modernization, two aft and two amidships mounts were removed to make room for the Tomahawk and Harpoon missile decks. Each ship now has six gun mounts.

Level 2

Combat Engagement Center (CEC)

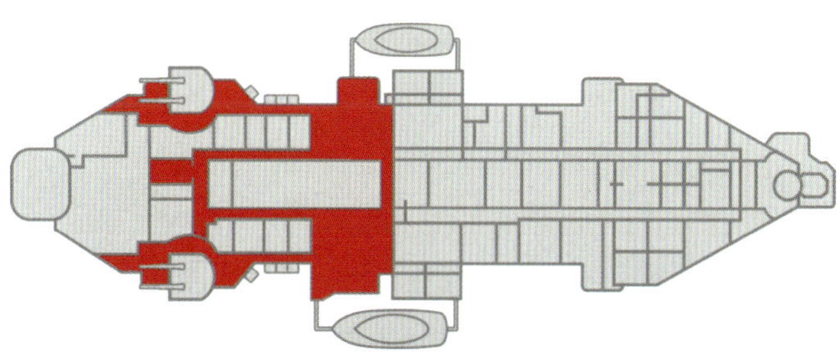

The CEC (here aboard *Iowa*) was added to the *Iowas* during the 1980s for use with the modern weapon systems including the control stations for the Tomahawks and Harpoons, the operator's console for the close-in weapon system (CIWS) as well as various radar stations. While the CEC was used specifically for control of modern weapon systems, the CIC (Combat Information System) on the fourth deck below was always used to control the main and secondary battery guns.

Level 3

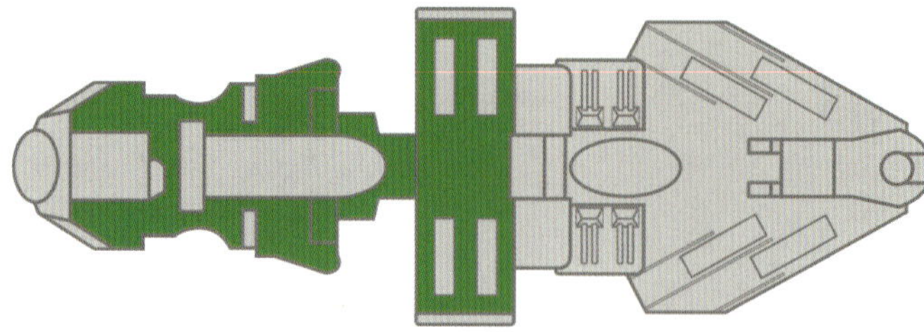

Tomahawk Deck

During the 1980s modernization, platforms were constructed on the superstructure amidships and aft to accommodate eight 4-missile armored box launchers (ABLs) for a total of 32 missiles, used for land attack warfare.

Harpoon Deck

Four 4-missile Harpoon launchers were also installed during modernization. The Harpoon (here fired from *Iowa*) is an over-the-horizon, anti-ship missile system.

Level 4

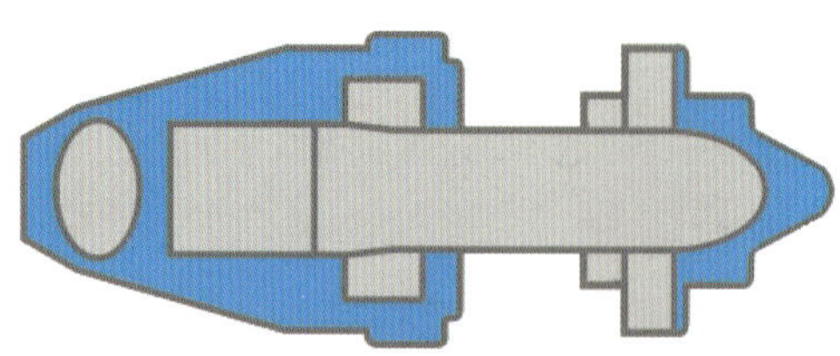

Navigation Bridge

This is the steering and control center of the ship during underway conditions and the command station for the commanding officer (CO) or officer of the deck (OOD). The navigation bridge contains the pilot house, command or conning station, chart house, meteorological facility and the captain's at-sea cabin. While the 04 navigation bridge is the steering and conning station for normal underway steaming, there is also a secondary steering and conning station in the 08 level above.

Conning Station

The central armored conning station, shown here during *Missouri's* modernization, called the "citadel" because of its 17-inch-thick steel armor, is the helmsman's station. Under combat conditions it served as the conning station where the commanding officer and all other personnel gathered.

Chart House

The chart house is located just aft (behind) of the helm. This is where the ship's navigators use maps to plot the ship's position and course according to directions provided by the CO or OOD.

Level 5

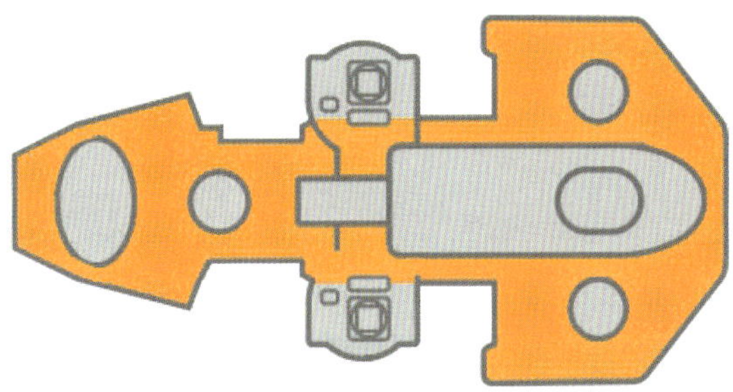

Phalanx Close-in Weapon System

During the 1980s modernization, all WWII-era 20-mm and 40-mm antiaircraft guns were replaced by four automated Phalanx CIWS rapid-fire Gatling guns protecting the ship against incoming missiles and other aerial threats.

Open Bridge

The open bridge is where the top level of the conning tower is located. In the 1940s and 1950s, the air defense officer would have been stationed here.

Second Deck

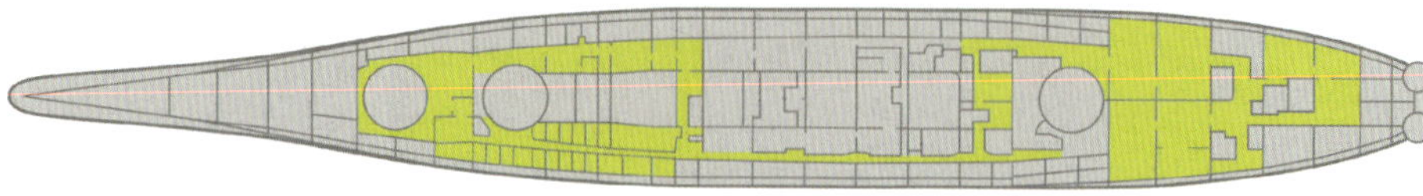

Crew's Mess

The enlisted mess decks are the largest dining area onboard the *Iowas* with four meals a day served: breakfast, lunch, dinner, and midnight rations.

Crew's Galley & Truman Line

The battleship has two chow lines: the *Missouri Express* line and the *Truman Line*. The former was where sailors could get fast food, such as hamburgers, hot dogs, french fries and sandwiches. The latter provided more selection and complete meals. The enlisted galley produced over 5,000 crew rations a day. The *Truman Line* is named after President Harry S. Truman, who stayed on board in 1947.

Bread Room & Bakery

The bakeshop worked round the clock to produce 1,800 loaves of bread a day. In addition to bread, the bakers made biscuits, pies, and donuts. The photo shows the mass production of lemon pies in the battleship's bakery during her shakedown period, summer 1944.

Machine Shop

This area helped keep the ship and its crew self-sustaining while underway by repairing or replacing machinery. American warships are considered American soil, so anything fabricated on board is *made in the USA*.

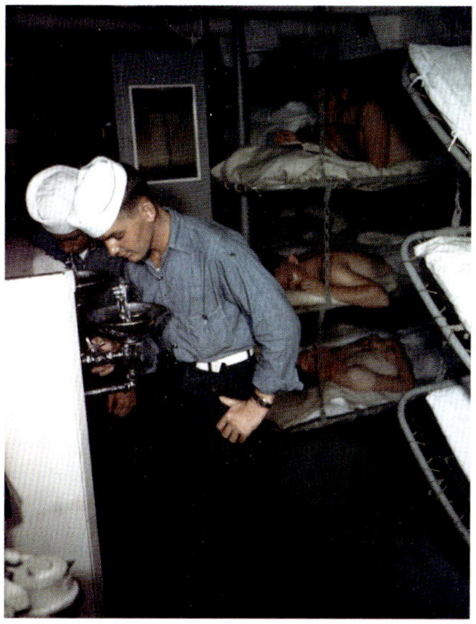

Enlisted Crew Berthing World War II

Berthing area during World War II. Note the water dispenser for enlisted men. There would be virtually no privacy. Officers had more comfortable cabins.

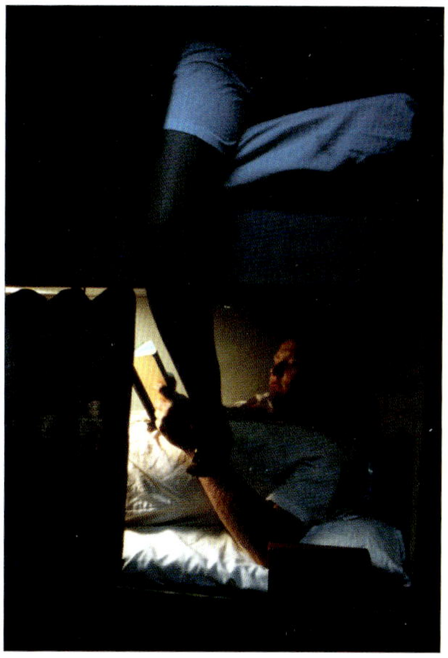

1980s berthing

Enlisted berthing area, modernized during the 1980s. The sleeping racks are referred to as "coffin racks" because many racks opened—like a coffin—to reveal storage space underneath. Each one has a reading light and privacy curtain. There are about 1,660 of these racks on each *Iowa*-class ship.

Post Office

The *Iowa*'s post office offered all the same postal services at sea as on land.

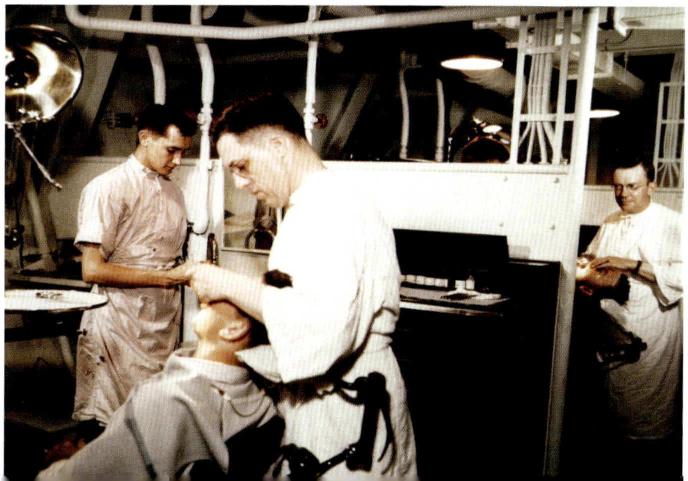

Dental Facilities

Dental facilities served the entire crew offering various services including routine cleanings to lost fillings to root-canal surgery. The *Iowas* also had a hospital with several doctors where even complex operations could be performed.

Preserved Battleships

After reading this book, you may ask "Where are they now?" There are no battleships or battlecruisers preserved outside the United States and Japan, although there were several of these veterans available after World War II. The British *Vanguard*, the French *Jean Bart*, or the Italian *Italia* (ex-*Littorio*) all would have made wonderful floating museums, but various factors including the financial situation after six years of war resulted in different priorities during the postwar period in these countries.

Mikasa, the world's last remaining pre-dreadnought battleship, has been preserved in Yokosuka, Japan, allowing us to walk the planks of one of the ships that fought in the famous battle of Tsushima. The only surviving battleship, which fought in both world wars in various theaters, the super-dreadnought *Texas*, can be visited at the San Jacinto Battleground State Historic Site near Houston, Texas. The wrecks of *Arizona* and *Utah*, sunk during the Japanese attack on Pearl Harbor in 1941, are designated historical landmarks and national grave sites. A visit to *Arizona*'s memorial, spanning its submerged wreck, and *Utah*'s memorial, located near its wreck, allows us to reflect on the sacrifice made by young sailors in wartime. The *North Carolina*, preserved in Wilmington, North Carolina, took part in almost every major naval offensive in the Pacific theater. Two ships of the subsequent *South Dakota*-class, *Massachusetts* and *Alabama*, are located in Fall River, Massachusetts, and Mobile, Alabama, respectively. Both served in the Atlantic and Pacific theaters of World War II. The U.S. Navy's last completed battleships of the *Iowa*-class, have been all preserved. *Iowa* is on display at the Los Angeles Waterfront in San Pedro, California, *New Jersey* in Camden, New Jersey, *Missouri* in Pearl Harbor, Hawaii, and *Wisconsin* in Norfolk, Virginia.

Opened to the public as a museum ship in 1999, U.S.S. *Missouri* watches over the sunken U.S.S. *Arizona*. Both ships represent the "book ends" of World War II—while *Arizona* stands for the initial defeat, *Missouri* represents the final victory in mankind's most brutal conflict.

Over the years, all the *Iowas* were turned into floating museums. In June 2102, U.S.S. *Iowa* arrived at the Los Angeles Waterfront in San Pedro, California, and was opened to the public under the direction of the Pacific Battleship Center. (Photo: Rich Abele/Battleship U.S.S. *Iowa* Museum)

Although most battleships are gone, their history lives on in books, films, museums, and surviving ships—and perhaps most importantly—in the (recorded) personal memories of those who served aboard them. When the British Admiral Jackie Fisher was created Baron Fisher in 1909, he chose the motto *"Fear God and dread nought"* on his coat of arms as a reference to HMS *Dreadnought.* For generations of sailors, battleships were the strongest warships afloat, bestowing on their crews exceptional pride and prestige. I salute them. Farewell, Dreadnought!

After the U.S. Navy had handed over the control of U.S.S. *New Jersey* to the Home Port Alliance of Camden, New Jersey, the battleship was opened to the public in October 2000 on the Camden Waterfront. (Battleship *New Jersey* Museum & Memorial)

Bibliography

Bauernfeind, Ingo (2011). *Schlachtschiffe der U.S. Navy*. Motorbuch-Verlag, Stuttgart.

Bauernfeind, Ingo (2016). *Prinz Eugen—Die Geschichte des legendären deutschen Kreuzers*. Motorbuch-Verlag, Stuttgart.

Bauernfeind, Ingo (2018). *U.S.S.* Arizona*—The Enduring Legacy of a Battleship*. Bauernfeind Press, Mülheim.

Breyer, Siegried (1990). *Schlachtschiffe und Schlachtkreuzer 1905–1970*. 2nd ed. Auflage. Bernard & Graefe, Koblenz.

Friedman, Norman (1984). *U.S. Battleships: An Illustrated History*. Naval Institute Press, Annapolis.

Lambert, Andrew (1984). *Battleships in Transition—The Creation of the Steam Battlefleet 1815–1860*. Conway Maritime Press, London.

Stilwell, Paul (2001). *Battleships*. MetroBooks, New York.

In 2009, the U.S. Navy officially transferred U.S.S. *Wisconsin* to the city of Norfolk, Virginia, after the city had maintained the ship since 2000. Today, the battleship is part of the Nauticus, a maritime-themed science center and museum at Norfolk's downtown waterfront.

Index